1006614505

Global Economic Prospects

Global Economic Prospects

Crisis, Finance, and Growth

201

ISBN: 978-0-8213-8226-4
eISBN: 978-0-8213-8227-1
DOI: 10.1596/978-0-8213-8226-4
ISSN: 1014-8906

Cover photos: © iStockphoto.com/burakpekakcan (sky); © iStockphoto.com/mikeuk (sea)
Cover design: Critical Stages

The cutoff date for the data used in this report was January 8, 2010. Dollars are current
U.S. dollars unless otherwise indicated.

Contents

Figures

Tables

Boxes

Foreword

This year, *Global Economic Prospects* is being released at a critical juncture for the world economy. A recovery from the financial crisis that rocked the world in the fall of 2008 is under way, but many challenges remain and much uncertainty continues to cloud the outlook.

In many respects, recent economic news has been encouraging. Industrial production and trade, after falling by unprecedented amounts worldwide, are growing briskly; financial markets have recovered much of the steep losses they incurred in late 2008 and early 2009; and developing countries are once again attracting the interest of international investors. However, the depth of the recession has left the global economy seriously wounded. Even as profitability returns to many of the firms that were at the heart of the crisis, industrial production and trade levels have yet to regain their pre-crisis levels, and unemployment has reached double digits in many countries and continues to rise.

Given the depth of the crisis and the continued need for restructuring in the global banking system, the recovery is expected to be relatively weak. As a result, unemployment and significant spare capacity are likely to continue to characterize the economic landscape for years to come. This poses a real challenge for policy makers, who must cut back on unsustainably high fiscal deficits without choking off the recovery. Similarly, the extraordinary monetary stimulus needs to be scaled back to avoid the creation of new bubbles. The medium-term strength of the recovery will depend both on how well these challenges are met and on the extent to which private-sector demand picks up. If policies are adjusted too slowly, inflationary pressures and additional bubbles could develop; too quick of an adjustment could stall the recovery.

Whatever the relative strength of the recovery in the next few months, the human costs of this recession are already high. Globally, and notwithstanding upward revisions to growth projections for 2010, the number of people living on $1.25 per day or less is still expected to increase by some 64 million as compared with a no-crisis scenario. The recession has cut sharply into the revenues of governments in poor countries. Unless donors step in to fill the gap, authorities in these countries may be forced to cut back on social and humanitarian assistance precisely when it is most required.

In addition to analyzing the immediate challenges for developing countries posed by the crisis, this year's *Global Economic Prospects* describes some of the longer-term implications of tighter financial conditions for developing-country finance and economic growth. While necessary and desirable, tighter regulation in high-income countries will result in less abundant capital (both globally and domestically) and increased borrowing costs for developing countries. As a result, just as the very loose conditions of the first half of this decade contributed to an investment boom and an acceleration in developing-country growth, so too will higher capital costs in coming years serve to slow growth in developing countries and provoke a decline in potential output.

Countries should not respond passively. Efforts to strengthen domestic financial systems and expand regional cooperation (including regional self-insurance schemes) can help to reduce the sensitivity of domestic economies to international shocks and counteract some of the longer-term negative effects of tighter international financial conditions. Such initiatives are most likely to benefit middle-income countries that already have reasonably well-developed regulatory and competitive environments and healthy financial sectors. Finally, both low- and middle-income countries should strengthen domestic financial regulations. Over time, such steps can improve domestic financial-sector efficiency and reduce borrowing costs—more than offsetting any negative impacts from tighter international conditions.

Overall, these are challenging times. The depth of the recession means that even though growth has returned, countries and individuals will continue to feel the pain of the crisis for years to come. Policy can help mitigate the worst symptoms of this crisis. However, there are no silver bullets, and achieving higher growth rates will require concerted efforts to increase domestic productivity and lower the domestic cost of finance.

Justin Yifu Lin
Chief Economist and
Senior Vice President
The World Bank

Acknowledgments

This report was produced by staff from the World Bank's Development Prospects Group. The report was managed by Andrew Burns, with direction from Hans Timmer. The principal authors of the report were Andrew Burns, William Shaw, and Theo Janse van Rensburg. The report was produced under the general guidance of Justin Yifu Lin.

Several people contributed substantively to chapter 1. Theo Janse van Rensburg was its main author. The Global Macroeconomic Trends team, under the leadership of Andrew Burns, was responsible for the projections. The projections and regional write-ups were produced by Dilek Aykut, Ivailo Izvorski, Eung Ju Kim, Annette De Kleine, Oana Luca, Israel Osorio-Rodarte, Theo Janse van Rensburg, Elliot (Mick) Riordan, Cristina Savescu, and Nadia Islam Spivak. These were produced in coordination with country teams, country directors, and the offices of the regional Chief Economists and PREM directors. The short-term commodity price forecasts were produced by John Baffes, Betty Dow, and Shane Streifel. The remittances forecasts were produced by Sanket Mohapatra, while Shaohua Chen from the Development Research Group and Dominique van der Mensbrugghe generated the long-term poverty forecast.

Andrew Burns, William Shaw, and Nikola Spatafora were the main authors of chapter 2, with written contributions from Mike Kennedy, Oana Luca, and Angel Palerm. Chapter 3 was written by Andrew Burns and William Shaw, with written contributions from Dilek Aykut, Jean-Pierre Chauffour, and Mariem Malouche. Both chapters 2 and 3 benefited from the expert research assistance of Augusto Clavijo, Yueqing Jia, Eung Ju Kim, Irina Kogay, Sergio Kurlat, Sabah Mirza, and Nadia Islam Spivak.

The accompanying online publication, *Prospects for the Global Economy* (PGE), was produced by a team led by Cristina Savescu and composed of Cybele Arnaud, Augusto Clavijo, Sarah Crow, Betty Dow, Ernesto McKenzie, Kathy Rollins, Ziming Yang, and Ying Yu, with technical support from Gauresh Rajadhyaksha. The translation process was coordinated by Jorge del Rosario (French and Spanish) and Li Li (Chinese). A companion pamphlet highlighting the main messages of the commodities section of the report was prepared by Kavita Watsa and Roula Yazigi.

Martha Gottron edited the report. Hazel Macadangdang managed the publication process, and Rebecca Ong and Merrell Tuck-Primdahl managed the dissemination activities. Book production was coordinated by Aziz Gökdemir along with Stephen McGroarty and Andrés Meneses, all from the World Bank Office of the Publisher.

Several reviewers offered extensive advice and comments throughout the conceptualization and writing stages. These included Shaghil Ahmed, Daniel Benitez, Cesar Calderon, Otaviano Canuto, Kevin Carey, Rodrigo Chavez, Jeff Chelsky, Mansoor Dailami, Jeff Delmon, Shahrokh Fardoust, Alan Gelb, Jack Glen, Arvind Gupta, Fernando Im, Jacqueline Irving, Ada Karina

Izaguirre, Ivailo Izvorski, Prakash Kannan, Auguste Tano Kouame, Robert Kahn, Doreen Kibuka-Musoke, Jean Pierre Lacombe, Atushi Limi, Justin Yifu Lin, Dominique van der Mensbrugghe, Celestin Monga, Mustapha Nabli, Fernando Navarro, Il Young Park, Maria Soledad Martinez Peria, Zia Qureshi, Hartwig Schafer, Luiz Pereira da Silva, Claudia Paz Sepulveda, Hans Timmer, and Augusto de la Torre.

Abbreviations

ASEAN	Association of Southeast Asian Nations
BIS	Bank for International Settlements
CDOs	collateralized debt obligations
CDSs	credit default swaps
CPI	consumer price index
DECPG	Development Economics Prospects Group (World Bank)
ECB	European Central Bank
EMBI	Emerging Markets Bond Index
EMBI+	Emerging Markets Bond Index Plus
FDI	foreign direct investment
GCC	Gulf Cooperation Council
GDP	gross domestic product
GIDD	Global Income Distribution Dynamics model
GNFS	goods and nonfactor services
GNI	gross national income
IBRD	International Bank for Reconstruction and Development
IDA	International Development Association
IMF	International Monetary Fund
IPO	initial public equity offering
Lao PDR	Lao People's Democratic Republic
LCU	local currency unit
LIBOR-OIS	London Interbank Offered Rate-Overnight Indexed Swap rate
M&A	mergers and acquisitions
MDG	Millennium Development Goal
MSCI	Morgan-Stanley Composite Index
NIEs	newly industrializing economies
ODA	official development assistance
OECD	Organisation for Economic Co-operation and Development
OPEC	Organization of the Petroleum-Exporting Countries
PPP	purchasing power parity
saar	seasonally adjusted annualized rate
T-bill	Treasury bill (U.S.)
TFP	total factor productivity
UAE	United Arab Emirates

Overview

The world economy is emerging from the throes of a historically deep and synchronized recession provoked by the bursting of a global financial bubble. The consequences of the initial bubble and the crisis have been felt in virtually every economy, whether or not it participated directly in the risky behaviors that precipitated the boom-and-bust cycle. And while growth rates have picked up, the depth of the recession means that it will take years before unemployment and spare capacity are reabsorbed.

This year's *Global Economic Prospects* examines the consequences of the crisis for both the short- and medium-term growth prospects of developing countries. It concludes that the crisis and the regulatory reaction to the financial excesses of the preceding several years may have lasting impacts on financial markets, raising borrowing costs and lowering levels of credit and international capital flows. As a result, the rate of growth of potential output in developing countries may be reduced by between 0.2 and 0.7 percentage points annually over the next five to seven years as economies adjust to tighter financial conditions. Overall, the level of potential output in developing countries could be reduced by between 3.4 and 8 percent over the long run, compared with its pre-crisis path.

The report further finds that the very liquid conditions of the first half of the decade contributed to the expansion in credit available in developing countries and that this expansion was responsible for about 40 percent of the approximately 1.5 percentage point acceleration of the pace at which many developing-country economies could grow without generating significant inflation.

While developing countries probably cannot reverse the expected tightening in international financial conditions, there is considerable scope for reducing domestic borrowing costs, or increasing productivity and thereby regaining the higher growth path that the crisis has derailed.

The acute phase of the crisis is over

The immediate impacts of the crisis (including a freezing up of credit markets, a sharp reversal of capital flows, and the precipitous equity market and exchange rate declines that ensued) are largely in the past. Since March 2009, stock markets in high-income and emerging economies have recovered roughly half the value they lost, with developing economies rebounding somewhat more strongly than high-income ones. Interbank lending rates have returned to normal levels, developing-country sovereign interest rate premiums have declined from a peak of more than 800 to around 300 basis points and stock market volatility has receded (figure O.1). In addition, bond flows to high-income corporate and emerging-market sovereigns have returned to more normal levels, and most developing-country currencies have regained their pre-crisis levels against the dollar. However, bond markets and bank lending have

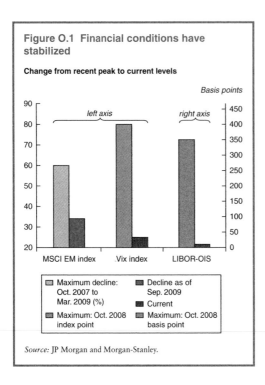

Figure O.1 Financial conditions have stabilized

Change from recent peak to current levels

Source: JP Morgan and Morgan-Stanley.

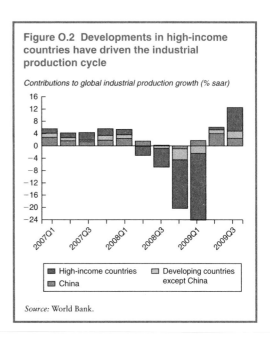

Figure O.2 Developments in high-income countries have driven the industrial production cycle

Contributions to global industrial production growth (% saar)

Source: World Bank.

begun only recently to reopen themselves to private sector borrowers in developing countries, with syndicated loans to developing countries totaling only $123 billion in 2009, compared with $236 billion during 2008.

The real side of the global economy is also recovering, with industrial production at the global level growing at more than 12 percent annualized pace in the third quarter of 2009. The recovery, which was initially concentrated in developing countries, has become more balanced recently as the drawdown of inventories in high-income countries slows and activity catches up to underlying demand trends (figure O.2). Nevertheless, the level of output remains depressed worldwide, with industrial production still 5 percent below pre-crisis peaks in October 2009.

Trade, which initially fell sharply, is also recovering; the exports of developing countries were expanding at a 36 percent annualized pace in October, but the volume of world trade remained 2.8 percent lower than its pre-crisis level and some 10 percent below the

level consistent with its pre-crisis trend growth rate. Overall, considerable slack remains in the global economy, with unemployment continuing to rise, disinflation widespread, and commodity prices between 50 and 25 percent lower than their levels in mid-2008.

A subdued recovery

Overall, after falling for two to three quarters, global GDP has begun recovering; output grew rapidly during the second half of 2009 and is expected to continue to do so during the first half of 2010. However, as the positive contribution to growth from fiscal stimulus and the inventory cycle wanes, growth will slow, in part because spending by households and the banking sector will be less buoyant as they rebuild their balance sheets. As a result, global GDP growth, which is projected to come in at 2.7 percent in 2010 (after an unprecedented 2.2 percent decline in 2009), is expected to accelerate only modestly to 3.2 percent in 2011 (table O.1).

A weak recovery is also anticipated in developing countries. Arguably the inventory cycle is somewhat more advanced in East Asia and the Pacific, and there are signs that the growth impact of fiscal stimulus in China may already be waning

Table O.1 A modest recovery
(real GDP growth, percentage change from previous year)

Region	2007	2008	2009ᵉ	2010ᶠ	2011ᶠ
World	3.9	1.7	−2.2	2.7	3.2
High-income countries	2.6	0.4	−3.3	1.8	2.3
Euro Area	2.7	0.5	−3.9	1.0	1.7
Japan	2.3	−1.2	−5.4	1.3	1.8
United States	2.1	0.4	−2.5	2.5	2.7
Developing countries	8.1	5.6	1.2	5.2	5.8
East Asia and Pacific	11.4	8.0	6.8	8.1	8.2
Europe and Central Asia	7.1	4.2	−6.2	2.7	3.6
Latin America and the Caribbean	5.5	3.9	−2.6	3.1	3.6
Middle East and North Africa	5.9	4.3	2.9	3.7	4.4
South Asia	8.5	5.7	5.7	6.9	7.4
Sub-Saharan Africa	6.5	5.1	1.1	3.8	4.6
Memorandum items					
Developing countries					
excluding transition countries	8.1	5.6	2.5	5.7	6.1
excluding China and India	6.2	4.3	−2.2	3.3	4.0

Source: World Bank.
Note: e = estimate; f = forecast; growth rates aggregated using real GDP in 2005 constant dollars.

(industrial production and import growth in the region are already slowing). Output is estimated to have picked up in virtually every other developing region in the final quarter of 2009 and should continue to do so early in 2010, before slowing toward more sustainable rates later in the year. The pace of the recovery is expected to be most subdued in the Europe and Central Asia region, partly because the pre-crisis level of demand in the region was well above potential and partly because the financial system in the region has been more acutely affected by the crisis.

Combined, GDP growth in developing countries is projected to grow by some 5.2 percent in 2010, after a modest 1.2 percent rise in 2009 (−2.2 percent if India and China are excluded), and by a relatively weak 5.8 percent in 2011. Despite these relatively robust growth rates, the unusual depth of the recession will mean that spare capacity and unemployment will continue to plague economies in 2011 and some sectors may well still be shrinking. Overall, the output gap (the difference between actual GDP and what GDP would be if capital and labor were fully employed) in developing countries will remain elevated at about 4 percent of potential output in 2011 (figure O.3).

The depth of the recession and the relative weakness of the expected recovery suggest that

Figure O.3 The downturn in developing countries has been deeper and more broadly based than during previous recessions

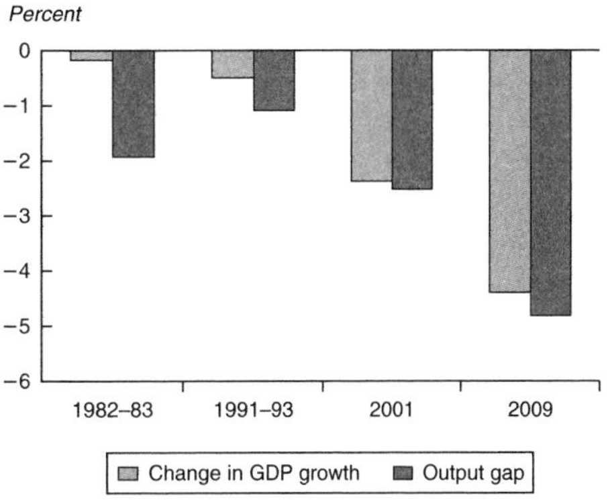

Source: World Bank.
Note: Change in GDP growth is the percentage change in the growth rate of developing-country GDP between the crisis year(s) and the previous year. The output gap is the percentage difference between GDP and potential output during the crisis year(s).

significant spare capacity, high unemployment, and weak inflationary pressures will continue to characterize both high-income and developing countries for some time. Already, the slowdown in growth is estimated to have increased poverty. Some 64 million more people around the world are expected to be living on less than $1.25 a day by the end of 2010 than would have been the

3

case without the crisis, and between 30,000 and 50,000 children may have died of malnutrition in 2009 in Sub-Saharan Africa because of the crisis (Friedman and Schady 2009). Moreover, the slowdown is expected to cut heavily into government revenues in poor countries. Countries eligible for soft loans and grants from the International Development Association of the World Bank may require as much as $35 billion to $50 billion in additional funding just to maintain 2008 program levels, never mind the resources necessary to fund additional demands brought upon by the crisis.

The outlook remains clouded by uncertainties and the challenge of unwinding the stimulus

Many uncertainties continue to surround the short-term outlook for developing countries. Principal among these is the extent to which private sector consumption and investment demand will respond to the pickup in activity prompted by fiscal and monetary stimulus and the inventory cycle. Should the response be weaker than expected in the baseline projection or should the stimulus be withdrawn too quickly, the recovery could stall. Although a double-dip recession in the sense of a return to negative global growth rates is unlikely, developing-country growth could come in as low as 5.1 percent in 2010 and 5.4 percent in 2011, with some countries potentially recording negative growth for one or more quarters.

A related but opposite risk is that the stimulus is not retracted quickly enough. In the case of fiscal policy, the risk is mainly one of increased indebtedness and unnecessary crowding out of private sector investment. On the monetary policy side, the risk is that the vast monetary expansion that has been undertaken begins to gain traction, potentially overinflating the global economy. This could recreate liquidity conditions similar to those that created the bubbles that precipitated the crisis, causing global imbalances to reemerge and forcing a much more abrupt tightening of policy—possibly even

a second recession. Indeed, in some middle-income countries, very loose monetary conditions may already be generating asset price bubbles in local real-estate and other asset markets.

Impact of the boom period on developing-country potential

In some ways, the crisis and recession from which the world economy is currently emerging resemble previous boom-bust cycles. Like many other major crises, the current one is characterized by a sharp reduction in economic activity following an extended period of rapid and ultimately unsustainable credit expansion, accompanied by excessive risk taking by financial institutions.

At the same time the current crisis differs from previous ones in fundamental ways. From a global perspective, this crisis is the most severe and widespread downturn since 1945. Global GDP is estimated to have contracted by 2.2 percent in 2009 (the first absolute decline in global GDP among the postwar crises). Even in 2011 demand is projected to remain 5 percent below the global economy's productive potential, which is almost twice the output gap during the next most severe recession (1982–83).

Moreover, in contrast with earlier downturns, the current crisis struck virtually every developing country hard, even though, with the important exception of many in Europe and Central Asia, most countries did not exhibit unsustainable macroeconomic imbalances (figure O.4). Outside of Europe and Central Asia, regional inflation rates averaged about 6 percent or lower (well below the double-digit rates in most regions during the early 1990s); most regional current account balances were near zero or strongly positive; and ratios of debt to gross national income were modest. The importance of prudent macroeconomic policies was revealed during the crisis, as the countries with the largest imbalances suffered the biggest declines in output (see chapter 3).

That the acute phase of the crisis was deeper than past ones may have important longer-term

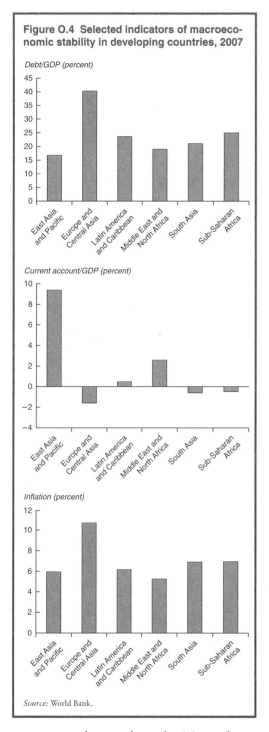

Figure O.4 Selected indicators of macroeconomic stability in developing countries, 2007

Debt/GDP (percent)

Current account/GDP (percent)

Inflation (percent)

Source: World Bank.

so many countries are affected, unemployment will remain high longer, skills will deteriorate, otherwise healthy firms may go bankrupt, and the overall level of economic dislocation and associated economic costs will remain high. Just passing through the crisis may have a sustained negative impact on productivity and the future path of economic growth. In some economies, prolonged weakness in demand could provoke the disappearance of whole sectors instead of just some companies. This could be especially the case for declining sectors. Similarly, an uneven recovery with growth and economic dynamism concentrated in one region versus another could sway the path of investment, making lagging countries look weaker and possibly creating new comparative advantages in the leading regions. Global trade patterns may be irrevocably altered.

How these forces will play out and the policies that should be put in place to respond to them merit in-depth exploration. However, dealing with all of the potential consequences of the crisis for developing countries lies outside of the scope of this publication.

The approach to the medium-term consequences of the crisis described in the pages that follow is more narrowly oriented toward the consequences for developing countries of the changes in financial conditions observed over the past decade and those that can be expected in the next 5–10 years. Initially, the focus is on how the boom in global financial markets affected credit conditions, investment, and growth prospects in developing countries and on the factors that help to explain which countries benefited most from the boom. It then switches to an examination of how changes in the regulatory environment, risk aversion, and the policy environment are likely to affect financial conditions, investment, and growth in developing countries.

Not all countries benefited fully from the liquidity boom

The liquidity boom in high-income countries during the first seven years of the 21st century

consequences for growth, productivity, and even the structure of the world economy going forward. Because the shock is so deep and because created favorable financial conditions in both high-income and developing countries. Much more intensive use of a range of financial innovations, including the securitization of loans and the development of off-balance-sheet vehicles, allowed banks to off-load an important portion of their loan portfolios onto capital and money markets. Effectively, these innovations allowed unregulated securities to support a portfolio of loans much like the traditional banking sector—but without capital requirements and under a much less stringent regulatory framework. That permitted an unprecedented leveraging of equity capital, and the rapid expansion of liquidity that ensued helped to drive down interest rates, interest rate premiums, and the cost of capital in both high-income and developing countries (figure O.5).

As a result, domestic banking sectors and the quantity of domestic credit available within developing countries increased quickly. At the global level, international banking sector credits grew twice as fast as nominal GDP, and the quantity of capital flowing to low- and middle-income economies surged. Overall private sector lending increased by 5.5 percent of GDP; the ratio of international capital inflows to GDP increased by about 5 percentage points; and stock market capitalization increased by 79 percent of GDP (table O.2).

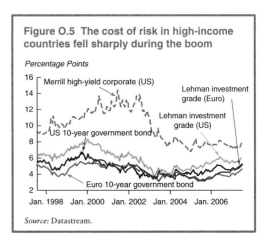

Figure O.5 The cost of risk in high-income countries fell sharply during the boom

Percentage Points

Merrill high-yield corporate (US)
Lehman investment grade (Euro)
Lehman investment grade (US)
US 10-year government bond
Euro 10-year government bond

Source: Datastream.

The ensuing investment boom boosted the supply potential of developing countries

The liquidity boom fed an investment boom in developing countries that prompted a rapid expansion in the supply potential of low- and middle-income countries but with limited impact on goods inflation in most countries. On average, investment-to-GDP ratios in developing countries increased by 5.5 percentage points, ranging from a 1.4 percentage point increase in Latin America and the Caribbean to an 8.1 percentage point rise in South Asia.

As a result, between 2000 and 2007 capital-to-output ratios in developing countries

Table O.2   Regional distribution of changes in financing conditions, 2000–07

Region	Cost of capital	Capital inflows	Stock market capitalization	Private credit by deposit money banks	Investment
	(basis points)	(percent of GDP)			
Developing countries	−400	5.0	79	5.5	5.5
Low-income countries					2.3
Middle-income countries					5.6
East-Asia and Pacific	−134	2.0	118	−10.7	5.5
Europe and Central Asia	−866	12.0	60	15.7	4.9
Latin America and the Caribbean	−471	2.0	40	2.2	1.4
Middle East and North Africa	269	2.0	36	6.2	5.0
South Asia	−142	7.0	107	14.8	8.1
Sub-Saharan Africa	−685	4.0	59	6.8	3.6

Sources: World Bank; Beck and Demirgüç-Kunt 2009.
Note: Regional values are simple averages of countries, except for investment rates, which are weighted averages.

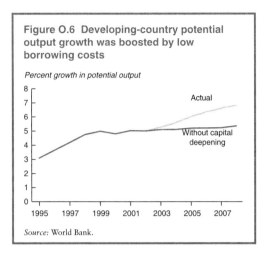

Figure O.6 Developing-country potential output growth was boosted by low borrowing costs

Percent growth in potential output

Source: World Bank.

Table O.3 Decomposition of increase in potential output growth directly attributable to capital deepening

Regions	Change in growth rate of potential output (2003–07 versus 1995–2003)		
	Total	Due to capital deepening	Share due to capital deepening
	(percentage points)		(percent)
Developing	1.5	0.6	40.3
Middle-income	1.5	0.6	39.8
Low-income	1.3	0.8	63.7
East Asia and Pacific (excluding China)	0.4	−0.1	−19.8
China	0.3	0.9	283.5
Europe and Central Asia	3.1	0.6	18.7
Latin America and the Caribbean	0.3	0.1	46.6
Middle East and North Africa	0.8	0.5	66.7
South Asia	1.4	1.1	78.5
Sub-Saharan Africa	1.9	1.5	79.5

Source: World Bank.

were about 10 percentage points higher than they would have been had investment rates held stable at their 2002 levels. The increase in capital services provided by the additional capital contributed to about 40 percent of the 1.5 percentage point increase in the rate of growth of potential output (the level of output if capital and labor were fully employed) during this period (figure O.6 and table O.3). In so far as the rising share of new capital embodying the latest technology contributed to the observed increase in total factor productivity growth during this period, the actual contribution of the boom to developing-country potential was even higher.

The notable exception was in the Europe and Central Asia region. Despite experiencing the largest increase in intermediation, much of the additional resources went into consumption. As a consequence, investment-to-GDP ratios in the region increased by only 4.9 percent, less than the 5.5 percent average for all developing countries considered as a whole. And in contrast with other regions, the expansion in domestic credit fueled a consumption binge that generated significant domestic and external imbalances and ultimately unstable macroeconomic conditions.

Economic policies are critical to understanding cross-country differences in intermediation

Lower borrowing costs were the largest identifiable factor behind the increase in intermediation in developing countries between 1998 and 2008. Nevertheless, other factors remain critical in understanding the cross-country differences in the level of intermediation (and in the increases observed since the 1980s). The quality of institutions and levels of market openness are associated with 56 and 37 percent of the variaion in the average level of intermediation between developing countries in the top and bottom quartiles according to the ratio of domestic credit to GDP, respectively. In practical terms, this finding suggests that an improvement in institutional quality in Sub-Saharan Africa to roughly the level observed in Latin America could generate an increase in the stock of domestic credit to the private sector of about 12 percent of GDP and in international finance of about 2 percent of GDP.

Countries with relatively open economies, strong institutions, and supportive investment climates enjoyed the largest increases in external flows during the boom. Resource-rich countries also fared well in attracting external capital, in part because their resources provided relatively secure collateral that partially compensated for the weak quality of their institutions.

Countries with good regulatory environments were also more successful in transforming increased financing into increased investment and, as a result, increased long-term supply potential. Inflows of foreign direct investment and domestic credit creation were associated with larger investment and growth effects than were equity or debt-creating inflows.

Medium-term implications of the bust for finance in developing countries

The short-term costs of the financial crisis have been severe and discouraging. In many countries, the sharp contraction in activity wiped out several years worth of the additional GDP gains that the above-average growth of the preceding years had produced. That a crisis rooted in regulatory failure in high-income countries has had such pronounced effects on developing countries may have caused a backlash against financial and trade liberalization, particularly among the many developing countries that implemented stricter fiscal policy regimes, improved regulatory institutions, and introduced more flexible exchange rates during the 1990s and 2000s. Although these measures likely prevented the buildup of domestic vulnerabilities during the boom period, which would have made the crisis much more serious, they did not entirely insulate developing countries from its effects.

Tighter financial conditions are in the offing, implying reduced levels of finance

The lessons and fallout from the crisis are likely to shape financial policies and market reactions for years to come. Beyond the immediate and unprecedented global recession that it has provoked, the crisis can be expected to significantly alter the global financial landscape over the next 5 to 10 years.

These changes may include:

- a tightening and broadening of the scope of financial market regulation;

- the introduction of rules and policies designed to isolate developing countries from excessive financial market volatility;
- increasing reliance on domestic intermediation and efforts to deepen regional financial markets;
- a generalized increase in risk aversion; and
- a step backward from some of the innovative financial instruments that were most associated with the financial crisis.

Anticipated regulatory changes in high-income countries are expected to broaden the range of financial institutions and activities that come under supervision, increase reporting criterion, reduce the scope for using derivatives and other innovative financial instruments, and pay greater attention to inter-bank dependencies and cross-border activities. These changes, plus increased risk aversion and the necessity for banks in high-income countries to rebuild their capital, suggest that liquidity will be more scarce and expensive in the years to come.

Possible impacts of scarcer and more expensive finance

The extent to which international financial conditions impinge on developing-country finance goes well beyond the traditional current account financing of developing countries (see below). Indeed, in aggregate, developing countries are net lenders to high-income countries. Once cross-border flows have been netted out, developing countries invested more of their savings into high-income countries than high-income countries invested in them between 2000 and 2008.

However, for many countries with capital shortages, external savings are still a critical source of finance for investment. Excluding China and the oil exporters, the remaining developing countries are, on average, net importers of capital. Of the 53 developing countries that faced an external financing gap in 2009, most had current account deficits of 5 percent

Table O.4 Contribution of private-source debt inflows to external finance of developing countries with current account deficits, average 2003–07

	Number of countries with current account deficits	Current account deficit (% of GDP)	Net debt inflows from private sources (% of GDP)
All countries	53	6.3	2.2
Low income	16	5.8	0.8
Lower middle income	20	6.1	0.8
Upper middle income	17	7.1	5.3
Of which: ECA	8	8.5	8.1

Source: World Bank.
Note: Data on current account deficits and debt inflows are simple averages of country numbers. Excludes small island economies.

of GDP or more, with private-source net debt inflows equal to about 2.2 percent of GDP (or almost half the deficit)—0.8 percent if the countries in Europe and Central Asia are excluded from the mix (table O.4). For these countries a significant withdrawal of external financing could have serious consequences for domestic investment and long-term potential output.

Weaker and more expensive capital at the global level also will affect financial conditions in developing countries indirectly by influencing conditions in domestic financial markets (changes in the cost of and rate of return on external investment and borrowing, increased competitive pressure, technology, and knowledge transfers).

Tighter regulations, along with the transformation of many investment banks into traditional banks, may reduce the supply of financial services, including the intermediation of developing countries' capital issuances (figure O.7). Over the past 10 years, American investment banks participated in 86 percent of the value of developing-country initial public offerings, or 32 percent of the number of deals, and the operation of mutual funds and other investment vehicles allowed individual and institutional investors in high-income countries to place money in developing markets. While developing-country competitors could pick up some of these activities and while high-income firms will almost certainly continue their involvement in this business, the likely result is that developing-country firms will have less access to capital. Moreover,

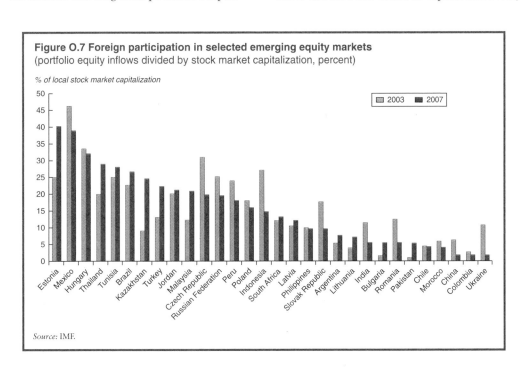

Figure O.7 Foreign participation in selected emerging equity markets
(portfolio equity inflows divided by stock market capitalization, percent)

% of local stock market capitalization

Legend: 2003, 2007

Source: IMF.

overall productivity will be affected if less active foreign investment banks have a comparative advantage in identifying firms and products with strong potential in global markets.

Tighter regulation in high-income countries and the need for parent banks to build up their capital may also impede foreign banks' participation in developing countries, which could have negative consequences for their development—especially for poorer countries with good regulatory regimes. Foreign banks can serve as a conduit for foreign savings into a developing country and can contribute to greater intermediation at lower cost by increasing competition. This can be especially important in less developed countries. However, the quality of domestic institutions is important. In the presence of weak institutions, foreign banks' participation may have no or even a net negative effect on intermediation and cost saving, if, as has happened in some regions, they cherry-pick the best clients and merely displace domestic banks.

Foreign direct investment (FDI) should be less constrained than debt flows by the rise in risk aversion and more stringent regulation. However, parent firms will face higher capital costs, and these are likely to reduce their ability to finance individual projects. As a result, FDI inflows are projected to decline from recent peaks of 3.9 percent of developing-country GDP to around 2.8–3.0 percent of GDP. The real-side consequences of such a decline could be serious because foreign direct investment represents as much as 20 percent of total investment in Sub-Saharan Africa, Europe and Central Asia, and Latin America (figure O.8).

Of course, access to foreign capital is not an unmixed blessing, as both this crisis and past crises serve to remind us. Historically, private capital flows into developing countries, notably debt flows such as bank and bond lending, have been very volatile (figure O.9). Because such capital flows can stop, or even reverse abruptly, countries that become heavily reliant upon them can be very vulnerable. From this point of view, a less integrated global financial

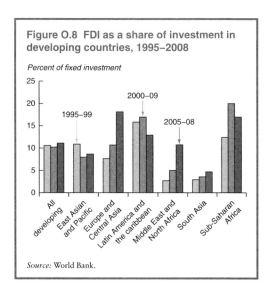

Figure O.8 FDI as a share of investment in developing countries, 1995–2008

Percent of fixed investment

Source: World Bank.

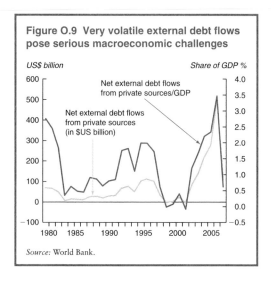

Figure O.9 Very volatile external debt flows pose serious macroeconomic challenges

Source: World Bank.

system could have some benefits if it reduced developing countries' dependence on volatile capital flows.

Indeed, a central lesson from this boom-bust cycle is that although the very loose financial conditions contributed to the growth boom in developing countries, the boom was not sustainable and the crisis, loss in output, and associated social dislocation were essential and arguably inevitable consequences of the boom. If better regulation of financial flows going forward suc-ceeds in reducing volatility and the frequency of boom-bust cycles, the benefits of more stable and sustainable conditions could outweigh the costs (see below) of more expensive and less abundant capital.

Countries may seek to insulate themselves from global financial markets. . .

Of course, the extent to which a given country experiences volatility in financial markets, as well as the consequences for the real economy, also depends on domestic policies. Despite the fact that countries with prudent and open policies tended to benefit from the boom and suffer least in the bust, the negative impacts of this crisis, which encompassed many devel-oping countries that had managed the inflows associated with the boom period in a very prudent manner, may induce authorities in de-veloping countries to take additional steps to reduce their economies' vulnerability to large changes in conditions outside their control.

In the past, developing countries have re-acted to crises by increasing their official re-serves or imposed capital controls as a means of reducing the domestic consequences of ex-ternal shocks. Such self-insurance mechanisms can be expensive. By some estimates, recent reserve holdings of developing countries have cost as much as 1 percent of GDP to maintain. Nor are such reserves necessarily effective. For example during the recent crisis, there was only a limited correlation between the sever-ity of the real-side downturn experienced by developing countries and the level of reserves they held going into the crisis period. This lack of correlation does not mean that reserves did not help cushion the shock—indeed, countries with low reserves and high current account deficits tended to be hardest hit by the crisis. However, it does suggest that beyond a point, additional reserves offer little additional pro-tection from this kind of international shock observed and that countries should carefully weigh the additional costs associated with

accumulating and maintaining even higher reserves.

Another strategy that has been followed after earlier crises has been the imposition of capital controls or a slowdown in liberaliza-tion. While such steps may reduce the risk that an economy develops a level of external in-debtedness that makes it vulnerable to a rapid shift in sentiment, it does so at the expense of the longer-term benefits (such as technol-ogy transfers, increased investment, and fur-ther integration into the global economy) that might have accompanied the excluded capital inflows. In addition, controls on capital are often ineffective, particularly when they are used to support substantial exchange rate misalignment.

. . . and increase the role of domestic and regional alternatives

Faced with a less active external financing sys-tem, authorities and entrepreneurs in developing countries may take steps to promote domestic financial intermediation as an alternative to re-liance on foreign capital. Given the importance that intermediation has for development, such a strategy could have significant benefits for those middle-income countries that already have a strong framework for financial intermediation, by increasing the efficiency of domestic financial intermediaries through learning by doing and economies of scale.

For low-income countries, the longer-run ef-fects of a weaker international system may be more serious. In the short run, low-income coun-tries may be less directly affected by the crisis-induced increase in borrowing costs—simply because their economies are not well intermedi-ated. However, a weaker international financial system could deny them investments critical to their development, particularly because defi-ciencies in domestic intermediation systems are likely to prevent them from compensating for a reduced foreign presence (figure O.10).

The crisis is also likely to result in greater regional cooperation, which could strengthen financial services by capturing economies of scale and facilitating risk sharing by

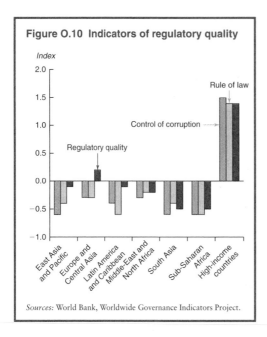

Figure O.10 Indicators of regulatory quality

Sources: World Bank, Worldwide Governance Indicators Project.

management strategies that contributed to boosting liquidity are all factors that are likely to increase borrowing costs in both high-income and developing countries.

The overall expansion of investment and growth during the boom period, without the creation of significant inflationary pressures or external imbalances in many developing countries, suggests that in these countries the boom relieved what may have been a binding capital constraint on growth, albeit in what proved to be a temporary and unsustainable manner. The necessary and desirable tightening of regulations will hopefully reduce the frequency of boom-bust cycles and provide a more stable financial environment for developing countries. However, higher borrowing costs are likely to mean a temporary decline in the rate of growth of developing-country potential output. Financial services are critical to the smooth functioning of an economy, and the level of domestic intermediation (for example, the ratio of domestic bank credit to GDP) is strongly correlated with economic development (figure O.11).

The extent to which anticipated changes in financial markets will increase borrowing

pooling reserves. Such cooperation may also help strengthen South-South financial flows, which are likely to be important in sustaining FDI flows to many developing countries. However, progress in regional financial cooperation has been slow in developing countries. Further, such arrangements are likely to be of greatest benefit to regions that already have relatively robust domestic financial systems, such as East Asia and the Pacific. Poor countries with weak institutions can benefit through integration with stronger regional economies, but the promotion of regional integration with other countries with weak institutions is unlikely to be beneficial.

Medium-term impact on the supply potential of developing countries

Increased risk aversion, the necessity for banks to recapitalize, increased borrowing requirements from high-income governments, and the falling into disrepute of many of the risk-

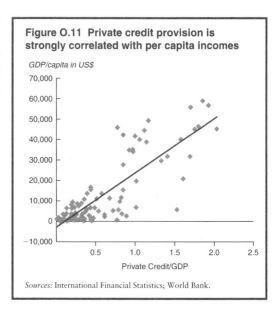

Figure O.11 Private credit provision is strongly correlated with per capita incomes

Sources: International Financial Statistics; World Bank.

costs in developing countries will depend on many factors, including the level of interest rates in high-income countries. Currently, under the influence of the extraordinary steps taken by the U.S. Federal Reserve Bank and other central banks, medium (1-year) and long-term (10-year) interest rates on U.S. government securities are 0.4 and 3.8 percentage points, respectively—some 290 and 60 basis points lower than during the boom period. Similarly, developing-country risk premiums have fallen and appear to have stabilized at close to their pre-crisis levels or about 150 basis points higher than during the boom period. If real interest rates in high-income countries return to their pre-boom levels and if the historical relationship between these base rates and interest rate spreads remain unchanged, the borrowing costs developing countries face could rise by between 110 and 220 basis points compared with their boom-period levels.

Just as the decline in borrowing costs during the first few years of this decade was associated with a marked pickup in investment activity and potential growth rates, higher borrowing costs going forward will tend to reduce investment rates and result in lower levels of potential output than would have been observed otherwise. Firms can be expected to react to higher capital costs by employing less capital and more labor and natural resources per unit of output, so economy-wide capital-to-output and investment-to-GDP ratios will decline. During the transition period to the new, lower capital-output ratio, the rate of growth of potential output could slow by between 0.2 and 0.7 percentage points from the average of 6.2 percent rate observed during the 2003–07 period (figure O.12). Over the long run, unless offset by other factors (notably improved domestic policies, see below), this substitution away from capital-intensive techniques could reduce the supply potential in developing countries by between 3 and 5 percent and potentially by as much as 8 percent.

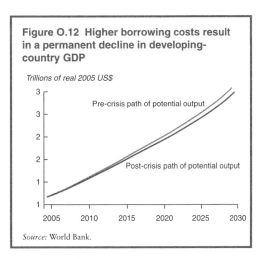

Figure O.12 Higher borrowing costs result in a permanent decline in developing-country GDP

Trillions of real 2005 US$

Pre-crisis path of potential output

Post-crisis path of potential output

Source: World Bank.

Developing countries can mitigate the effects of weaker international conditions

Although there is little that developing countries can do to prevent a deterioration in global financial conditions, they should not stand by passively. Much can be done to mitigate the costs of a tightening of global financial conditions by reducing the domestic cost of intermediation through strengthening regional and domestic institutions or by improving long-term productivity growth.

Inefficiency of domestic financial sectors resulting from corruption, weak regulatory institutions, poor protection of property rights, and excessive limits on competition can make borrowing costs in developing countries 1,000 basis points higher than in high-income countries (even more so if the even higher costs imposed by informal lenders are taken into account).

Improvements in the policies and institutions governing the financial sector can thus have a significant impact in boosting domestic financial intermediation, one that can outweigh any potential negative impact of higher global risk premiums. Simulations suggest that if developing countries continue to improve policies and other fundamentals, so that their interest spreads fall by an average of 25 basis points a year, they would more than offset the long-term effects of the financial crisis—producing a 13 percent increase in long-term potential output and increases in potential output growth of about 0.3 percent per year by 2020.

Efforts to increase domestic financial intermediation should focus on strengthening institutions, not on discriminating against foreign capital. Especially in countries with poor regulations or weak enforcement capacities, discouraging foreign capital could have the detrimental effect of forcing firms to rely on more expensive domestic sources of finance and potentially reducing the overall level of intermediation. Suppressing foreign capital also could reduce firms' access to new technology, expertise, and international market contacts.

Conclusion

The international financial conditions of the boom period were unsustainable and resulted in the extremely disruptive and costly crisis from which the global economy is only now emerging. At the same time they demonstrated that, when exposed lower capital costs, developing countries were capable of sustaining significantly higher growth rates without generating higher inflation.

Over the medium term, international capital costs are going to be higher than they were during the boom period. As a result, developing-country growth potential will remain well below recent highs, which is likely to be a source of frustration for many countries. While some prudent reforms to reduce the sensitivity of domestic economies to some of the more volatile forms of international capital may be advisable, policy makers need to remain mindful of the benefits that financial openness and improved intermediation can bring.

Looking forward, it is not desirable to recreate the unstable and unsustainable international conditions of the boom period. However, the domestic savings in developing countries represent an enormous growth potential that is waiting to be released through reforms aimed at reinforcing and growing domestic intermediation. Although such reforms will take time to bear fruit over the longer term they may once again place developing countries on the higher growth path that the crisis has derailed.

References

Beck, Thorsten, and Asli Demirgüç-Kunt. 2009. "Financial Institutions and Markets across Countries and over Time: Data and Analysis." Policy Research Working Paper 4943. World Bank, Washington, DC.

Friedman, Jed, and Norbert Schady. 2009. "How Many More Infants Are Likely to Die in Africa as a Result of the Global Financial Crisis?" Policy Research Working Paper 5023. World Bank, Washington, DC.

1

Prospects for Developing Economies

The acute phase of the financial crisis has passed and a global economic recovery is under way. Moreover, the recovery is fragile and expected to slow in the second half of 2010 as the growth impact of fiscal and monetary measures wane and the current inventory cycle runs its course. Indeed, industrial production growth is already slowing (albeit from very high rates). As a result, employment growth will remain weak and unemployment is expected to remain high for many years. The overall strength of the recovery and its durability will depend on the extent to which household- and business-sector demand strengthens over the next few quarters. While the baseline scenario projects that global growth will firm to 2.7 percent in 2010 and 3.2 percent in 2011 after a 2.2 percent decline in 2009, neither a double-dip scenario, where growth slows appreciably in 2011, or a strengthening recovery can be ruled out.

Financial markets have stabilized and are recovering, but remain weak. Interbank liquidity as measured by the difference between the interest rates commercial banks charge one another and what they have to pay to central bankers have declined from an unprecedented peak of 366 basis points in dollar markets to less than 15 basis points—a level close to its "normal" pre-crisis range. Currencies, which fell worldwide against the U.S. dollar in the immediate aftermath of the crisis, have largely recovered their pre-crisis levels. And international capital flows to developing countries have recovered—with a rapid run-up during the last months of 2009. Also, borrowing costs for emerging market borrowers have stabilized over the last few quarters, but remain elevated.

However, private sector firms remain shut out from international banking markets. Moreover, the Dubai World event and ripple effects to credit downgrades for Greece and Mexico can be expected to once again raise concerns about sovereign debt sustainability and will impact risk assessments, capital flows, and financial markets in 2010.

The real economy is recovering as well. Although global industrial production in October 2009 remained 5 percent below its level a year earlier, it is recovering, with output in both high-income and developing countries expanding at more than a 12 percent annualized rate (or saar) in the third quarter of 2009. Just as a sharp drop in inventories contributed to a precipitous initial decline in industrial production, the stabilization of inventory levels has contributed to a strong rebound in production, and this factor is expected to support industrial production, even as growth rates start to come down.

Trade too is recovering but remains depressed. Quarterly growth rates have moved into positive territory in recent months, but the U.S. dollar value of trade was still off 17 percent from its September 2009 level. Lower commodity prices mean that the volume of trade has fared better, but it is nevertheless down by 3 percent from a year ago.

The most marked increases have been in developing East Asia, and reflect, at least partly, the 4 trillion renminbi (or 12 percent of GDP) fiscal stimulus put into place by the Chinese authorities extending through 2010 (roughly half spent).

Much of that stimulus has found its way into imported raw commodities and investment goods. Indeed, partly because of restocking, Chinese demand for key metals has been supportive of commodity prices, which have recovered about one-third of their earlier declines. Nevertheless, international metal prices, measured in U.S. dollars, are 20 percent below their July 2008 levels, oil prices are 44 percent lower, and food prices 24 percent lower, with global oil demand some 2 percent lower than its peak level of 87 million barrels a day in 2007.

The combination of the abrupt fall in commodity prices and ample spare capacity worldwide has resulted in median inflation in developing countries falling from more than 10 percent in August 2008 to about 1 percent in October 2009.

Global imbalances narrowed further during the crisis. This trend may be largely cyclical, as it relates to substantial declines in the U.S. trade deficit, the Chinese trade surplus, and the price of oil. The durability of the narrowing will depend on the speed with which the United States can unwind its fiscal and monetary stimulus and the extent to which stimulus-based infrastructure investment in China contributes to higher domestic demand rather than additional export capacity.

Although the real-side effects of the crisis have been large and serious, economic activity in most developing countries is recovering and overall growth is expected to pick up from the anemic performance of 1.2 percent in 2009 to 5.2 percent in 2010 and to 5.8 percent in 2011 (table 1.1). Although much lower than the 6.9 percent growth rate that developing countries averaged between 2003 and 2008, these rates are well above the 3.3 percent average performance during the 1990s. Excluding China and India, the remaining developing countries are projected to grow at a 3.3 and

4.0 percent rate in 2010 and 2011, respectively, compared with 5.4 percent growth on average between 2003 and 2008. Countries in developing Europe and Central Asia have been hardest hit by the crisis and are expected to have the least marked recovery, with GDP expanding by only 2.7 percent in 2010 and by 3.6 percent in 2011.

The combination of the steep decline in activity in 2009 and the relatively weak projected recovery means that developing economies will still be operating about 3 percent below their level of potential output[1]—and unemployment, although on the decline will still be a serious problem. Moreover, the impacts on poverty and human suffering in these countries will be very real. Some 30,000–50,000 additional children may have died of malnutrition in 2009 in Sub-Saharan Africa because of the crisis (UNSCN 2009; Friedman and Schady 2009), and globally by the end of 2010, 90 million more people are expected to be living in poverty than would have been the case without the crisis.

Few of the poorest countries will have the fiscal space to respond to the economic dislocation caused by the crisis without significant additional financial assistance. It is estimated that IDA countries (those eligible for soft loans and grants from the International Development Association of the World Bank) will require an additional $35 billion to $50 billion in funding just to maintain current levels of programming, let alone come up with the additional funding required to meet the needs of those additional individuals thrown into poverty.[2] Worse, the recession may cause donors to reduce aid flows precisely at the moment the flows need to rise.

Great uncertainty continues to surround future prospects. Even the weak recovery outlined above is not certain. If the private sector continues to save in order to restore balance sheets, a double-dip, characterized by a further slowing of growth in 2011 is entirely possible—especially as the growth impact of fiscal stimulus wanes. A stronger recovery is also possible, if the massive traditional and

Table 1.1 The global outlook in summary

(percentage change from previous year, except interest rates and oil price)

	2007	2008	2009[h]	2010[i]	2011[i]
Global Conditions					
World trade volume	7.2	3.0	−14.4	4.3	6.2
Consumer prices					
G-7 countries[a,b]	2.0	3.1	−0.2	1.1	1.7
United States	2.9	3.8	−0.5	1.6	2.4
Commodity prices (US$ terms)					
Non-energy commodities	17.1	21.0	−21.6	5.3	0.7
Oil price (US$ per barrel)[c]	71.1	97.0	61.8	76.0	76.6
Oil price (percent change)	10.6	36.4	−36.3	23.1	0.8
Manufactures unit export value[d]	5.5	6.0	−4.9	1.5	0.7
Interest rates					
$, 6-month (percent)	5.2	3.2	1.2	1.8	2.8
€, 6-month (percent)	4.3	4.8	1.5	2.2	3.0
Real GDP growth[e]					
World	**3.9**	**1.7**	**−2.2**	**2.7**	**3.2**
Memo item: World (PPP weights)[f]	5.0	2.7	−1.0	3.5	4.0
High income	**2.6**	**0.4**	**−3.3**	**1.8**	**2.3**
OECD Countries	2.5	0.3	−3.3	1.8	2.3
Euro Area	2.7	0.5	−3.9	1.0	1.7
Japan	2.3	−1.2	−5.4	1.3	1.8
United States	2.1	0.4	−2.5	2.5	2.7
Non-OECD countries	5.4	2.6	−2.3	2.9	3.9
Developing countries	**8.1**	**5.6**	**1.2**	**5.2**	**5.8**
East Asia and Pacific	11.4	8.0	6.8	8.1	8.2
China	13.0	9.0	8.4	9.0	9.0
Indonesia	6.3	6.1	4.5	5.6	5.8
Thailand	4.9	2.6	−2.7	3.5	4.0
Europe and Central Asia	7.1	4.2	−6.2	2.7	3.6
Russia	8.1	5.6	−8.7	3.2	3.0
Turkey	4.7	0.9	−5.8	3.3	4.2
Poland	6.7	4.9	1.6	2.2	3.4
Latin America and Caribbean	5.5	3.9	−2.6	3.1	3.6
Brazil	5.7	5.1	0.1	3.6	3.9
Mexico	3.3	1.4	−7.1	3.5	3.6
Argentina	8.7	6.8	−2.2	2.3	2.4
Middle East and North Africa	5.9	4.3	2.9	3.7	4.4
Egypt[g]	7.1	7.2	4.7	5.2	6.0
Iran[g]	7.8	2.5	1.0	2.2	3.2
Algeria	3.0	3.0	2.1	3.9	4.0
South Asia	8.5	5.7	5.7	6.9	7.4
India[g]	9.1	6.1	6.0	7.5	8.0
Pakistan[g]	5.7	2.0	3.7	3.0	4.0
Bangladesh[g]	6.4	6.2	5.9	5.5	5.8
Sub-Saharan Africa	6.5	5.1	1.1	3.8	4.6
South Africa	5.5	3.7	−1.8	2.0	2.7
Nigeria	6.3	5.3	4.3	4.8	5.1
Kenya	7.1	1.7	2.8	3.7	4.8
Memorandum items					
Developing countries					
excluding transition countries	8.1	5.6	2.5	5.7	6.1
excluding China and India	6.2	4.3	−2.2	3.3	4.0

Source: World Bank.

Note: PPP = purchasing power parity; h = estimate; i = forecast.
a. Canada, France, Germany, Italy, Japan, the United Kingdom, and the United States.
b. In local currency, aggregated using 2005 GDP Weights.
c. Simple average of Dubai, Brent, and West Texas Intermediate.
d. Unit value index of manufactured exports from major economies, expressed in USD.
e. Aggregate growth rates calculated using constant 2005 U.S. dollar GDP weights.
f. Calculated using 2005 PPP weights.
g. In keeping with national practice, data for Egypt, Iran, India, Pakistan and Bangladesh
   are reported on a fiscal year basis. Expressed on a calendar year basis, GDP growth in these countries is as in the table just above.

	2008	2009[h]	2010[i]	2011[i]
Egypt	6.8	5.7	5.1	5.6
Iran	2.5	1.0	2.2	3.2
India	7.3	6.4	7.6	8.0
Pakistan	3.8	2.9	3.3	3.5
Bangladesh	6.3	6.1	5.7	5.7

untraditional monetary stimulus that has been put into place in high-income countries begins to gain traction.

Recent developments in financial markets

The unprecedented steps that were taken by policy makers in both developed and developing countries following the collapse of Lehman Brothers in September 2008 have gone a long way toward normalizing financial markets and restoring capital flows to developing countries (see World Bank, 2009c for a summary of such measures).

The immediate outflow of international capital from developing countries to safe havens in the United States and Europe has reversed itself. As a result, a large number of emerging-market exchange rates have recovered their pre-crisis levels vis-à-vis the U.S. dollar, equity markets have recovered much of their initial losses, and, capital flows to developing countries have begun to recover.

Toward the end of 2009, gross capital inflows to developing countries began to gain momentum as uncertainty subsided and risk aversion declined. On an annualized basis, total gross inflows to developing countries reached a $435 billion pace in the five months ending November 2009, up from $218 billion in the first half of the year. Although capital flows for the year as a whole remain 20 percent below their 2008 levels and well below their peaks in 2007, this recent surge in portfolio flows has raised concerns that if sustained, it could reinflate some of the asset bubbles in stock, currency, and real estate markets among developing countries that the crisis had only just begun to unwind. However, risk appetites may have been tempered by the Dubai World event and the credit rating downgrades of Greece and Mexico at the end of 2009.

Policy interest rates around the globe remain very low, although some central banks have begun tightening (e.g., Australia has already tightened by 75 basis points) or signaled their intention to begin to do so soon. In the United States, the Federal Reserve Board's federal fund rate has been hovering around 12 basis points, compared with close to 550 basis points in mid 2007. The European Central Bank's (ECB) policy rate remains in the 100-basis-point range, compared with a level of more than 400 basis points in 2008. Short-term market rates are also very low, reflecting the reduced opportunity cost of borrowing money from the monetary authority and increased confidence in the creditworthiness of counterparties within the international banking system. Reflecting policy steps to recapitalize banks and restore confidence in the international financial system, the spread between the price that commercial banks charge one another for overnight lending and the overnight rate charged by central banks—a common measure of banks' confidence in one another—has fallen from an unprecedented 365 basis points at the peak of the crisis to a more normal level of less than 15 basis points (figure 1.1, panel a). As a part of these efforts, central banks have taken a number of extraordinary steps including lending directly to private firms and intervening in secondary mortgage markets. As a result, their balance sheets have ballooned.

As a result of these and other measures, the freeze-up of financial markets that characterized the autumn of 2008 has eased considerably, and the spreads facing emerging-market borrowers have declined as well (figure 1.1, panel b), with commercial borrowers able to access funds for a premium of 359 basis points and sovereign borrowers at a premium of about 300 basis points. While these spreads are higher than the pre-Lehman average of about 180 basis points, they remain substantially lower than their long-term averages, the fruit of improved fundamentals of many developing countries and years of policy reform.

As spreads declined and the acute risk aversion of the immediate post-crisis period eased, investors started moving back some of the money that had been withdrawn from developing-country capital markets. As a

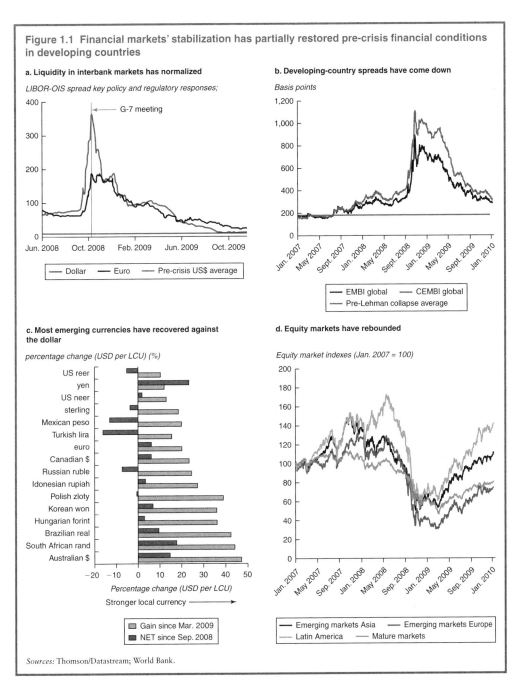

Figure 1.1 Financial markets' stabilization has partially restored pre-crisis financial conditions in developing countries

a. Liquidity in interbank markets has normalized

LIBOR-OIS spread key policy and regulatory responses;

— Dollar — Euro — Pre-crisis US$ average

b. Developing-country spreads have come down

Basis points

— EMBI global — CEMBI global
— Pre-Lehman collapse average

c. Most emerging currencies have recovered against the dollar

percentage change (USD per LCU) (%)

US reer
yen
US neer
sterling
Mexican peso
Turkish lira
euro
Canadian $
Russian ruble
Idonesian rupiah
Polish zloty
Korean won
Hungarian forint
Brazilian real
South African rand
Australian $

Percentage change (USD per LCU)

Stronger local currency ⟶

☐ Gain since Mar. 2009
☐ NET since Sep. 2008

d. Equity markets have rebounded

Equity market indexes (Jan. 2007 = 100)

— Emerging markets Asia — Emerging markets Europe
— Latin America — Mature markets

Sources: Thomson/Datastream; World Bank.

result, beginning roughly in March 2009 developing-country currencies began appreciating against the dollar (figure 1.1, panel c), their stock markets began rebounding, recovering between one-third and one-half of their initial losses (figure 1.1, panel d), helping to

restore global confidence by restoring some of the wealth initially destroyed in the crisis.

The revival in stock market activity has supported new equity placements by emerging economies, which totaled $98 billion in the first eleven months of 2009, up sharply from

$66 billion during the same period in 2008. Although initial public offering (IPO) activity remained subdued during the first half of 2009, there were signs of a sharp rebound in the third quarter, on the strength of large deals by China, Brazil, and India, which together accounted for about 85 percent of all emerging-market transactions year-to-date, compared with an average share of 65 percent in the five years through 2007. The relatively strong fundamentals in these countries appear to have raised investor preference for these economies. Gross equity flows to the remaining developing countries were still compressed at 0.15 percent of their GDP in 2009, versus 0.42 percent (of GDP) on average during the five years ending 2007.

Developing countries' access to international capital markets has also revived. Both sovereign and corporate borrowers have benefited from rising global liquidity, improved market conditions, and better long-term fundamentals of emerging economies vis-à-vis advanced economies. The recovery in corporate bond issuance by developing countries reached $109 billion during 2009, up almost $45 billion compared with 2008. During the first trading week of 2010, Turkey and the Philippines tapped international bond markets for $2 billion and about $1.5 billion, respectively, taking advantage of continuing favorable conditions. The improved bond and equity markets reflect a normalization of financial markets and, to an unknown extent, the opening up of a carry trade precipitated by low real interest rates in high-income countries. Some middle-income countries (notably Chile and Brazil) are attracting very large inflows, which if sustained at current rates, pose real policy challenges and could generate significant stress. Some countries have sought to use increased intervention or other measures such as a financial operational tax (Brazil)—even as the effectiveness of these measures is unknown.

In stark contrast to the recovery in bond and equity markets, cross-border bank lending remains weak as global banks continue to consolidate and deleverage in an effort to

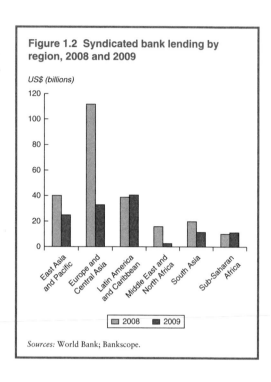

Figure 1.2 Syndicated bank lending by region, 2008 and 2009

Sources: World Bank; Bankscope.

rebuild their balance sheets. In 2009, syndicated loan deals involving developing countries amounted to $123 billion, compared with $236 billion in 2008. There was a surprising jump in December 2009, when loans amounted to $27 billion, mostly led by $10 billion lending for energy-related projects in Papua New Guinea and $6.5 billion trade finance loan to the Brazilian government (figure 1.2). Overall, banks' external claims on developing countries reported to the Bank of International Settlements (BIS) expanded by only $10 billion in the second quarter of 2009 (exchange rate adjusted), after contracting $126 billion in the first quarter of 2009 and $279 billion in the fourth quarter of 2008.

Prospects for a resurgence in bank lending in the near term are likely to be muted (longer-term prospects are discussed in chapter 3), especially in regions such as Europe and Central Asia where mounting nonperforming loans and large domestic adjustments are likely to restrain both the demand and supply side for lending. At the same time, lending to natural-resource-rich countries is likely to remain robust.

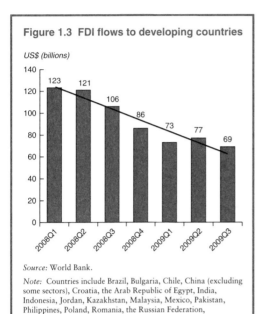

Figure 1.3 FDI flows to developing countries

US$ (billions)

Source: World Bank.

Note: Countries include Brazil, Bulgaria, Chile, China (excluding some sectors), Croatia, the Arab Republic of Egypt, India, Indonesia, Jordan, Kazakhstan, Malaysia, Mexico, Pakistan, Philippines, Poland, Romania, the Russian Federation, South Africa, Thailand, Turkey, Ukraine, and R. B. de Venezuela.

In contrast with debt-creating flows, foreign direct investment (FDI) has yet to show signs of rebounding. FDI tends to be the most stable source of international capital, but inflows nevertheless have declined by 40 percent since the first quarter of 2008 and stood at $69 billion in 2009Q3 (figure 1.3). Although these flows are expected to have recovered during the last quarter, inflows to all developing countries for the year as a whole are expected to come in at $385 billion, only 30 percent of their 2008 values. While resource-related investment has picked up in 2009 after the pause in late 2008, investment in the banking sector, which led the surge in recent years, remains limited.

The recent decisions of the Dubai World holding company to ask its creditors for a six-month standstill on debt payments, and of rating agencies to downgrade Greece and Mexico's credit rating, remind that the echoes of the crisis continue to be felt. Global markets have largely been unaffected by these developments and capital flows to emerging markets have strengthened in recent months. So far,

these stronger inflows have only partially offset the sharp reduction in flows following the crisis and have not re-created bubble conditions. However, should these strong inflows persist or strengthen, asset bubbles could begin to reinflate, leaving countries vulnerable to a second sudden stop in external finance.

Prospects and implications for developing-country financing needs

Overall, net private capital flows to developing countries in 2009 are estimated to have fallen by $795 billion (relative to their high in 2007), or by almost 70 percent. Even with recovery on the horizon, projected flows in 2010 are only $517 billion, or 3.2 percent of GDP. Lower-income countries will suffer the most from this shrinkage, because their already miniscule share of total private capital flows (i.e., 2.6 percent in 2007) is expected to dwindle to almost nothing in 2010. Even though small in absolute terms, the capital inflows to these low-income countries represent a significant share of national income and investment, and their loss will certainly have a severe impact on the ability of these countries to meet their financing needs in the short to medium term (see chapter 3).

While capital inflows have declined sharply, the ex ante financing needs of developing countries have not changed significantly. Based on the current account deficit projections for 2010, along with schedules of private foreign debt coming due, the total external financing needs of developing countries are expected to be on the order of $1.1 trillion in 2010, compared with an estimated $1.2 trillion in 2009.[3] Countries in Europe and Central Asia and Latin America and the Caribbean face the largest external financing needs in 2010, projected at $447 billion and $280 billion, respectively (figure 1.4). Although smaller in magnitude, Sub-Saharan Africa's financing needs are also large, standing at nearly 12 percent of GDP.

Combining these projections with country-specific estimates of the amount of private sector financing likely to be forthcoming suggests

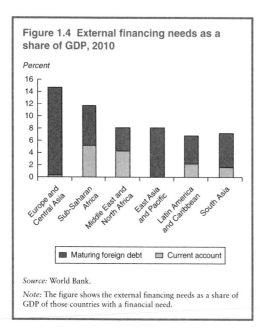

Figure 1.4 External financing needs as a share of GDP, 2010

Percent

Legend: ■ Maturing foreign debt   ▨ Current account

Source: World Bank.

Note: The figure shows the external financing needs as a share of GDP of those countries with a financial need.

However, since SDRs are allocated according to country quotas, the benefits of this move for the neediest developing countries are small.

Global growth

After a deep global recession, economic growth has turned positive, as a wide range of policy interventions has supported demand and reduced uncertainty and systemic risk in financial markets. However, the recovery is expected to be slow, as financial markets remain impaired, stimulus measures will need to be withdrawn in the not too distant future, and households in countries that suffered asset-price busts are forced to rebuild savings while struggling with high unemployment. Although global growth is expected to return to positive territory in 2010, the pace of the recovery will be slow and subject to uncertainty. After falling by an estimated 2.2 percent in 2009, global output is projected to grow 2.7 and 3.2 percent in 2010 and 2011, respectively (−1.0, 3.5, and 4.0 percent when aggregated using purchasing-power-parity weights).

The main drag on global growth is coming from the high-income countries, whose economies are expected to have contracted by 3.3 percent in 2009. Japan, which felt the consequences of the global crisis more severely than other high-income countries, experienced the sharpest growth contraction (−5.4 percent). Growth rates of 2.5 and 2.9 percent are expected in 2010 for the United States and for high-income countries that are not members of the Organisation for Economic Co-operation and Development (OECD), respectively.

The global economic crisis affected developing countries first and foremost through a sharp slowdown in global industrial activity due to a sudden cut in investment programs, consumer durable demand, and a widespread effort to reduce inventories in the face of uncertain future conditions. Falling export demand, commodity prices, and capital flows exacerbated and extended the downturn. Overall, growth in developing countries declined to an

that developing countries could face a total financing gap of as much as $315 billion in 2010.

In 2009 those countries whose ex ante financing needs exceeded private capital inflows were forced to bridge the gap either by cutting into domestic demand and via exchange rate depreciation—thereby reducing their trade deficits via lower imports, or by using other resources such as drawing down international reserves or drawing upon official assistance (or both). Overall, developing countries consumed some $362 billion worth of their international reserves during the initial phases of the crisis, while a wide range of countries increased borrowing from the International Monetary Fund (IMF), the World Bank, and various regional and bilateral development agencies. Currently, an overall count of the increase in official flows is unavailable, but the World Bank (International Bank for Reconstruction and Development, or IBRD, and IDA) alone increased its lending commitments by some $12.8 billion, while the IMF made an additional commitment of $70 billion by October 2009.

The IMF's lending resources are being tripled, to $750 billion, including a new special drawing right (SDR) allocation of $283 billion.

estimated 1.2 percent in 2009, down from 5.6 percent in 2008.

Among developing-country regions, economies in Europe and Central Asia were hit hardest by the crisis, with GDP falling 6.2 percent (with the Russian Federation contracting 8.7 percent). The main causes were lower oil prices (Russia) and difficulties in funding large current account deficits in a risk-adverse environment.

Growth in the East Asia and Pacific region (particularly in China) as well as in South Asia (particularly India) has been resilient, buoyed by a massive fiscal stimulus package in China and by India's skillful macroeconomic management. Between 2008 and 2009, growth in the East Asia and Pacific region is estimated to have eased by only 1.2 percentage points to 6.8 percent, while South Asian growth has remained stable at 5.7 percent. GDP growth in China is estimated to have slowed from 9 percent in 2008 to 8.4 percent in 2009, but is expected to recover toward 9 percent over the remainder of the forecast period.

These developments have also been reflected in global industrial production, which declined sharply in the aftermath of the global financial crisis. In February 2009, world industrial production was falling at a 27 percent annualized pace, but by the beginning of April/May, production began recovering (figure 1.5), initially led by accelerating growth in China following the implementation of the $575 billion (over five quarters) fiscal stimulus package. Increased import demand from China quickly spread to other countries, with industrial production registering positive growth in emerging countries (excluding China) by March 2009 and high-income countries by May 2009. As the benefits of the stimulus measures and inventory restocking began to wane, industrial production growth rates have started to moderate. Whether this deceleration signals a transition to slower growth, more in line with underlying demand patterns, or the beginnings of a double-dip growth recession will largely depend on the extent to which consumer and business demand picks up in the months ahead (see the Risks section below).

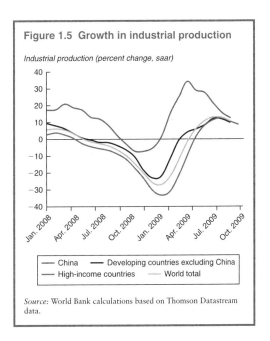

Figure 1.5 Growth in industrial production

Industrial production (percent change, saar)

Source: World Bank calculations based on Thomson Datastream data.

Prospects for high-income countries

Output among high-income economies in 2009 is estimated to have contracted by 3.3 percent, the first time since 1960 that the aggregate GDP of these countries has declined. Industrial production and trade flows among high-income countries were particularly distressed, with the former registering peak-to-trough declines in excess of 20 percent in countries such as the United States, the United Kingdom, Germany, and Japan.

A pronounced growth rebound is under way. The initial turnaround was driven by an investment rebound in developing countries, particularly China and the newly industrialized economies of East Asia, which has spread to high-income capital-equipment-exporting countries such as Germany and Japan. High-income countries have now started making larger contributions to world output and trade growth, as the effects of stimulus measures bear fruit in fostering domestic demand and imports, and a turn in the inventory cycle underpins production gains.

Supported by large stimulus programs, Japan, Germany, and France all started growing in the second quarter of 2009, while GDP in the United States expanded 2 percent in the third quarter. Recent data releases also indicate a continued rise in output in Japan, growing by 1.3 percent during the third quarter (seasonally adjusted rate).

The growth rebound in high-income countries is projected to remain relatively strong over the next several months but should lose strength during the course of 2010 as the growth impact of stimulus measures and the rebuilding of depleted inventories cease to bolster growth. During the depths of the recession, changes in stock building shaved off 2.4 percent (first quarter of 2009) from annualized growth (figure 1.6). The inventory cycle is expected to be an especially important element feeding the recovery in the United States and the newly industrialized economies because the destocking during the acute phase of the crisis was particularly strong in these economies. In Europe, although slower inventory accumulation had acted as a drag on growth, inventories continue to build up,

albeit slowly. As a result, the inventory cycle in Europe is expected to be shallower and shorter-lived.

In the United States, notwithstanding the recovery of growth in the second half, whole year GDP is estimated to have declined by 2.5 percent in 2009. The recovery is expected to continue into 2010, supported by the inventory cycle, the bottoming out of the housing sector downturn, and fiscal and monetary stimulus. However, the pace of recovery should slow toward the middle of 2010 as the growth impact of these forces wanes and as banking sector balance sheet consolidation, and still large negative wealth effects weigh on domestic demand. Overall, growth is projected to come in at 2.5 percent in 2010 and stabilize at a relatively modest 2.7 percent in 2011.

The IMF estimates that even though global bank write-downs amounted to $1.3 trillion through the first half of 2009, further write-downs of some $1.5 trillion may be required as U.S.-domiciled banks have recognized only about 60 percent of anticipated write-downs.

In high-income *Europe,* GDP is expected to decline by 3.9 percent in 2009 and to increase by only 1.0 percent in 2010. The support from fiscal and monetary policy for domestic demand, as well as improving global demand is likely to support growth in the region. However, ongoing balance-sheet problems of Euro Area banks are likely to remain a drag on financing conditions. So far, commercial banks have made little use of the governments' rescue packages, and governments have yet to amend rescue plans. As a result lending restrictions are likely to remain a drag for capital expenditure. According to the latest ECB *Financial Stability Review* (2009) only two-thirds of potential losses in major European banks have been provisioned or written off so far, with some 187 billion euros of potential losses still remaining.

Outturns in *Germany* have been key to developments in the Euro Area more generally. The German economy grew at an

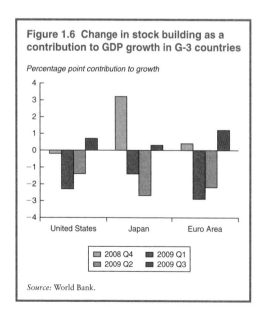

Figure 1.6 Change in stock building as a contribution to GDP growth in G-3 countries

Percentage point contribution to growth

Legend: 2008 Q4, 2009 Q1, 2009 Q2, 2009 Q3

Source: World Bank.

annualized pace of 2.9 percent in the third quarter of 2009, with growth largely driven by corporate investment and construction, while private consumption waned. Looking forward, the strong recovery in foreign orders for manufactured goods suggests that net exports will come to support growth. In addition, increasing public capital expenditures will support activity in the second half of 2009 and most of 2010. However, rising unemployment will be a drag on private consumption.

In *France* output in the third quarter benefited from a rise in exports even as private spending remained stagnant and fixed investment continued to fall. In general, France suffered less than other rich nations, because it was neither a large supplier of international credit nor reliant on borrowing, and when private demand suddenly plunged, the French government stepped in. Although the recession in the *United Kingdom* has been deeper than most initially expected, positive GDP growth is expected to resume in the fourth quarter, thereby ending six consecutive quarters of falling GDP.

Japan's economy grew by a revised 1.3 percent (saar) in the third quarter. The recovery results mainly from stimulus efforts at home and abroad. Tax incentives, as well as a reward program for purchasing green products, are encouraging Japanese consumers to switch to low-emission cars and energy-saving home appliances. At the same time, export volumes have benefited from increased demand for Japanese products from abroad, such as cars and related products in the United States and electronic goods in China.

Over the next few quarters, growth is forecast to benefit from an end to the sharp inventory liquidation in both domestic and overseas markets and the continued support emanating from the stimulus packages. Growth may come under renewed pressure later in 2010/11, as the effect of the stimulus package ebbs and the anticipated recovery in major trading partners remains modest.

Prospects for developing economies

Most developing countries were not directly involved in the risky behaviors that precipitated the financial crisis, and the banking systems in most regions carried only limited exposure to subprime loans. Nonetheless, economic activity in virtually all countries were sharply affected. By the first quarter of 2009, 25 of 31 developing countries (for which quarterly national account data are available) had reported negative growth rates (figure 1.7).

Domestic demand in developing countries was particularly affected by the sharp slowdown in fixed investment growth, which fell from 13.4 percent in 2007 to 8.5 percent in 2008 and to an estimated 1.3 percent in 2009. In response to falling domestic and external demand, industrial production came under pressure. By the end of the first quarter of 2009, industrial production was down by 12.9 percent from its level a year earlier, the volume and value of developing-country exports had declined by 30.2 percent and 17.6 percent, respectively, and the commodity prices that had supported growth in the boom years in many countries had fallen sharply. Moreover, the freezing of capital flows in high-income countries and

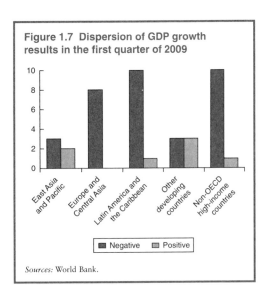

Figure 1.7 Dispersion of GDP growth results in the first quarter of 2009

Sources: World Bank.

increased borrowing costs generated a huge $690 billion financing gap that had to be met by reduced imports, layoffs, and in some instances substantial injections of foreign capital through official agencies such as the IMF, World Bank and various regional development banks.

As a result, GDP growth in developing countries decelerated sharply, coming in at only 1.2 percent for the year as a whole. Developing Europe and Central Asia, which went into the crisis period with large current account deficits due to a consumption boom financed by international credit and FDI, was hardest hit. GDP there fell an estimated 6.2 percent in 2009. Excluding these countries and China and India, which were able to weather the worst effects of the turmoil through large fiscal and monetary stimulus packages, GDP in the remaining developing countries fell by an estimated 2.2 percent in 2009—well below the 3 percent trend growth rate of these countries going into the crisis. While overall developing-country growth remained positive, the deceleration and dislocation that it has caused has been brutal. Unemployment is rising, an additional 90 million people are expected to remain in poverty (less than $1 a day) by the end of 2010 as a result of the slower growth, and as many as 30–50 thousand additional children are expected to have died of malnutrition in 2009 in Sub-Saharan Africa (Friedman and Schady 2009).

Prospects for developing countries are for a relatively robust recovery in 2010, with growth of 5.2 percent in aggregate or 3.7 percent if China, India, and Europe and Central Asia are excluded. Output should strengthen further in 2011, but only modestly, rising to 5.8 percent for the developing aggregate as a whole and 4.1 percent for developing countries excluding China, India, and Europe and Central Asia.

Regional outlooks

More detailed descriptions of prospects for developing regions, including country-specific projections, are available in the regional appendix to this report and online at http://www.worldbank.org/globaloutlook.

East Asia and the Pacific

East Asian economies were less adversely affected by the crisis than other regions, although as a key durable- and investment-goods-producing region it experienced dramatic declines in trade and production between September 2008 and March 2009.

The direct fallout from the financial crisis in high-income countries was limited. Although equity markets declined steeply and rapidly, the region's financial system held relatively few toxic assets and its overall resilience had been improved by banking reforms following the East Asian financial crisis of the 1990s.

Regional industrial production was declining at a 9 percent annualized pace toward the end of 2008, but started recovering early in 2009 under the influence of the 4 trillion renminbi (12 percent of GDP) fiscal stimulus package and monetary easing introduced by the Chinese government. Regional exports plummeted more sharply still, falling at a 50 percent annualized pace in the first quarter of 2009. Since then export volumes have been recovering, up 18 percent during the third quarter. Beginning in March 2009, regional trade partners started to benefit from the surge in Chinese imports associated with its fiscal stimulus (figure 1.8), and overall export volumes have been growing at a 10 percent annualized pace in recent months.

Overall, GDP resisted the global recession to a fair degree, expanding by 6.8 percent in 2009. Excluding China, the deceleration in growth was sharper. GDP in these countries grew at an estimated 1.3 percent, down from 4.8 percent in 2008. Regionwide fiscal and monetary stimulus plus the weakness of external demand have raised the contribution of domestic demand to overall growth.

Looking forward, the stabilization of international financial markets and renewed capital inflows, coupled with a strong inventory cycle, particularly among the newly industrialized economies in the region, are expected to boost growth in 2010 to 8.1 percent, with China leading the recovery with growth of 9 percent. Continuing

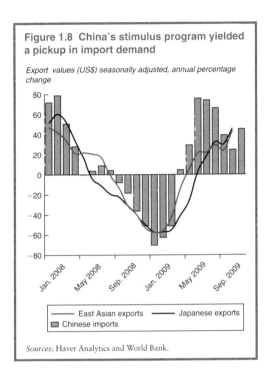

Figure 1.8 China's stimulus program yielded a pickup in import demand

Export values (US$) seasonally adjusted, annual percentage change

Legend:
— East Asian exports — Japanese exports
▦ Chinese imports

Sources: Haver Analytics and World Bank.

excess capacity in manufacturing and only moderate advances in world trade growth (in historic context) will restrain GDP growth from accelerating much faster than 8.2 percent in 2011.

Europe and Central Asia

Preexisting vulnerabilities in developing Europe and Central Asia, including large current account deficits, excessive reliance on foreign capital to finance domestic consumption, and sizable fiscal deficits in some countries, exposed the region to a particularly sharp adjustment when international sentiment reversed with the onset of the crisis.

Faced with the dramatic tightening of external financing conditions, authorities responded with a mix of domestic macroeconomic adjustment initiatives and extensive resort to official financing from the IMF, the World Bank, and the European Union to replenish foreign reserve holdings, support budget initiatives, and resist downward pressure on local currencies.

Notwithstanding these efforts, the crisis hit the region hardest of all developing regions. GDP is estimated to have fallen 6.2 percent

regionwide. In Russia, GDP in the third quarter was 9.0 percent lower than a year earlier, as the drop in commodity prices (particularly oil) and the sudden reversal of capital flows led to a substantial decline in revenues and fixed investment. Industrial activity is now recovering, growing at a 9.3 percent annualized pace in the three-month period ending November 2009. In November, industrial output shifted to positive annual growth of 1.3 percent following 12 consecutive months of decline over prior year levels. In Poland industrial production was more robust and GDP growth remained positive, supported by relatively resilient domestic demand and recent cuts to income taxes and improved retirement benefits. Production in Turkey, while down 1.8 percent as of November 2009 from a year earlier, has also been resilient and is recovering. In the Baltic States, industrial production declined between 15 and 20 percent. Among other smaller countries, such as Armenia, Kyrgyz Republic, and Tajikistan, the depth of the slowdown in Russia has cut into remittances, whose U.S. dollar value declined by between 15 percent and 33 percent in the first half of 2009.

The recovery in the region is expected to remain weak, given the substantial adjustment in domestic demand levels required and extensive financial weakness. Because of the depth of the crisis, the number of nonperforming loans has increased substantially and can be expected to continue to rise for some time. This, in combination with higher interest rates and weak international capital flows, may dampen investment growth (figure 1.9). Overall, the recovery is projected to be anemic, with GDP growth of only 2.7 percent in 2010 and 3.4 percent in 2011. Moreover, given substantial weaknesses and remaining needs for balance-sheet consolidation, substantial downside risks persist, including the possibility of a secondary regional financial crisis or a double-dip recession.

Latin America and the Caribbean

Owing to sound macroeconomic fundamentals, the Latin America and Caribbean region

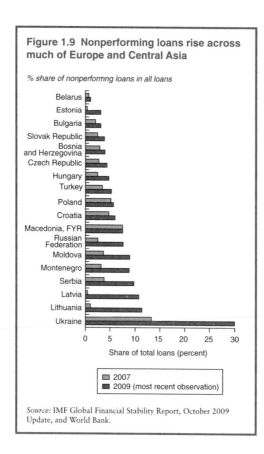

Figure 1.9 Nonperforming loans rise across much of Europe and Central Asia

% share of nonperformng loans in all loans

Share of total loans (percent)

2007

2009 (most recent observation)

Source: IMF Global Financial Stability Report, October 2009 Update, and World Bank.

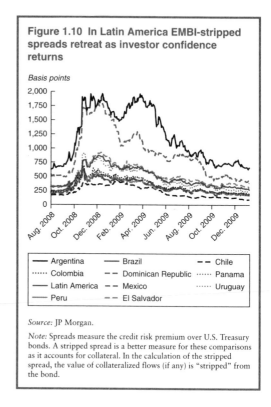

Figure 1.10 In Latin America EMBI-stripped spreads retreat as investor confidence returns

Basis points

Argentina — Brazil — Chile

Colombia — Dominican Republic — Panama

Latin America — Mexico — Uruguay

Peru — El Salvador

Source: JP Morgan.

Note: Spreads measure the credit risk premium over U.S. Treasury bonds. A stripped spread is a better measure for these comparisons as it accounts for collateral. In the calculation of the stripped spread, the value of collateralized flows (if any) is "stripped" from the bond.

has been able to weather the crisis much better than earlier ones. Indeed, risk spreads in the region have declined to near pre-crisis levels as investor confidence returned (figure 1.10). As elsewhere, both industrial production and international trade volumes declined sharply in the face of the abrupt contraction in global demand. By October 2009 industrial production was 5.3 percent below its August 2008 level, even as it has been recovering at a 9.8 percent annualized pace in recent months. Similarly, the volume of regional exports fell by 25 percent in the first several months of the crisis and is only now beginning to recover. Falling commodity prices meant that the value of exports fell even more sharply, contributing to lower incomes in many countries in the region.

Notwithstanding these circumstances, exchange rates have held up well, with virtually all of the countries in the region having regained their pre-crisis exchange rate level relative to the U.S. dollar. Equity markets too have been recovering, and spreads on regional sovereigns have come down. Partly as a result, many countries in the region have successfully accessed international capital markets.

However, stronger capital inflows, in part attributable to still high interest rate differentials, have put upward pressure on real effective exchange rates in some countries. In the case of Brazil the government levied a 2 percent financial transaction tax on foreign portfolio inflows, but that action may not be able to stem capital inflows or the real appreciation of the *real*. Some economies may be faced with appreciating real currencies, because of a weaker U.S. dollar, higher commodity prices, and strong capital inflows, losing external competitiveness at a time when external demand recovery is still fragile.

Within the region, the *Mexican* economy suffered the deepest contraction, with quarterly GDP down 9.7 and 6.3 percent in the second and third quarters of 2009. The depth of the fall in activity reflects Mexico's close ties to the U.S economy and its specialization in those sectors most deeply affected by the crisis (construction, automotive manufacturing, and electric appliances). Moreover, it is estimated that the outbreak of the AH1N1 flu virus, which caused declines in air transport volumes of 80 percent in some months and hotel vacancies in tourist areas of 80 or more percent, shaved 0.7 percentage point off GDP.

In *Brazil*, GDP fell by 0.2 percent year-on-year in the first two quarters of the crisis period, but rebounded in the second and third quarter of 2009. A robust fiscal policy package, including support for the automotive sector and a reversal of the inventory cycle, boosted industrial production, which was strong at a 22.2 percent annualized pace in October 2009. At the same time, lower policy interest rates and a decline in interest rate spreads helped prompt a recovery in private credit that has bolstered domestic demand.

In *Argentina*, GDP increased by 0.5 and 0.2 percent on an annualized basis in the second and third quarters of 2009. Policy-related uncertainties, including export restrictions, contributed to a sharp 17.3 percent decline in industrial production and trade. The pace of recovery has also been held back by a severe drought, which caused agricultural output to plunge.

Output in the region is expected to continue strengthening into 2010. Industrial production is currently growing at a 22.2 percent annualized pace in Brazil and the contraction in Mexico is beginning to moderate. This should be further supported by ongoing fiscal stimuli, the lagged benefits of strong monetary policy support, a shift in the inventory cycle and improvements in the terms of trade. But many of the smaller countries in Central America, which are highly dependent on migrant workers' remittances are likely to lag the overall recovery in output. As a result, regional GDP is projected to increase by 3.1 percent in 2010, and 3.6 percent is expected in 2011.

Key challenges facing the region include winding down of monetary and fiscal stimulus without undermining the recovery, providing adequately for the unemployed in a fiscally sustainable manner, and maintaining an open attitude toward international trade and investment.

The Middle East and North Africa

The developing economies of the Middle East and North Africa region were adversely affected by the crisis to varying degrees. At the onset of crisis, equity markets among the high-income Gulf Cooperation Council (GCC) economies and several bourses in the developing region plummeted—by more than the average for emerging markets. Recovery in these markets has been hesitant, given uncertainties surrounding financial conditions in Dubai and the United Arab Emirates that have played a major role in funneling FDI into the developing region.

GDP growth in 2009 for the developing economies is estimated to have eased from 4.3 percent in 2008 to 2.9 percent. Despite continuing large infrastructure development programs, the growth rate of developing oil exporters effectively halved from 2.9 percent in 2008 to 1.6 percent in 2009, mainly because of oil production cutbacks to support OPEC (Organization of Petroleum-Exporting Countries) price floors (figure 1.11).

Growth for the diversified economies faltered by almost 2 percentage points in the year, from a strong 6.6 percent outturn in 2008 (powered by growth of more than 7 percent in the Arab Republic of Egypt), to 4.7 percent. The virtual collapse of key export markets (notably the Euro Area), yielded sharp declines in goods exports from countries such as Egypt, Jordan, Morocco, and Tunisia. At the same time, remittances in 2009 dropped by 6.3 percent and tourism revenues by 5 percent—both

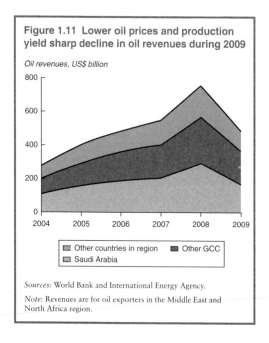

Figure 1.11 Lower oil prices and production yield sharp decline in oil revenues during 2009

Oil revenues, US$ billion

Sources: World Bank and International Energy Agency.

Note: Revenues are for oil exporters in the Middle East and North Africa region.

important sources of foreign income that support household consumption and job creation for these countries.

Looking forward, economic recovery will depend on global demand for oil and gas, which may not gain momentum until late in the forecast period. On balance, growth among developing countries in the region is anticipated to move moderately higher, to 3.7 percent during 2010, before firmer recovery sets in the following year. Nonetheless GDP gains of 4.4 percent in 2011 will remain below the 5 percent growth attained earlier in the 2000s.

The recent difficulties of Dubai World holding company, an entity of the government of Dubai, indicate that institutions in the region were not entirely unaffected by the global financial crisis. Given the very high investment levels of the past several years, as well as asset inflation (property prices increased particularly sharply in Egypt and Morocco), there may be large-scale financial losses within the region that have yet to be realized. Should these materialize, they could adversely affect market confidence, financial conditions, and employment and investment in the region, to the detriment of medium-term growth prospects.

South Asia

South Asia appears to have escaped the worst effects of the crisis, with GDP growth in the region estimated at 6.0 percent in 2009, down from 6.9 percent in 2008. The slowdown in GDP growth mainly reflected weaker investment and private sector demand, which were only partially offset by an increase in public expenditures. Several countries (Maldives, Pakistan, and Sri Lanka) faced serious challenges financing large current account deficits.

Despite enduring a 5 percent decline in goods and services export volumes, an even sharper decline in import demand (partly explained by weaker investment demand) and lower food and oil prices meant that trade and current account balances improved in 2009 (figure 1.12). Remittance flows to the region, which equal some 4.7 percent of GDP, fell an estimated 1.8 percent, representing a significant drop in household incomes and foreign currency earnings.

The region experienced sizeable capital outflows at the onset of the crisis, particularly in Pakistan and Sri Lanka, where outflows were driven by investor concerns about rising domestic and external imbalances. Improved investor sentiment, particularly related to relatively strong growth outturns (India) and ongoing or new IMF stabilization programs

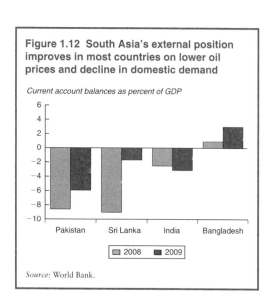

Figure 1.12 South Asia's external position improves in most countries on lower oil prices and decline in domestic demand

Current account balances as percent of GDP

Source: World Bank.

(Pakistan and Sri Lanka) as well as improved political stability (with the ending of the decades-old civil war in Sri Lanka) led to renewed capital inflows during the second and third quarters of 2009. Partly as a result, exchange rates and local equity markets have regained strength as both domestic and foreign investors have become less risk averse.

The recovery in the region is expected to be less marked than elsewhere, partly reflecting the relative shallowness of the downturn. Growth is expected to rebound to 7.0 and 7.4 percent in 2010 and 2011, respectively, compared with 6.0 percent in 2009.

Sub-Saharan Africa

The collapse of global trade slowed growth in Sub-Saharan Africa markedly, to 1.1 percent in 2009 from an average of 5 percent in the preceding five years. Initially, as global capital inflows reversed, the impact of the global crisis was felt most acutely by countries such as South Africa, whose financial markets are more integrated into global financial markets. Subsequently, as trade collapsed, the impact spread to oil exporters (such as Angola) and commodity exporters (such as Botswana and Zambia). Lower tourism volumes, falling remittances, and lower levels of official development assistance also affected the region adversely. Overall, GDP growth is estimated to have decelerated by 4 percentage points, and gross national income (a measure that includes terms-of-trade effects) fell by 3.7 percentage points between 2008 and 2009.

South Africa recorded three consecutive quarters of negative growth, with output declining at a 2.8 percent annualized pace in the second quarter of 2009. But South African growth rebounded to positive territory in the third quarter, rising 0.9 percent, while in Kenya GDP increased by 5.8 percent (saar) in the second quarter of 2009, suggesting that recovery is under way (figure 1.13). Nigeria's growth performance has been helped by a relatively strong performance in the agriculture sector as well as in gas and oil. Given the high level of nonperforming loans, however, the financial

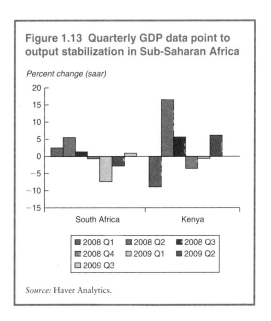

Figure 1.13 Quarterly GDP data point to output stabilization in Sub-Saharan Africa

Percent change (saar)

Legend:
- 2008 Q1
- 2008 Q2
- 2008 Q3
- 2008 Q4
- 2009 Q1
- 2009 Q2
- 2009 Q3

Source: Haver Analytics.

sector is likely to be a drag on Nigeria's growth in the near future.

The sharp decline in oil prices that accompanied the recession has caused current account balances in the region's oil exporters to fall (by more than 10 percent of GDP in countries such as Angola, Gabon, and Nigeria).

The recovery is expected to be modest, with GDP expanding by 3.8 and 4.6 percent in 2010 and 2011, respectively. However, the outlook is very uncertain and the strength of the recovery will depend to a large extent on growth performance in key export markets. A growth rebound there should translate into stronger external demand, while also triggering a recovery in FDI flows. Incomes in countries dependent on workers' remittances are expected to remain subdued, largely owing to continued high unemployment in the United States and the European Union.

Commodity markets

An extended period of strong developing-country growth, coupled with specific supply-side factors, resulted in uncomfortably low levels of spare capacity in the oil sector and low stocks of many grains and limited stockpiles of many traded metals in the mid-2000s (see World Bank 2009b for an in-depth discussion of the commodity boom and bust). These fundamental factors were also supported by financial investments associated with the global liquidity boom (see chapter 2), which may well have exacerbated the effect of the tight supply situation on commodity prices. Consequently, between 2003 and 2008 real non-energy commodity prices doubled, while real energy prices rose 170 percent.

Although commodity prices began falling before the onset of the acute phase of the financial crisis, both the financial contraction associated with the crisis itself and the spectacular contraction in economic activity that it provoked generated a sharp decline in global demand for commodities. Between July 2008 and February 2009, the U.S. dollar price of energy plummeted by two-thirds, and that of metals dropped by more than 50 percent, from earlier highs. Dollar prices of agricultural goods retreated by more than 30 percent, with the prices of fats and oils dropping 42 percent.

Dollar prices of energy and metals commodities began to recover in March 2009 broadly in tandem with global economic activity. The price increases partly reflect the depreciation of the dollar that has since reversed almost all of the appreciation that was associated with the immediate flight of capital from the rest of the world to the United States. Indeed, the real local-currency price of international commodities (a measure that corrects for currency fluctuations and inflation differentials) increased much less than dollar prices (figure 1.14). For instance, although energy prices measured in U.S. dollars rose 57 percent between February and October 2009, the increase over the same period in trade-weighted real local-currency terms was only 33 percent.

Crude oil

World oil demand, which grew on average by 1.7 percent a year over the 2000–2007 period, declined by nearly 3 percent during the last

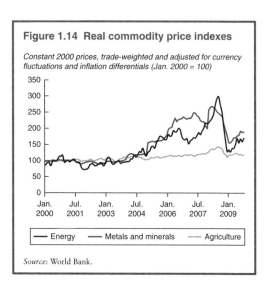

Figure 1.14 Real commodity price indexes

Constant 2000 prices, trade-weighted and adjusted for currency fluctuations and inflation differentials (Jan. 2000 = 100)

— Energy   — Metals and minerals   - - - Agriculture

Source: World Bank.

quarter of 2008 and the first quarter of 2009—a result of reduced economic activity and induced conservation and substitution toward other energy sources in response to high oil prices. Oil demand in OECD countries began declining in the fourth quarter of 2005 (when oil prices surged above $50 a barrel) and has been falling for more than four years now, with little or no growth expected in 2010. Demand in non-OECD countries also declined in the first quarter of 2009, but has since increased and is projected to resume its trend growth rate in 2010.

OPEC responded to the fall in global demand by reducing its production by nearly 4 million barrels a day in an effort to maintain prices at around $75 a barrel. As a result, OPEC spare capacity—one measure of global slack in oil markets—has increased to around 6.5 million barrels a day, equivalent to about five years of demand growth, and roughly the same level as in 2003 when oil prices were $20 a barrel (figure 1.15). Moreover, inventories of already extracted oil and oil products remain very high with some 150 million barrels currently being stored on ships at sea owing to weak demand and saturation of some land-based storage facilities.

While immediate-term supply is ample, the longer-term prospects are more clouded. Over

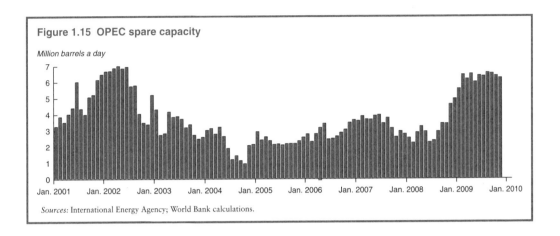

Figure 1.15 OPEC spare capacity

Million barrels a day

Sources: International Energy Agency; World Bank calculations.

the past decades non-OPEC supply (outside the former Soviet Union where output rose strongly in the early 2000s) has been fairly stagnant, with increased production in Brazil, Canada, and West Africa offset by large declines in U.S. and North Sea output. Although much higher prices now have prompted increased investment, growth from new developments has been sluggish, partly because of high costs in 2007–08 caused by shortages of equipment and skilled labor, and because of numerous project delays. Moreover, some three-fourths of known reserves are in the control of national oil companies (OPEC-controlled or otherwise), which forces major international oil companies to invest in higher-cost developments (such as oil sands and deepwater), increasing their costs and the amount of lead time needed before projects come on stream.

Given the large inventory overhang and the modest increases in oil demand expected over the next few years, real oil prices are not expected to rise substantially. However, the sector remains sensitive to both demand and supply developments, and a significant disruption to global supply could result in a sharp, if temporary, rise in prices once again.

Unless significant additional reserves are discovered over the longer term, OPEC's pricing power will continue to increase. Ultimately, however, alternative energy sources such as coal, natural gas, nuclear power, and various renewables are likely to prevent real oil prices from rising without end. Industry estimates suggest that at current real oil prices, demand and supply should remain in balance for the foreseeable future.

Metals

The global recession prompted a sharp decline in demand for metals. During the first half of 2009, global consumption of aluminum and copper, the most important metals in terms of volume, fell by 19 percent and 11 percent, respectively. Restocking by Chinese companies (China is the world's largest consumer of metals) and the government's State Reserves Bureau resulted in strong demand growth in the first half of the year, but during the second half of the year the restocking waned, and a similar restocking in industrial countries has yet to materialize. As a result, global demand for aluminum and copper in 2009 is estimated to have declined by 11 percent and 9 percent respectively from 2007 peaks, with world demand outside China down by more than 20 percent for both metals.

On the supply side, cutbacks at mines and smelters were significant early in the downturn of the cycle. In addition, project cancellations, tight scrap markets, and numerous strikes (in Canada and South America, for example) have helped tighten markets. Over the next two years, metals prices are expected to continue to rise moderately as the global recovery progresses and metal demand expands. Prices are, however, not expected to rise substantially, partly because of the large price appreciation to date, but mainly because of substantial idle capacity in many sectors that can be profitably brought back into production at current prices. Once demand growth returns to trend and idle capacity is eliminated, the industry will again be challenged to add sufficient capacity in the face of strong growth in developing countries—partly because new mines will be more expensive (underground versus open pit, for example) and often in geopolitically difficult regions. The mining industry will also have to contend with declining ore grades, environmental and land rehabilitation, as well as water, energy, and labor pressures. However, metals prices are not expected to reach the nominal peaks attained earlier this decade over the forecast period.

Agriculture

Although agricultural prices have declined by 22 percent since their peak in June 2008, they nevertheless remain almost twice as high as the lows reached in the early 2000s. The recent fall in agricultural prices (relative to previous peaks) reflects lower oil prices—a key cost component—and larger stockpiles of key agricultural commodities, including rice, maize, and wheat (figure 1.16), resulting from favorable harvests and area expansion of key agricultural commodities.

Barring unforeseen production problems, agricultural markets are likely to remain well supplied. As a result, agricultural prices are projected to decline by 13.8% in 2009, compared with 2008. Over the medium- to longer terms, agriculture prices are expected to remain broadly stable in real terms, reflecting two opposing forces. On the one hand, a stronger link between energy and agricultural prices (higher costs of production plus demand for biofuel) will exert upward pressure on prices; on the other hand, continued gains in total factor productivity (which tends to be stronger in agriculture than in manufacturing) should constrain production costs.

Short-term food security concerns have subsided, and most countries have reduced or eliminated the export bans and other export restrictions that were put in place during the commodity price spike of 2008. However, the poverty challenges posed by higher food prices remain. Over the longer term, productivity gains at the global level should ensure long-term food supply. However, advances in agricultural productivity in many poor countries is not keeping pace with population growth. As a result, there is a rising risk of increasing dependence on imported food to meet basic needs. For example, between 1980 and 2004, per capita agricultural GDP in Sub-Saharan Africa grew by less than 1 percent a year (versus more than 3 percent per year in East Asia).

Prospects

Over the medium term, real commodity prices are projected to remain relatively stable, with up- and downside risks more or less in balance (figure 1.17). Recent price rises reflect dollar weakness and some overshooting associated with the slowdown in global economic activity. Long term there is some concern that non-industrial commodities may become more procyclical and volatile than in the past. If the influence of financial investors in commodity markets rises, then the procyclical nature of their activity could raise volatility in affected markets. Similarly, the use of agricultural products as an alternative fuel source may introduce

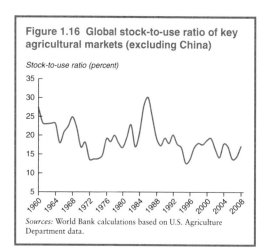

Figure 1.16 Global stock-to-use ratio of key agricultural markets (excluding China)

Stock-to-use ratio (percent)

Sources: World Bank calculations based on U.S. Agriculture Department data.

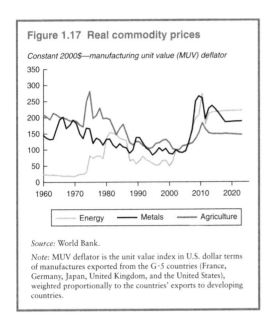

Figure 1.17 Real commodity prices

Constant 2000$—manufacturing unit value (MUV) deflator

Source: World Bank.

Note: MUV deflator is the unit value index in U.S. dollar terms of manufactures exported from the G-5 countries (France, Germany, Japan, United Kingdom, and the United States), weighted proportionally to the countries' exports to developing countries.

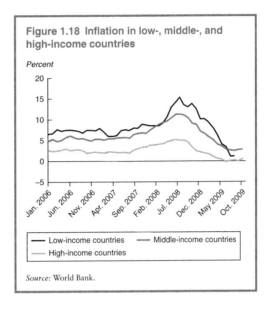

Figure 1.18 Inflation in low-, middle-, and high-income countries

Percent

Source: World Bank.

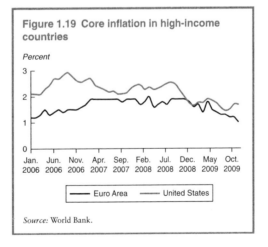

Figure 1.19 Core inflation in high-income countries

Percent

Source: World Bank.

an element of cyclicality into some food prices that was not previously there.

Inflation

Just as the sharp rise in food and fuel prices generated a rapid acceleration of headline inflation in both high-income and developing countries during 2008, the fall of commodity prices during the course of 2009 and the unprecedented slowdown in the global economy has led to a dramatic fall in headline inflation (figure 1.18). The median rate of year-over-year consumer price inflation in high-income countries, which peaked at 5.2 percent in mid-2008, turned negative in July, but was 0.6 percent in November 2009. The median inflation rate in developing countries has declined from a peak of 12.4 percent in mid-2008 to only 2.6 percent. Notwithstanding the declines in headline inflation, core inflation has remained relatively stable in high-income countries (figure 1.19). Only in Japan has core inflation dropped below zero. The bulk of the commodity price deflation has now passed through the system; therefore headline inflation can be expected to rise toward core inflation rates in coming months. Headline inflation in the United States

and Group of Seven countries is expected to average 1.6 percent and 1.1 percent in 2010, respectively.

Inflation developments have changed drastically among middle- and low-income countries. Median inflation in low-income countries peaked at 15.4 percent in the middle of 2008, but as of October 2009 it was 1.2 percent—well below the levels observed before the food and fuel boom. However, food inflation in developing countries has not been

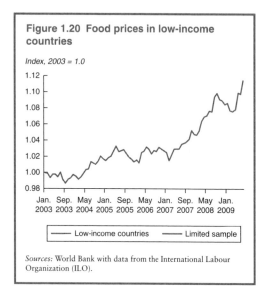

Figure 1.20 Food prices in low-income countries

Index, 2003 = 1.0

Sources: World Bank with data from the International Labour Organization (ILO).

falling as rapidly as overall prices in the two-thirds of developing countries for which data are available through May 2009 (figure 1.20).

As a result, by the end of May 2009, food prices in developing countries had risen about 8 percent faster than nonfood prices, when compared with January 2003. This suggests that the poor in these countries may not be

benefiting from lower international food prices to the same degree as the poor in richer countries and that a significant portion of the 130 million pushed into extreme poverty during the food-price spike (World Bank 2009b) may not have exited poverty as might have been expected given the fall in international food prices.

World trade

In general, global trade has followed a broadly similar pattern similar to industrial production, albeit the fall was deeper and the recovery lagged somewhat. The dollar value of world trade plummeted 31 percent between August 2008 and its low point in March 2009 (figure 1.21). The decline in volume terms was somewhat less pronounced when falling commodity prices and exchange rate fluctuations were taken out of the equation; nevertheless, by March 2009 global trade volumes were down by 22 percent. Although global trade has recovered from these troughs, as of October 2009 it was still 2.8 percent below its pre-crisis level.

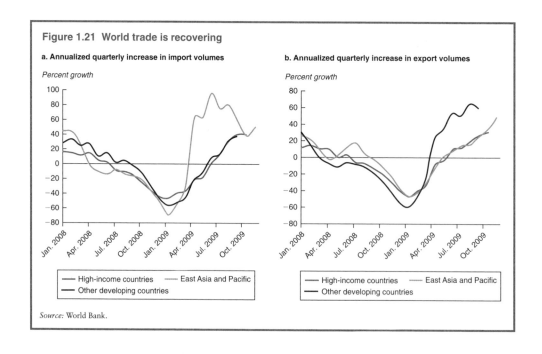

Figure 1.21 World trade is recovering

a. Annualized quarterly increase in import volumes

Percent growth

b. Annualized quarterly increase in export volumes

Percent growth

Legend: High-income countries — East Asia and Pacific — Other developing countries

Source: World Bank.

The lag in the trade rebound does not appear to be wholly a reflection of weak trade finance (although doubtless it has played some role). Rather, the lag appears to reflect the still-depressed level of investment activity (investment goods generally are heavily traded). Global investment fell by an estimated 9.7 percent in 2009 and even in 2010 investment is forecast to grow by only 4.9 percent.

The initial fall-off in import volumes was relatively stronger in high-income countries, partly reflecting the growth slowdown that had already begun before the failure of Lehman Brothers. With the crisis, the decline accentuated and broadened, with global import volumes falling at a 40 percent annualized pace in the first quarter of 2009. At the trough, imports in high-income countries were 24 percent off their August 2008 level; in developing countries they were also down by 25 percent.

The trade slump was less marked in Asian countries, in part because of fiscal stimulus in China. Most Chinese trade partners benefited from the rebound in Chinese imports. By the third quarter, import demand had strengthened among most countries. After a period of some weakness, reflecting faltering domestic demand, the United States' import volume growth jumped to 29 percent in October (saar), in Germany to 27 percent, and in Japan to 31 percent as of November.

In general, services trade has been more resilient than merchandise trade, in part because a larger share is destined for personal consumption rather than investment expenditures. Tourism represents something of an exception—such expenditures tend to be luxury goods and therefore more volatile. The World Tourism Organization reports that compared with 2008, tourism arrivals were off 7 percent in the first six months of 2009 (figure 1.22). Regionally, Central and Eastern European nations recording the largest fall in tourism (11 percent), while Africa registered a modest increase in tourist arrivals. Mexico was particularly hard hit, with arrivals down 19 percent (year-over-year) in

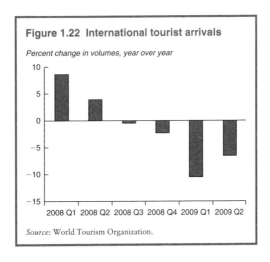

Figure 1.22 International tourist arrivals

Percent change in volumes, year over year

Source: World Tourism Organization.

the second quarter, where the effects of the global recession were magnified by the outbreak of AH1N1 in that country and efforts by individuals worldwide to avoid infection. Most recently, global tourism arrivals appear to be picking up, with July volumes only 4 percent lower than a year earlier. Notwithstanding widespread efforts to support tourism through special tax deductions, the easing of visa restrictions, and investment plans, the World Tourism Organization expects global tourist volumes to have declined by between 4 and 6 percent during 2009.

Overall, world merchandise trade volumes are estimated to have contracted by 17.6 percent in 2009, with goods and services down some 14.4 percent. Given the expected weak recovery and weak base effects, trade is projected to expand by only 4.3 percent in 2010 and by 6.2 percent in 2011. As a result even two years into the recovery, the overall volume of goods and services traded is forecast to be 5 percent lower than its 2008 peak.

Remittances are another important source of external currency for developing countries, representing as much as 20 percent of GDP in some countries. Remittances have been more stable than capital flows and merchandise trade, but have nevertheless declined by an estimated 6.1 percent in 2009 (box 1.1).

Box 1.1 Prospects for remittances

Officially recorded remittance flows to developing countries reached a peak of $338 billion in 2008, up 16.7 percent from 2007, despite a slowdown in several remittance corridors during the final quarter of 2008. Based on monthly and quarterly data released by some central banks and in line with the World Bank's global economic outlook, it is estimated that remittance flows to developing countries will fall by 6.1 percent in 2009, before recovering in 2010. Weaknesses in the U.S. job market led to a significant decline in recorded remittances to Latin America, particularly Jamaica and Mexico, where year-to-date remittances fell by 16 and 13 percent, respectively. In contrast, remittances to some South Asian countries such as Bangladesh and Pakistan have continued to record positive growth in 2009, where year-to-date remittances have increased 16 percent and 27 percent respectively. The latter is in part a result of measures by the Pakistani authorities to increase flows through formal channels including subsidies for marketing expenses to providers of remittance services (see the Pakistan Remittance Initiative); in addition, some migrants are returning with accumulated savings.[a]

However, in all regions, remittance flows are expected to weaken from 2008 levels, with Europe and Central Asia likely to record the largest deterioration

in flows (−15 percent), while remittances to South Asia are expected to drop by a more modest 2 percent. Remittance flows to South Asia grew strongly in 2008 despite the global economic crisis, but now there are risks that they may slow in a lagged response to a weak global economy. East Asia and Sub-Saharan Africa also face similar risks. In contrast, remittance flows to Latin America and the Caribbean and to the Middle East and North Africa have been weaker than expected in 2009; however, they appear to have reached a bottom already, with the expectation of a recovery in 2010 and 2011.

Overall, migration and remittance flows are expected to recover in 2010 and 2011, but the recovery is likely to be shallow, with remittances not expected to reach the level of 2008 even in 2011. In all developing regions, remittance flows are likely to face three downside risks: a jobless economic recovery, tighter immigration controls, and unpredictable exchange rate movements. Despite these risks, remittances are expected to remain more resilient than private capital flows and will become even more important as a source of external financing in many developing countries. Policy responses could involve efforts to facilitate migration and remittances to make these flows cheaper, safer and more productive for both the sending and the receiving countries.[b]

a. See http://www.pri.gov.pk/.
b. Ratha 2009.

Narrowing global external payment imbalances

In aggregate, the crisis has prompted a narrowing of global imbalances attributable to an overall decline in the volume of trade (for a given percentage imbalance between imports and exports, weaker trade will reduce the global imbalance), falling oil prices, and a narrowing of China's and the United States' trade imbalances. Overall, the absolute value of global current account balances (the sum of all surpluses plus the absolute value of all deficits) is estimated to have declined from a peak of 5.9 percent of world GDP in 2008 to around

3.9 percent in 2009. Given continued relatively large gaps in global output and the absence of strong excess demand pressures (particularly in high-income countries)—which should keep oil prices in check—this narrowing is projected to be broadly stable, with imbalances rising only slightly to around 4.1 percent of GDP in 2011 (figure 1.23).

The decline in the U.S. current account deficit reflects the continuation of a preexisting narrowing of the non-oil trade balance that was masked by rising oil prices. It also reflects a sharp increase in household savings rates as the wealth effect of the housing bubble ceased to support high levels of consumer

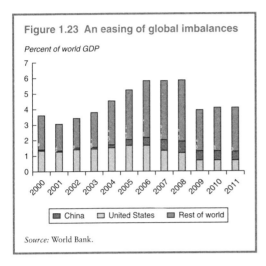

Figure 1.23 An easing of global imbalances

Percent of world GDP

Source: World Bank.

demand. The most recent small increase in the U.S. trade deficit mainly reflects high oil prices as public sector deficits have only partially offset the increase in consumer saving. The sharp narrowing of the Chinese surplus is more directly related to the drop in global trade and China's large fiscal package, which has bolstered imports at a time that global export demand was weaker (figure 1.24).

Whether the narrowing of these trade balances persists will depend importantly on how

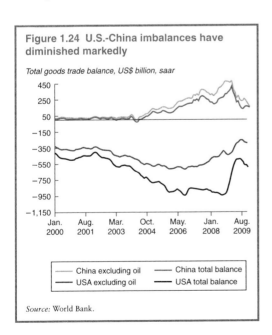

Figure 1.24 U.S.-China imbalances have diminished markedly

Total goods trade balance, US$ billion, saar

Source: World Bank.

the fiscal and monetary stimuli in both of these countries are unwound. In the case of the United States, if household savings rates fall as the recovery takes hold, but public sector spending is not cut back, the trade deficit can be expected to rise once again. Although growth in the United States is still in the early stages of recovery, recent improvements in the current account have been maintained in the third quarter of 2009, as the marginal increase in the current account deficit from 2.8 to 3 percent of GDP is largely related to higher oil import costs.

In China, the success of the authorities in stimulating domestic demand will determine whether or not its trade surplus begins to rise as world trade recovers. So far, most of the stimulus has gone into additional infrastructure investment. If, as some fear, this merely bolsters the economy's export competitiveness without promoting an expansion of domestic spending, then as global trade revives, China's trade surplus could reemerge. While additional exchange rate flexibility could help increase the attractiveness of domestic markets for Chinese producers, such a move is unlikely to eliminate China's tendency toward large trade surpluses unless it is accompanied by structural changes to decrease household and firm savings rates.

In the baseline forecast, a further modest unwinding of global imbalances is projected over the medium term. China's current account surplus is expected to decline from an estimated 5.6 percent of GDP in 2009 to 4 percent of GDP by 2011, while the U.S. current account deficit is projected to rise only marginally from an estimated 2.9 percent in 2009 to 3.1 percent of GDP by 2011. Overall, the extent of global imbalances, measured as the absolute value of current account balances as a percent of world GDP, is projected to decline from its peak of 5.9 percent in 2008 to 4.5 percent in 2011.

Uncertain prospects

As emphasized above the economic rebound that is currently under way is likely to continue for several months, supporting relatively rapid growth. However, a great deal of uncertainty clouds the outlook for the second half of 2010 and beyond. The waning growth impact of the fiscal stimulus, a progressive end to the inventory cycle, uncertainty about the extent to which private sector confidence will step in and sustain the recovery, and the possibility of a second round of bank failures either in developed or developing countries are among the factors that could contribute to a more pronounced slowdown of growth in the second half of 2010 and into 2011—potentially yielding a double-dip growth recession.

On the upside, if private sector confidence does return, there is a risk that the huge traditional and nontraditional monetary stimulus that has been put into place will begin to gain traction, potentially reflating some of the bubbles that have only recently burst. Indeed, some (Roubini 2009) are already arguing that very loose monetary policy in high-income countries has produced a carry-trade opportunity that is underpinning in an unsustainable manner the resurgence of capital flows to developing countries, which may ultimately regenerate the kind of global imbalances that precipitated the crisis in the first place.

The following pages address some of these issues and present simulations designed to illustrate potential alternative outcomes should these pressures, which exist in the baseline, hold greater or lesser sway in the months to come. These alternative scenarios are not meant to quantify the result of worst- or best-case scenarios, but to illustrate a reasonable range of possible outcomes given the uncertainties prevailing today.

A deeper growth recession

Table 1.2 reports the results of two scenarios. The first outlines growth prospects for GDP under the assumption that the progressive improvement in global financial markets implicit in the baseline scenario is not as strong as projected and is exacerbated by the beginning of efforts to unwind the fiscal and monetary stimulus already in place. In this scenario, the

Table 1.2 Prospects remain uncertain
Real GDP growth

Region	2008	2009	2010	2011
Baseline scenario				
World	1.7	−2.2	2.7	3.2
High-income countries	0.4	−3.3	1.8	2.3
Developing countries	5.6	1.2	5.2	5.8
East Asia and Pacific	8.0	6.8	8.1	8.2
Europe and Central Asia	4.2	−6.2	2.7	3.6
Latin America and the Caribbean	3.9	−2.6	3.1	3.6
Middle East and North Africa	4.3	2.9	3.7	4.4
South Asia	5.7	5.7	6.9	7.4
Sub-Saharan Africa	5.1	1.1	3.8	4.6
Deeper recession scenario				
World	1.7	−2.2	2.5	2.7
High-income countries	0.4	−3.3	1.6	1.8
Developing countries	5.6	1.2	5.1	5.4
East Asia and Pacific	8.0	6.8	7.9	7.5
Europe and Central Asia	4.2	−6.2	2.6	3.2
Latin America and the Caribbean	3.9	−2.6	3.0	3.2
Middle East and North Africa	4.3	2.9	3.7	4.4
South Asia	5.7	5.7	6.9	7.3
Sub-Saharan Africa	5.1	1.1	3.8	4.4
Stronger growth scenario				
World	1.7	−2.2	3.1	3.4
High-income countries	0.4	−3.3	2.2	2.4
Developing countries	5.6	1.2	5.8	6.3
East Asia and Pacific	8.0	6.8	9.0	8.8
Europe and Central Asia	4.2	−6.2	3.1	4.0
Latin America and the Caribbean	3.9	−2.6	3.6	4.2
Middle East and North Africa	4.3	2.9	4.1	4.6
South Asia	5.7	5.7	7.4	7.6
Sub-Saharan Africa	5.1	1.1	4.0	5.1

Source: World Bank.

combination of a modest tightening of monetary and fiscal policy and ongoing restructuring in the banking sector causes investment growth to be more subdued than in the baseline. The results in the second panel of the table are based on a simulation that assumes that 10 percent of the 2009 increase in structural deficits is withdrawn[4] in 2010 and a further 20 percent in 2011 and that the rebound in investment is only 80 percent as strong as in the baseline.

In this scenario, global growth comes in about 0.2 percentage points lower in 2010 and 0.5 percentage points lower in 2011 than in the baseline forecast. Growth rates in high-income countries decline by 0.2 and 0.5 percentage points in 2010 and 2011, respectively. This is more than the 0.1 and

0.4 percentage points decline projected for developing countries, mainly because the fiscal stimulus in high-income countries was much bigger than in developing countries. Indeed in many developing countries financial constraints precluded any real countercyclical increase in spending.

Global imbalances narrow in this scenario mainly because of weaker consumer demand in high-income countries, and disinflation, unemployment and high output gaps become even more pronounced problems.

A more buoyant private sector reaction

The reaction of the private sector to the recovery is one of the major uncertainties underlying the outlook. In the baseline scenario, the negative wealth effect from the crash plus the indebtedness incurred during the boom period are expected to dampen consumer demand for several years. In addition, the weakened banking sector is not expected to be able to support the kind of investment rebound that normally follows a serious recession.

However, with monetary policy as loose as it currently is in high-income countries, there is a reasonable probability that household saving rates will decline more quickly than is assumed in the baseline. By the same token, investment may react more forcefully to low interest rates and improved confidence.[5]

The third panel of table 1.3 reports the results of a simulation that assumes that the savings rate in the United States declines over time from its current level of 3.4 percent of household income to about 2.7 percent of household income—close to its average level in the 2000s. Savings rates in high-income European countries are assumed to fall by about the same amount.

In this scenario, the combination of stronger consumption and investment throughout the global economy increases GDP growth by about 0.4 percentage points for high-income countries and 0.6 percent for developing countries in 2010. As a result global trade is close to 0.2 percentage points higher in 2011 than in the baseline, and output gaps are about

0.6 percentage points lower. Lower savings in the United States serve to push up its current account deficit by about 0.2 percent of GDP.

The impact of the crisis on the very poor

The financial crisis has taken its toll on achieving the 2015 poverty Millennium Development Goal (MDG). Newly updated World Bank estimates suggest that the crisis will leave an additional 50 million people in extreme poverty in 2009 and some 64 million by the end of 2010 relative to a no-crisis scenario.[6] These depressing statistics notwithstanding, the relatively rapid rebound in developing countries, their future medium term prospects as described in the first part of this chapter combined with the significant progress in most regions since 1990, the poverty MDG is likely to be met at the global level.

The current projection of the percentage of developing-country population living on $1.25/day or less (a standard measure of poverty) in 2015 is 15 percent (table 1.3), well below the target rate of 20.8 percent (one-half the 1990 headcount index). This translates into around 920 million people living under the international poverty line, which coincidentally is around 50 percent of the estimated number of poor in 1990. There is significant regional variation. East Asia and the Pacific will largely surpass its regional target, in large part because of the significant success in reducing poverty in China, by far the region's most populous country. Sub-Saharan Africa is projected to miss its target (by over 9 percentage points) as will Europe and Central Asia. Africa's poor performance reflects mainly weak growth in the 1990s. The economic adjustments required by the transition from planned economies to market economies led to a rise in poverty in Europe and Central Asia, albeit from a low level. Significant progress in reducing poverty is anticipated in both regions between 2005 and 2015.

Progress on poverty using the broader $2/day definition is projected to be somewhat less promising, with the headcount index dropping

Table 1.3 Poverty in developing countries by region, selected years

Region or country	1990	2005	2015[f]	2020[f]
Percentage of the population living on less than $1.25/day				
East Asia and Pacific	54.7	16.8	5.9	4.0
China	60.2	15.9	5.1	4.0
Europe and Central Asia	2.0	3.7	1.7	1.2
Latin America and the Caribbean	11.3	8.2	5.0	4.3
Middle East and North Africa	4.3	3.6	1.8	1.5
South Asia	51.7	40.3	22.8	19.4
India	51.3	41.6	23.6	20.3
Sub-Saharan Africa	57.6	50.9	38.0	32.8
Total	41.7	25.2	15.0	12.8
Percentage of the population living on less than $2.00/day				
East Asia and Pacific	79.8	38.7	19.4	14.3
China	84.6	36.3	16.0	12.0
Europe and Central Asia	6.9	8.9	5.0	4.1
Latin America and the Caribbean	19.7	16.6	11.1	9.7
Middle East and North Africa	19.7	16.9	8.3	6.6
South Asia	82.7	73.9	57.0	51.0
India	82.6	75.6	58.3	51.9
Sub-Saharan Africa	76.2	73.0	59.6	55.4
Total	63.2	47.0	33.7	29.8
Number of people living on less than $1.25/day (millions)				
East Asia and Pacific	873	317	120	83
China	683	208	70	56
Europe and Central Asia	9	16	7	5
Latin America and the Caribbean	50	45	30	27
Middle East and North Africa	10	11	6	6
South Asia	579	595	388	352
India	435	456	295	268
Sub-Saharan Africa	296	387	366	352
Total	1,817	1,371	918	826
Number of people living on less than $2.00/day (millions)				
East Asia and Pacific	1,274	730	394	299
China	961	473	220	168
Europe and Central Asia	32	39	22	18
Latin America and the Caribbean	86	91	67	62
Middle East and North Africa	44	52	30	26
South Asia	926	1,091	973	926
India	702	828	728	686
Sub-Saharan Africa	391	555	574	595
Total	2,754	2,557	2,060	1,926

Source: World Bank.
f: Forecast.

to a still high one-third of the total developing-country population and more than 50 percent of the 1990 level, leaving some 2 billion people living with $2/day or less.

As is the case each year, the new poverty forecast is a combination of two changes—new and more recent household surveys and a new forecast of per capita income growth. Beyond the methodological advances in more recent surveys, they also reflect changes in the underlying distribution of income that are not measured by changes in mean income (or consumption). Since last year's report, the new poverty forecast integrates 31 new household surveys. Combining these new surveys with last year's growth forecast implies a 0.5 percentage point decline in the aggregate headcount index from 15.5 percent to 15.0 percent (figure 1.25). The largest single change is for China where the new survey causes the projected 2015 headcount index to drop by about 2 percentage points. Sub-Saharan Africa shows a small rise of 0.3 percentage point for the same reason. The new economic forecast, compared with 2008, has no net effects at the aggregate level, but raises slightly the headcount index for Sub-Saharan Africa and East Asia and the Pacific.[7]

As 2015 is rapidly approaching, it is useful to look a bit further ahead and assess the needs of developing countries 10 years forward. This year's forecast for 2020 suggests that 826 million or 12.8 percent of developing-country citizens will be living on $1.25/day or less and that there will be almost 2 billion poor people using the $2/day poverty line. The five additional years would still leave Sub-Saharan Africa short of the poverty MDG.

Policy implications for developing countries

Although the financial crisis has passed and the global economic recovery seems to be under way, many challenges for policy makers and international financial institutions remain. Paramount among these is the management of the unwinding of the fiscal and monetary stimulus that has played such a critical role in avoiding a much more serious downturn.

Timing the tightening of fiscal and monetary policy to avoid killing off the recovery is one clear consideration. But so too is the risk that the very loose monetary and fiscal conditions in high-income countries could

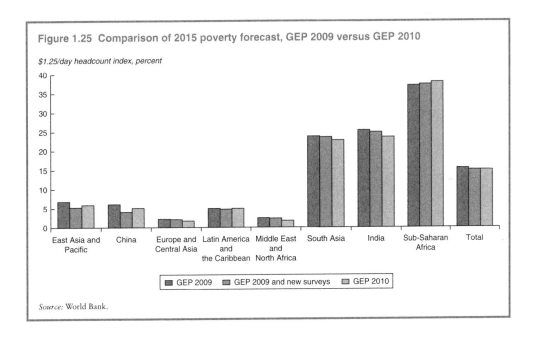

Figure 1.25 Comparison of 2015 poverty forecast, GEP 2009 versus GEP 2010

$1.25/day headcount index, percent

Source: World Bank.

create dangerous conditions for developing countries. Already very low interest rates in high-income countries are promoting carry trades that may be promoting destabilizing capital inflows into developing countries that could create new asset bubbles and the potential for future crises. For developing countries, the management of the recovery in capital flows is a critical challenge. Warding off new asset price bubbles may call for greater exchange rate flexibility. If these inflows are enduring and effectively channeled into productive investment, they could present a major boon to developing countries (see the analysis in chapter 2). However if they exceed the absorptive capacity of countries or are cut off abruptly, the costs could be very high.

Given the slow growth and associated real-side adjustments that are expected over the medium term (see chapters 2 and 3), government policies should focus on productivity-enhancing growth strategies. For low-income countries, these strategies may involve simultaneously addressing underlying structural problems such as the quality of institutions, regulatory reform, and openness—all critical factors in promoting faster productivity growth. To the extent that these

measures succeed in generating additional output and government revenues, associated expenditures will be more sustainable than more traditional expenditure-oriented ones. Countries with sufficient fiscal space may seek to target measures to reduce (infrastructure) bottlenecks. Invested wisely in human and physical capital, such steps can position a country to take better advantage of the global recovery when it comes, by more effectively exploiting existing comparative advantages and helping to generate new ones.

Notes

1. Potential output is the level of output commensurate with the level of production when all factors of production, i.e., labor, capital, and technology, are fully employed.

2. Total revenues in IDA countries is estimated (based on IMF 2009) to have fallen from an average of 26.2 percent of GDP over the 2000–08 period to 21.9 percent of GDP in 2009. This 4.3 percent (as a share of GDP) decline in revenues is equivalent to nearly $35 billion. When 2009 revenues are compared to the year before (when total revenues were equivalent to 28.1 percent of GDP), the fall in revenue is equivalent to nearly $50 billion.

3. The external financing need and gap projections are based on the methodology developed in

World Bank (2009a) and assess the extent to which capital flows from private sources will meet developing countries' external financing needs defined as current account deficit and scheduled principal payment on private debt. Private short-term debt is projected to decline further in 2010, while medium and long term debt increase slightly.

4. The fiscal stimulus for the G-20 countries was taken as the change in the discretionary measure of the fiscal deficit from Horton, Kumar, and Mauro (2009). For the remainder of developing countries, it was estimated as the change in the structural deficit (in those countries where structural expenditures increased as a percent of GDP)—using IMF estimates for general government expenditures and revenues.

5. In the early 2000s investment grew about 1.6 times as quickly as GDP in developing countries, but the elasticity has occasionally been as high as 2 during upswings. In the baseline, this investment-GDP elasticity is roughly consistent with the trends earlier in this decade—about 1.4 times GDP growth in most countries. Applying the larger historical elasticity of 2 during upswings suggests that investment could grow as fast as 10.9 percent on average over 2010–11 versus the 7.8 percent in the baseline scenario.

6. These calculations update those in Ravallion (2009) and World Bank (2009c) and are consistent with new survey evidence and the revised forecasts for growth presented in this report.

7. We have not decomposed these changes into changes in the growth forecast itself and changes to the poverty elasticity with respect to growth as emerges from the new surveys.

References

Agriculture, U.S. Department of. 2009. "Production, Supply and Distribution" [online], available at http://www.fas.usda.gov/psdonline/ [Accessed: December 9, 2009].

Chen, S., and M. Ravallion. "The Impact of the Global Financial Crisis on the World's Poorest." Vox: Research-based policy analysis and commentary from leading economists [Accessed: December 9, 2009], www.voxeu.org/index.php?q=node/3520.

ECB (European Central Bank). 2009a. "What Triggers Prolonged Inflation Regimes? A Historical Analysis," by Isabel Vansteenkiste. Working Paper Series.

_____. 2009b. December 2009 Financial Stability Review. Frankfurt, Germany. http://www.ecb.europa.eu.

Friedman, Jed, and Norbert Schady. 2009. "How Many More Infants Are Likely to Die in Africa as a Result of the Global Financial Crisis?" Policy Research Working Paper 5023, World Bank, Washington, DC.

Horton, Mark, Manmohan Kumar, and Paolo Mauro. 2009. "The State of Public Finances: A Cross-Country Fiscal Monitor." IMF Staff Position Note SPN/09/25, International Monetary Fund, Washington, DC.

IMF (International Monetary Fund). 2009. World Economic Outlook. Washington, DC.

International Energy Agency. 2009. Oil Market Report. Paris.

Ratha, Dilip. 2009. "Dollars without Borders: Can the Global Flow of Remittances Survive the Crisis?" Foreign Affairs, October 16. http://www.foreignaffairs.com/articles/65448/dilip-ratha/dollars-without-borders.

Ratha, Dillip, Sanket Mohapatra, and Ani Silwal. 2009. "Migration and Remittance Trends 2009: A Better-Than-Expected Outcome So Far, But Significant Risks Ahead." In Migration and Development Brief. World Bank, Washington, DC.

Ravallion, Martin. 2009. "The Crisis and the World's Poorest." Development Outreach, World Bank, Washington, DC. December.

Roubini, Nouriel. 2009. "Mother of All Carry Trades Faces an Inevitable Bust." The Financial Times, November 1.

UNSCN (United Nations Standing Committee on Nutrition). 2009. "Global Recession Increases Malnutrition for the Most Vulnerable People in Developing Countries. Pregnant Women and Children Are Hardest Hit." In Nutrition Impacts of the Global Food and Financial Crises. Geneva.

World Bank. 2009a. Global Development Finance 2009. Washington, DC: World Bank.

_____. 2009b. Global Economic Prospects: Commodities at the Crossroads. Washington, DC.

_____. 2009c. "Protecting Progress: The Challenge Facing Low-Income Countries in the Global Recession," Background paper prepared for the G-20 Leaders' Meeting, Pittsburgh, PA, Sept 24–25, 2009. http://siteresources.worldbank.org/NEWS/Resources/WorldBankG20PaperonLICs-Sept2009.pdf.

World Bureau of Metal Statistics. World Metal Statistics Yearbook. London.

2

The Impact of the Boom in Global Finance on Developing Countries

The first seven years of the 21st century were very good for developing countries. GDP growth continued to accelerate as it had done in the 1990s but at an even faster pace, while economic volatility was far lower than in previous periods of rapid growth (IMF 2007). And while large countries with very fast growth rates, such as China and India, tended to attract the most attention, most of the acceleration in developing-country growth during this period occurred among smaller countries that in the past had been growing much less quickly.

Somewhat surprisingly and in contrast to popular perceptions, this growth spurt occurred during a period in which external demand conditions for developing countries were not that strong. Growth in high-income countries was actually slower during the boom years 2003–07 than during the preceding 13 years. Moreover, import demand from high-income countries was growing only 5.6 percent a year, marginally slower than during the preceding 13 years. More than all of the acceleration in developing-country exports came from an expansion in their share in high-income country imports and very rapid growth in South-South trade.

Financial conditions were, however, very favorable. Interest rates and interest rate premiums were low (for example, the average secondary market spread on developing countries' sovereign bonds fell to about 200 basis points by mid-2007, down from

about 700 basis points in January 2003), and global credit expanded twice as fast as nominal GDP.[1] A range of financial innovations, including the securitization of loans and the development of off-balance-sheet vehicles, allowed banks to fund an important portion of their loan portfolios through capital and money markets, leveraging equity capital in a way never before possible. Partly as a result, the amount of finance—both domestic and international—available to developing countries expanded very rapidly, and countries enjoyed a sustained investment boom.

That boom came to an abrupt end in the fall of 2008 with the failure of Lehman Brothers and the financial crisis that ensued (see chapter 1). Although clouded by uncertainty, the longer-term consequences of the crisis could be far-ranging. The sharp scaling back of global production may result in permanent and long-lasting adjustments in global production patterns. Firms and regional specializations may fail and disappear in a way that they would not have had adjustment occurred more gradually. Global trade patterns may be irrevocably altered, and the depth of the recession in some regions and countries relative to others may change the future pattern of growth in the world. The temporary weakness of the financial sector in high-income countries may create opportunities for financial firms in developing countries, allowing them to grow and expand in ways that might not have been possible otherwise. Although each of these possible consequences merits in-depth exploration, dealing with all of the potential consequences of the crisis for developing countries lies outside the scope of this publication.

The analysis presented in this and the next chapter focuses more narrowly on the medium-term consequences of recent and anticipated changes in financial conditions for developing-country finance, investment, and supply potential, both over the past decade and that can be expected in the next 5 to 10 years. This orientation was chosen partly because, contrary to popular perceptions, real-side external factors do not appear to have played a major role in the boom. Most important, this focus on the financial aspects of the crisis was chosen because of the important role that finance played in causing the crisis and because the likely regulatory and market-based changes in the sector are somewhat less speculative than those that might surround other important elements of the post-crisis world.

Within this overall context, this chapter examines the link between the global expansion of liquidity and the improvement in developing countries' growth before the financial crisis. It begins with a review of the credit boom and its implications for the pricing of risk and borrowing costs. It then describes how the global boom contributed to the rapid expansion of domestically supplied credit and international capital flows in developing countries, discusses the factors that helped to determine which countries most benefited from the liquidity glut, and examines the extent to which different countries were able to translate these more liquid conditions into increased investments. The chapter concludes with some model-based measurements of the impact of the investment boom on growth and potential output in developing countries. All of this serves as a prelude to chapter 3, which analyzes the extent to which, in the future, tighter financial regulation, increased risk aversion, and higher interest rates and interest rate premiums are likely to constrain investment and potential growth in developing countries and the scope for developing countries to pursue policies to mitigate these impacts.

A number of key messages emerge from the discussion in chapter 2:

- The acceleration in developing-country growth during the 2003–07 period arose despite relatively lackluster GDP and import growth among high-income countries. Developed-world GDP grew on average 0.2 percentage point slower than during the 1990s and import demand increased 0.4 percentage point less quickly.

- The fall in borrowing costs during the 2003–07 period was associated with almost 70 percent of the increase in capital flows into developing countries and 80 percent of the increase in domestic intermediation.

- While the biggest apparent contribution to the changes in the extent of intermediation in developing countries was driven by lower borrowing costs and the overall expansion of global liquidity, cross-country differences in the level of intermediation remain very large and are best explained by fundamental factors such as the quality of regulatory frameworks and the business environment, inflation rates, and levels of government debt.

  o Country-specific differences in the quality of institutions and the degree of market openness of the top and bottom performing 25 percent of countries are associated with 56 and 37 percent of the cross-country variation in levels of domestic intermediation, respectively, and 1/3 and 1/5 of the cross-country difference in international capital flows.

  o Countries with good regulatory environments were also more successful in transforming increased financing into increased investment and GDP growth. More than one-quarter of the 11.5 percent of GDP difference between the investment rates of the top and bottom 25 percent of developing countries appears to reflect differences in the quality of institutions.

o Countries with high levels of financial openness and well-developed domestic intermediation systems also had higher investment rates. About 3 percentage points of the difference between the investment-to-GDP ratio of the top 25 percent of developing countries and the bottom 25 percent is associated with differences in the size of foreign capital inflows. For domestic intermediation, the same figure is just under 2 percent of GDP.

o These results suggest that if Sub-Saharan Africa could improve its institutions to roughly the levels observed in Latin America, the overall extent of financial intermediation would rise substantially, perhaps by as much as 12 percent of GDP in the case of domestic credit to the private sector and 2 percent of GDP in the case of international financial flows.

- Different forms of finance had different effects on investment.

  o Bond flows had significant impacts on investment in middle-income countries.

  o Bank lending, which dominated flows into Europe and Central Asia, were associated with a larger increase in current account deficits and consumer demand.

  o Foreign direct investment (FDI) funded as much as 20 percent of total investment in some regions, with low-income countries tending to be more reliant on this form of financing than richer countries.

- Overall, more than half of the 1.4 percentage point increase in potential output growth rates in developing countries between 2003 and 2007 is directly attributable to the capital deepening that was observed during this period, even under the conservative assumption that higher investment had no role in the rise in productivity.

- The expansion of investment and growth during the boom period, without the creation of significant inflationary pressures or external imbalances in many developing countries, suggests that in these countries the boom relieved what may have been a binding capital constraint on growth. That in turn implies that such stronger growth rates for developing countries may be achievable over the long term if sufficient finance (domestic or external) is forthcoming. Of course there were exceptions, notably in the Europe and Central Asia region, where the strongest expansions in credit boom contributed to macroeconomic instability.

Financial innovation, high-income finance, and the liquidity boom

The liquidity boom that preceded the financial crisis of 2008 was broadly based and rooted in a number of factors. Like other booms and busts, this one was prompted by a rapid increase in credit and investment that ultimately proved unsustainable and the ensuing bust provoked a sudden contraction in GDP (box 2.1).

Data from the Bank of International Settlements (BIS) indicates that from 2002 through 2007 international bank credit expanded about twice as fast as nominal GDP and more than twice as fast as it had during the previous decade (figure 2.1). Long-term interest rates were only between 1.5 and 2 percentage points higher than inflation in the major industrial countries (table 2.1), compared with about 3.5 percentage points (in the United States) during the global expansion in the second half of the 1990s.

The proximate cause of the credit boom is a question of considerable debate—a debate that is unlikely to be resolved anytime soon. Among the competing and not necessarily contradictory explanations are:

A savings glut. According to this argument (see Bernanke 2005, among others), high

Box 2.1 Comparing this boom-bust cycle with other major cycles

This boom-bust cycle shares many characteristics with earlier financial crises: an extended period of rapid and ultimately unsustainable credit expansion, accompanied by excessive risk taking by financial institutions, followed by a sharp reduction in economic activity. However, this crisis differs in three important respects from earlier crises.

First, this crisis is the most severe and widespread downturn since 1945. Global GDP is estimated to have declined by 2.2 percent in 2009 (the only absolute decline in global GDP during the postwar period), and GDP is projected to remain well below potential output for years to come, with estimates of the developing-country output gap peaking at 4.8 percent of GDP—almost 50 percent larger than during the next most severe modern-day recession (1982–83).

Second, for the majority of developing countries this is a crisis that originated in high-income countries. Moreover, with the notable exception of many countries in Europe and Central Asia, it was

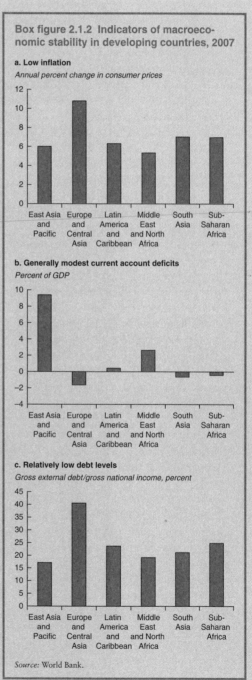

Box figure 2.1.2 Indicators of macroeconomic stability in developing countries, 2007

a. Low inflation
Annual percent change in consumer prices

b. Generally modest current account deficits
Percent of GDP

c. Relatively low debt levels
Gross external debt/gross national income, percent

Source: World Bank.

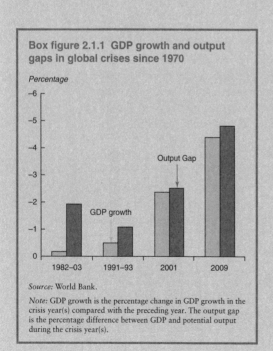

Box figure 2.1.1 GDP growth and output gaps in global crises since 1970

Percentage

Source: World Bank.

Note: GDP growth is the percentage change in GDP growth in the crisis year(s) compared with the preceding year. The output gap is the percentage difference between GDP and potential output during the crisis year(s).

not preceded by the buildup of serious domestic and external imbalances, and domestic actors largely did not participate directly in the unsustainable activities that precipitated the crisis.

During earlier global or large-scale crises triggered by changes in high-income countries, major impacts tended to be limited to developing countries with preexisting vulnerabilities. The tightening of U.S. monetary policy in 1979–80 boosted real interest rates and brought on a global recession, which hit hardest those developing countries with excessive levels of private-source debt. The depreciation of the yen against the dollar in the mid-1990s reduced the competitiveness of East Asian economies that pegged their currencies to the dollar, which may have contributed to the onset of the 1997 crisis. By contrast, the current crisis struck virtually every developing country hard, even though, outside Europe and Central Asia, most countries did not exhibit unsustainable macroeconomic balances (box figure 2.1.2). In most countries regional inflation rates averaged about 6 percent or lower (well below the double-digit rates in most regions during the early 1990s); most regional current account balances were near zero or strongly positive; and ratios of debt to gross national income were modest. However, the quality of policies still affected the impact of the crisis—the countries with the largest imbalances suffered the most (see chapter 3).

Third, this crisis has struck many more countries than earlier recessions did, a factor that complicates recovery for individual countries because there are few fast-growing external markets with which to engage in an export-led recovery strategy.

savings relative to investment in East Asia kept global interest rates low, fueling rapid increases in investment and consumption in high-income countries.

An extended period of loose monetary policy. Very loose monetary conditions in the United States, Japan, and Europe over an extended period of time bled through into longer maturities, provoking an unprecedented expansion in global credit (BIS 2006).

An excessive loosening of regulatory oversight. The reduction of regulatory barriers to speculation and excessive reliance on self-regulation of the banking sector in industrial countries generated and failed to curb excessive risk taking by financial institutions (Crotty 2009).

Financial innovations. In this loosely controlled environment, the use of new financial innovations expanded rapidly; these innovations increased risk taking and helped to circumvent those regulatory barriers that remained (Calvo 2009).

Finally, in contrast to popular thinking, unusually strong developed-country demand

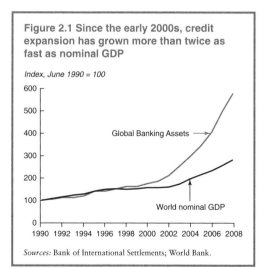

Figure 2.1 Since the early 2000s, credit expansion has grown more than twice as fast as nominal GDP

Index, June 1990 = 100

Global Banking Assets

World nominal GDP

Sources: Bank of International Settlements; World Bank.

Table 2.1   Interest rates and inflation in industrial countries, January 2002–June 2007
(percent)

	Consumer price inflation	Average long-term interest rate
Euro Area	2.2	4.1
Japan	−0.1	1.4
United States	3.0	4.4

Source: OECD.
Note: CPI inflation is expressed as the average annual percentage change over the period, and the average long-term rate is in percent.

was not a major factor behind the acceleration in developing-country growth or exports. Indeed, the boom period 2003–07 was actually one of relatively slow growth for high-income countries in terms of both GDP and imports. Developed-country GDP grew on average 2.3 percent during the period versus an average of 2.5 percent between 1990 and 2003 (figure 2.2). Moreover, notwithstanding the somewhat heated rhetoric surrounding trade issues, high-income-country import demand, which grew an average of 5.6 percent during the boom period, actually expanded less quickly than during 1990–2003, when it

rose an average of 6.0 percent annually. The strong performance of developing-country exports during this period reflected three main factors: rapidly expanding supply capacity in developing countries, an increase in their share of the imports of high-income countries, and rapidly expanding South-South trade.

Novel channels for credit creation

Whatever the fundamental reason for the long credit boom, the increased availability of a number of new financial instruments (box 2.2) gave investors what ultimately proved to be a false sense that the risks of rapid credit expansion had been reduced. This false sense of security contributed to the reductions of interest rates and interest rate spreads, thus facilitating the expansion of credit.

The expanded use of a number of these financial innovations boosted the growth of what has been called the "shadow banking system"—comprising institutions that do not have access to deposit insurance or central bank rediscount operations and that are not subject to the same prudential regulations as banks (Farhi and Cintra 2009). These institutions nevertheless actively sold and marketed instruments that leveraged the savings of households in a manner akin to the credit creation process of more traditional banks. The institutions involved included investment banks, hedge funds, investment funds, private equity funds, special investment vehicles (including those operated off balance sheet by banks), pension funds, and insurance companies. The quasi-banking activities of these entities were actively supported by ratings agencies, which markedly increased their revenues by rating the structured products these entities sold.

It is difficult to measure the contribution of the shadow banking system to the financial boom, compared with more traditional balance-sheet transactions of the commercial

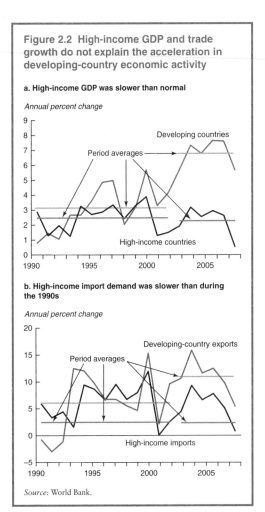

Figure 2.2 High-income GDP and trade growth do not explain the acceleration in developing-country economic activity

Source: World Bank.

Box 2.2 Recent and systemically important financial innovations

Securitization is not a recent innovation, but its use skyrocketed during the boom. It refers to the issuance of new securities backed by a pool of debt instruments. By this mechanism, a relatively illiquid stream of future cash flows (such as a standard loan with fixed repayment terms) is converted into a security that can be traded in the marketplace.

Credit default swaps (CDSs) are agreements in which the buyer makes a series of payments to the seller, in return for which the seller is obligated to compensate the buyer if the underlying bond or loan goes into default. Effectively, these instruments provided insurance against default—although the regulatory environment for such swaps and insurance are very different. More extensive use of credit default swaps also increased arbitraging opportunities by making it easier for speculators to take positions in securities that they did not own (Guttmann 2009).

Interest rate and currency swaps are instruments that allow investors to effectively change the payment scheme associated with a loan or an asset. For example, interest rate swaps often involve contracting to make a fixed series of payments by one counterparty in exchange for receiving a second series of payments based on a floating rate. Other swaps involve

swapping payment obligations from one currency to another. These transactions are often used to protect a portfolio in the face of uncertain changes in interest or exchange rates or to speculate on such changes.

Collateralized debt obligations (CDOs) are securities backed by collateral in the form of a portfolio of bonds, bank loans, or other debt (such as credit card debt). Repayments to the pool of investors are typically allocated according to some prioritization; for example, senior CDO notes are paid first. Other tranches earn higher returns but are only paid out if funds *are* remaining. This structure permits issues that satisfy differing trade-offs between risk and return: more speculative investors can purchase the lower-rated tranches, while more risk-averse investors can purchase higher-rated tranches.

Other credit derivative products. U.S. financial markets have generated several, more exotic approaches to securitizing debt transactions. For example, credit-linked notes are sold with an embedded credit default swap, where the issuer is not required to repay the debt if a specified event occurs (essentially eliminating the need for third-party insurance). Specialty finance companies have been created where transactions involve both securitization and lending.

banking system—in large part because it faced much less comprehensive reporting requirements and oversight. One indication of its importance can be gleaned from the rise in the share in total U.S. domestic credit of mortgage pools (issued by Fannie Mae and Freddie Mac) and asset-backed securities. In 1995 these securities accounted for 16 percent of credit assets held by the U.S. financial sector or 30 percent of GDP. By 2007 the value of these securities had increased more than fivefold, reaching 23 percent of credit assets and 63 percent of GDP—almost as large as the total of commercial bank assets (figure 2.3).

The credit expansion was also reflected in the phenomenal rise in derivative swap

transactions, the notional value of which quadrupled between 2002 and 2008 (figure 2.3), reaching more than 25 times U.S. GDP (figure 2.4). The gross notional value of the derivative market involves considerable double counting (the net exposure of counterparties is much smaller because of offsetting transactions); moreover the actual associated flows involved in these transactions are typically a very small percentage of the notional values. Nevertheless, the notional value provides a sense of how pervasive and far reaching these instruments had become in intermediating economic activity. Moreover, the notional values provide a sense of the systemic vulnerability represented by these instruments, especially during the acute phase of the crisis when the ability of

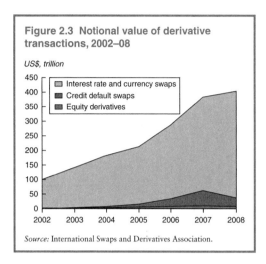

Figure 2.3 Notional value of derivative transactions, 2002–08

US$, trillion

Legend: Interest rate and currency swaps; Credit default swaps; Equity derivatives

Source: International Swaps and Derivatives Association.

counterparties to meet their commitments was called into question and default payments under derivative contracts mushroomed.

The impact of the expansion of the shadow banking system was to greatly expand the amount of credit available and reduce its cost. Shadow banking effectively performed the same functions as banks, increasing assets to several times their equity by funding long-term assets with short-term liabilities (by

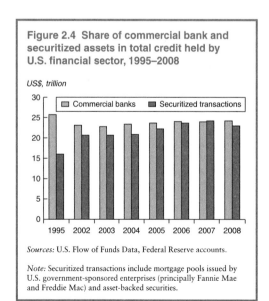

Figure 2.4 Share of commercial bank and securitized assets in total credit held by U.S. financial sector, 1995–2008

US$, trillion

Legend: Commercial banks; Securitized transactions

Sources: U.S. Flow of Funds Data, Federal Reserve accounts.

Note: Securitized transactions include mortgage pools issued by U.S. government-sponsored enterprises (principally Fannie Mae and Freddie Mac) and asset-backed securities.

raising funds in the commercial paper market, for example). The instruments it employed (such as collateralized debt obligations—see box 2.2) had the perceived virtue (compared with bank loans) of spreading the risk of lending. Large, risky investments could be divided efficiently among investors and thus increase the feasibility of such projects. And investors could more easily diversify their risk portfolio, allowing them to undertake higher risk and return projects.

However, these instruments were either loosely or not at all regulated and may have induced banks to reduce their lending standards more than they would have otherwise because the long-term risk associated with loans was being held by others. Moreover, in the event, ownership was concentrated in some systemically important hands. Banks were left with large holdings—often the lower-quality, higher-yielding tranches. In addition, banks that relied on secondary markets to buy and sell loans tended to increase their leverage (Duffie 2007), which contributed to increasing systemic risk to the extent that the buyers of these securitized loans lacked sufficient information to accurately evaluate the risks involved.[2] The extreme complexity of some of these instruments and the lack of standardized exchanges made it difficult for both purchasers and sellers to evaluate them and exacerbated the difficulties in debt renegotiations in the case of financial distress. Ex post, it appears clear that these instruments generated substantial further systemic risks by multiplying in a nontransparent manner the interdependencies in the financial system.

On balance, the growth of the shadow banking system and the expanded use of securitization and derivatives products worldwide (see box 2.2) contributed to the expansion of credit in developing countries during the boom period. Several factors underpinned the increased use of these instruments in developing countries. Their expanding use in high-income countries made more investors familiar with their benefits, while efforts to standardize derivative contracts (by the International Securities Dealers Association, for example, to develop standard documentation for credit default swaps) helped reduce their costs and improved confidence in derivative transactions. Growth in spot markets also encouraged greater use of derivatives for hedging purposes. In addition, the expansion of the size and length of maturities in local currency bond markets facilitated the creation and pricing of developing-country interest rate derivatives (Saxena and Villar 2008).

The expanded use of these products helped to disperse risk, improve diversification among investors, and increase the pool of developing-world investors, thereby increasing capital flows to developing countries. For example, banks were able to expand lending to developing-country borrowers—even high-risk borrowers—and transfer the risk to capital markets through credit default swaps (World Bank 2007) and by pooling loans and selling them to investors in high-income countries. Between 2003 and 2008, CDS spreads were quoted widely for 40 developing countries, in addition to a number of privately negotiated deals that were not widely reported.[3] The proliferation of securitized and derivative products enabled pension funds and insurance companies, many of which face regulatory restrictions on the kinds of investments they can make, to take indirect positions in developing-country loans by purchasing the more highly rated tranches of securitized loans.

The secondary sale of developing-country loans to nonbank investors, or the banks' own off-balance-sheet vehicles, contributed to overall credit expansion by replenishing banks' reserves and allowing them to provide new additional loans to developing countries. Increased availability of derivatives also boosted the supply of FDI by providing investors with a mechanism to hedge the short-term foreign exchange risk involved in projects, particularly in those targeting production for the domestic market (Griffith-Jones and Leape 2002).

Not all derivative transactions involving developing-country instruments increased the availability of capital to developing countries. For example, synthetic collateralized debt obligations were mainly a vehicle to facilitate speculation on developing-country returns. Investors purchase a synthetic CDO, the return on which was tied, say, to changes in the credit default swap spread on bonds issued by the Brazilian government. Because these synthetic CDOs did not involve the repackaging of existing bank loans, they did not reduce banks' exposure to developing-country debt and therefore did not enable them to increase lending. Indeed, some observers argue that by facilitating speculation, these instruments increased volatility in developing-country financial markets.[4]

Developing-country finance during the boom

The expansion of liquidity in high-income countries, the financial innovations, and the consequent fall in the price of risk dramatically changed developing-country finance. Net capital inflows quintupled, and spreads on foreign debt fell from 656 basis points in 2000 to 168 basis points at the end of 2007. Equally important, domestic credit as a share of GDP increased by 5 percentage points on average, with much larger increases in several regions, while domestic interest rates declined across the board. These developments were accompanied by an unprecedented tripling in the valuation of equities traded on developing-economy stock markets.

The rise in financial intermediation increased the supply of finance available to entrepreneurs to undertake productive investment, thereby contributing to capital accumulation and the expansion of potential output. Moreover, the influx of new investments, embodying newer technologies, facilitated an overall acceleration in technological progress in developing countries that was also supported by macroeconomic and institutional reforms in many countries.[5] Finally, the acceleration in growth itself likely triggered a further deepening of financial markets (see box 2.3 for the positive interaction between financial intermediation and growth).

Of course, while a rapid increase in global liquidity can facilitate economic growth, in some circumstances it can also cause macroeconomic instability. Easy access to finance can lead to excessive consumption and unsustainable current account deficits, as was the case in many countries in emerging Europe and Central Asia. More generally, international finance tends to be especially procyclical for developing-country borrowers. Weak institutions (including protection of property rights) and low-income levels make them less creditworthy on average. As a result, when both global and domestic conditions are good,

middle-income borrowers (and those low-income borrowers with market access) may see a surge of inflows that reverse especially sharply when prospects deteriorate.

Historically, this "stop-go" quality of finance, particularly external debt and portfolio equity flows, has exacerbated booms and painful busts in many developing countries. The source of instability is not always foreign, however. In many instances, large swings in international capital flows have been ascribed to the behavior of domestic investors.[6] In the East Asian financial crisis, much of the capital flight that contributed to the large currency depreciations and macroeconomic instability was the result of domestic investors fleeing local currency instruments in favor of foreign-denominated instruments that were expected to be better stores of value (Kawai, Newfarmer,

Box 2.3   Financial intermediation and economic development

Several empirical studies find that the size and efficiency of financial intermediation has a causal affect on growth: Measures of financial development are found to be correlated with growth in a subsequent period in a cross-section of countries (King and Levine 1993, Levine and Zervos 1998 for developed economies). Financial market deepening is found to be related to productive efficiency in cross-section data, including both developed and developing countries (Nourzad 2002). Financial development is associated with poverty reduction (Jalilian and Kirkpatrick 2002; Beck, Demirgüç-Kunt, and Levine 2007) and is found to precede growth in tests of Granger causation on time series data (Neusser and Kugler 1998; Rousseau and Wachtel 1998). Instrumental variables (English, French, German, or Scandinavian legal origin) as well as other econometric techniques are used to isolate the causal impact of financial development (Levine, Loayza, and Beck 2000). Financial development also is found to raise growth principally through its effects on total factor productivity (Beck, Levine, and Loayza 1999). Several country studies also show that financial development has a major impact on growth over time (Levine 1997).

But the literature is not unanimous in identifying a causal relationship between financial development and growth. Growth also has an impact on financial development. Moreover, third factors (such as technological innovations in communications and data processing, as well as the quality of institutions) affect both growth and financial development. Several economists find a bidirectional relationship between financial development and growth (Luintel and Kahn 1999; Al-Yousif 2002; Demetriades and Hussein 1999). Hurlin and Venet (2008) find a robust causality from growth to financial development in a sample of developed and developing countries but little evidence of causality from financial development to growth. Arestis and Demetriades (1997) find that financial development causes growth in only a few countries in their sample; Shan (2005) and Shan and Morris (2002), using time series data (covering OECD countries plus China), find little evidence that financial development leads economic growth; and Al-Taimimi and others (2001) find no evidence of Granger causation between financial development or economic growth in either direction from a sample of Arab countries.

and Schmukler 2001; World Bank 1998). A similar dynamic underlay the crisis in Mexico in 1994–95 (Frankel and Schmukler 1996). In the case of Chile following the East Asian and Russian crises, however, foreign investors were the main sources of capital flight (Cowan and others 2005).

As discussed in chapter 1, during the recent crisis a rapid reversal in capital flows adversely affected virtually every developing country, even those that had pursued prudent macroeconomic policies and accumulated large stocks of foreign currency reserves. That said, the countries (notably many in the Europe and Central Asia region[7]) that were hardest hit were precisely those in which the additional liquidity had been channeled into domestic consumption and that had accumulated significant domestic and external imbalances during the boom period.

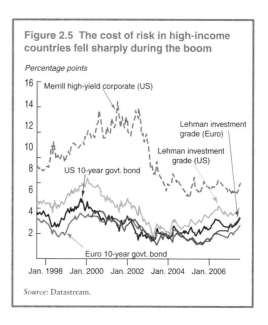

Figure 2.5 The cost of risk in high-income countries fell sharply during the boom

Percentage points

Source: Datastream.

The reduction in the price of risk

The rapid expansion of global credit and the low interest rates that accompanied it were reflected in a sharp fall of secondary-market spreads on investment grade and high-risk debt in industrial countries. For example, the risk premium on AAA corporate bonds in the United States fell from 490 to 65 basis points between 2002 and 2007, while that on BBB grade European corporate debt fell from 390 to 55 basis points. The simultaneous fall of spreads on a wide variety of risky assets is consistent with a significant reduction in the price of risk itself, either because of a decline in risk aversion on the part of investors or because of the emergence of a view that derivatives and other hedging mechanisms had lowered the likely financial cost of holding a given level of risk (figure 2.5).

The decline in interest rates and the fall in the price of riskier assets at the beginning of the decade were initially treated as a temporary cyclical phenomenon. However, as the boom period continued, commentators increasingly began to argue that financial market innovations such as credit default swaps and the securitization of loans in secondary

markets had permanently reduced long-term interest rates and risk premiums.

Falling interest rates internationally, lower risk premiums, and, especially toward the end of the boom period, rising commodity prices also meant that financial conditions within developing countries relaxed. Reflecting both these developments and the influence of policy improvements and political factors, interest rate premiums and the interest rates paid by developing-country borrowers fell sharply in several regions (figure 2.6).

The expansion in domestic credit

The decline in borrowing costs was associated with a rapid increase in financial flows, domestic intermediation, and capital market valuations throughout the developing world (table 2.2). Banking intermediation, as measured by claims of deposit money banks on the private sector, expanded on average from 29 percent of GDP in 2000 to 35 percent in 2007—greatly boosting the funds available to firms for investment (see table 2.2). In some regions, a growing participation by foreign banks in domestic financial systems

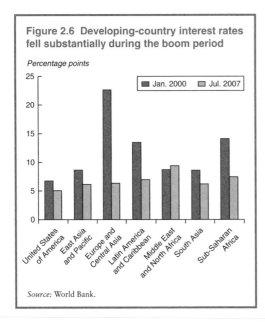

Figure 2.6 Developing-country interest rates fell substantially during the boom period

Percentage points

Legend: ■ Jan. 2000 □ Jul. 2007

Source: World Bank.

supported the rapid rise in domestic financial intermediation (box 2.4). Firms in developing countries also benefited from a surge in stock market capitalization, which rose from 35 percent of GDP in 2000 to 114 percent in 2007.[8] Moreover, lower interest rates and interest rate spreads reduced the cost of capital facing investors in developing countries. Partly as a consequence, ratios of investment to GDP adjusted for inflation jumped by 5 percent of GDP on average, with an 8 percent GDP jump in South Asia.

All regions participated in the financial boom to some extent, although the increase in

financial intermediation and the levels reached varied significantly:

- In Europe and Central Asia, bank credit almost doubled and stock market capitalization more than quadrupled (relative to GDP), reflecting very low initial levels attributable to the region's communist past (despite 10 years of transition), the prospects for accession of several countries to the European Union, and the boom in oil prices. Of the 25 countries with sufficient data, 12 registered increases in credit to the private sector of more than 10 percent of GDP.
- Financial intermediation also rose strongly in South Asia. In India the ratio of bank credit to GDP increased by 15 percentage points and the stock market capitalization nearly quintupled relative to GDP. Other countries in the region had more moderate increases (for example, the ratio of bank credit to GDP increased 12 percentage points in Bangladesh and 6 percentage points in Pakistan).
- The increase in credit to the private sector in the Middle East and North Africa was smaller but still robust—partly reflecting the fact that as measured the cost of capital in the region actually increased (see table 2.2). Credit in Algeria, Morocco, and Tunisia registered gains of 5–6 percentage points of GDP. Despite the near tripling of stock prices, the increase as a percentage

Table 2.2 Changes in domestic intermediation, 2000–07

Region	Private credit by banks			Stock market capitalization		
	2000	2007	Change	2000	2007	Change
	(percent of GDP)		(% points)	(percent of GDP)		(% points)
Developing countries	29.3	34.8	5.5	35.3	113.9	78.6
East Asia and Pacific	66.1	55.4	−10.7	47.1	165.1	118.0
Europe and Central Asia	16.8	32.5	15.6	17.5	77.3	59.8
Latin America and the Caribbean	24.9	27.1	2.2	31.6	71.4	39.8
Middle East and North Africa	33.0	39.2	6.2	19.9	56.1	36.2
South Asia	25.6	40.4	14.8	26.1	133.4	107.2
Sub-Saharan Africa	34.8	41.6	6.8	89.9	149.0	59.1

Source: World Bank calculations using Beck and Demirgüç-Kunt 2009.
Note: For private credit, the regional numbers are simple averages of available country data. For stock market capitalization, the averages are weighted by GDP.

Box 2.4   The role of foreign banks in domestic intermediation

Foreign banks play an important and growing role in domestic intermediation among developing countries. As of 2005, their share in total banking assets in developing regions ranged from a low of 7.4 percent in South Asia to a high of 54.4 percent in Europe and Central Asia (box table 2.4.1). Moreover, during the boom period foreign banks increased their share in total assets in all of the regions where they already had relatively large presences. Indeed, the extent of the expansion in domestic credit is loosely related to the extent to which foreign banks increased their market shares. The two regions with the smallest foreign presence (East Asia and the Pacific and South Asia) actually saw the market share of foreign banks decline.

The contribution of foreign banks to intermediation in developing countries is not straightforward. In some countries they can serve as an important conduit that facilitates the importation of external

capital to expand lending, and if they are more efficient and improve domestic bank efficiency (see below), they can reduce the cost of financial intermediation and encourage higher volumes. In these instances, foreign banks by stimulating intermediation may, in turn, encourage more rapid development. For example, in Europe and Central Asia, the acquisition of local banks by foreign banks was associated with increased lending to small and medium-size enterprises and retail markets (de Haas and Naaborg 2006), even though foreign banks lent predominantly to multinational corporations, large domestic firms, and governments—potentially squeezing out smaller players (see Gormley 2005 for the theoretical model). Indeed, the entrance of foreign banks in a market tended to cause local banks to increase lending to small enterprises in part because of increased competition in lending to larger firms (Jenkins 2000).

In some cases foreign banks may reduce the level of financial intermediation. Research suggests that especially among low-income countries with weak regulatory frameworks and competition law, foreign banks may enter into a market and cherry-pick the best local clients (Detragiache, Tressel, and Gupta 2006). In such circumstances, a larger presence of foreign banks may be associated with less credit to the private sector.

Overall, the evidence is mixed. Survey data indicate that entrepreneurs in countries with larger participation by foreign banks face less binding credit constraints (Clarke, Cull, and Martinez Peria 2001). Moreover, when domestic conditions are propitious (a solid local banking sector, and good regulatory and competitive protections), foreign banks can contribute to an overall expansion of credit and a lowering of costs for borrowers. However, foreign bank participation is not critical to increasing financial intermediation in developing countries and can, in some regions with weakly contested and poorly regulated markets, result in the crowding out of local providers and no net increase in intermediation.

Box table 2.4.1   Foreign bank participation and credit expansion

Region	Share of assets owned by foreign banks, 2001	Share of assets owned by foreign banks, 2005	Change in ratio of bank credit to the private sector over GDP, 2000–07
East Asia and Pacific	13.0	11.1	−10.7
Europe and Central Asia	42.0	54.4	15.7
Latin America and Caribbean	30.4	35.6	2.2
Middle East and North Africa	8.3	10.9	6.2
South Asia	8.9	7.4	14.8
Sub-Saharan Africa	46.2	49.5	6.8

Source: World Bank database on Financial Institutions and Structure.

of GDP and the level in 2007 were smaller than in the other developing regions

- The 7 percentage point increase in bank credit (relative to GDP) in Sub-Saharan Africa mainly reflects a 12 percentage point rise in South Africa, rather than a more generalized increase in domestic financial intermediation. Of the 30 countries with complete data, 9 experienced declines in domestic intermediation relative to GDP, and 12 countries experienced increases of less than 5 percentage points. Sufficient data on stock market capitalization are reported for only 13 countries. The strong increase is attributable to capitalization more than tripling relative to GDP in Côte d'Ivoire, Kenya, Mauritius, and Nigeria. The high level of stock market capitalization relative to output, however, is attributable to South Africa, where the level reached nearly three times output in 2006. Because South Africa attracts investment from other economies in the region that lack stock markets and are hence not included in the average, the average tends to overstate the level of capitalization for the South African economy per se. Excluding South Africa, the region has the lowest level of stock market capitalization relative to output of the six developing regions.

- The small average increase in credit to the private sector relative to output in Latin America and the Caribbean reflects very different outcomes across countries, ranging from a decline of more than 26 percentage points in Bolivia and Uruguay to an increase of 17 percentage points in Colombia and Costa Rica. Macroeconomic policies in Latin America have improved greatly since their boom-and-bust experiences over the last decades of the 20th century, and many countries avoided an excessive buildup of private credit and achieved steady growth in incomes. Compared with most other regions, the doubling of stock market capitalization was modest and may have reflected policy prudence by authorities in the region seeking to avoid an asset-price bubble.

- The drop in private credit relative to GDP in East Asia and the Pacific stems in part from adjustments following the East Asia crisis, with particularly significant declines in Malaysia (27 percentage points) and the Philippines (14 percentage points). However, East Asia is the developing region with the deepest domestic financial systems, and the region's ratio of bank credit to GDP exceeded that of the United States (although remaining below that of the more bank-based systems in Western Europe). The further deepening of financial markets was reflected in the more than tripling of stock market capitalization over the period.

The rise in foreign flows

The increase in domestic financial intermediation during the liquidity boom was accompanied by a rapid expansion of capital inflows (figure 2.7). Similar to increases in domestic credit, higher capital inflows can boost investment and efficiency (box 2.5).

While virtually every country saw inflows rise, they did not rise by the same amount in all countries, and not all forms of international capital flow increased to the same degree. *Portfolio equity flows* to developing countries increased rapidly before the financial

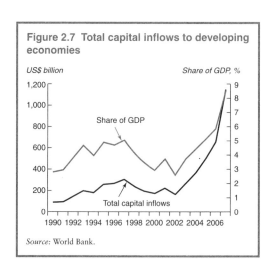

Figure 2.7 Total capital inflows to developing economies

Source: World Bank.

Box 2.5   Capital flows can boost investment and efficiency

Most developing countries relied on external finance during the 2003–07 boom. Developing countries' aggregate current account surplus (which averaged almost $243 billion during this period) mainly reflected large surpluses of savings over investment in a few countries, notably China, and developing oil and mineral exporters. Three-fourths of the remaining developing countries for which data are available were net importers of capital, with current account deficits that averaged more than 6 percent of their GDP and 28 percent of their total investment spending (box table 2.5.1).

External finance can improve efficiency by enhancing the transfer of technology from more developed economies, helping firms achieve larger size and thus benefit from economies of scale, building reputations in global markets, and establishing business and marketing contacts for developing countries' exports (World Bank 2006). These effects can be indirect or arrive more directly, as can be the case with some forms of foreign direct investment, if the result is the importation of more sophisticated machines or business techniques.

Box table 2.5.1   Developing countries with current account deficits, 2003–07

	Number of countries with current account deficits	Current account deficit (% of GDP)	Current account deficit (% of investment)
All countries	53	6.3	26.8
Low income	16	5.8	29.1
Lower middle income	20	6.1	23.4
Upper middle income	17	7.1	28.3

Source: World Bank.
Note: Data on current account deficits are simple averages of country numbers. Small island economies are excluded.

crisis, from near zero in 2001 to $160 billion in 2007, followed by a total collapse in 2008 (figure 2.8).

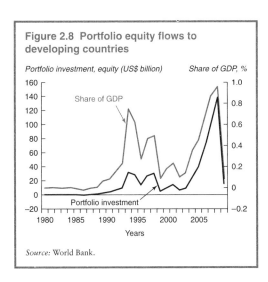

Figure 2.8 Portfolio equity flows to developing countries

Portfolio investment, equity (US$ billion)   Share of GDP, %

Share of GDP

Portfolio investment

Years

Source: World Bank.

Developing countries' access to external *bond markets and foreign bank lending* increased markedly during the liquidity boom, reaching a peak of 4 percent of developing-country GDP in 2007. *Net FDI inflows* increased from about 2.5 percent of GDP in 2001 to 3.9 percent in 2007 before falling slightly in 2008, along with the reduction in global investment in general (figure 2.9). *Official flows*, in contrast, reversed from net inflows of $26 billion in 2001 to net outflows of $0.1 billion in 2007.

At the regional level, Europe and Central Asia, East Asia and the Pacific, and Latin America were the largest recipients of capital inflows, receiving more than 80 percent of net inflows over 2001–07, with the first two regions together accounting for 65 percent of the total. However, expressed as a share of GDP, the differences in inflows across regions were

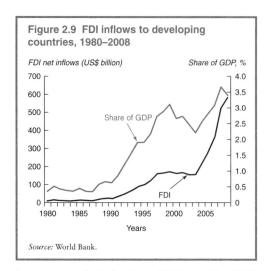

Figure 2.9 FDI inflows to developing countries, 1980–2008

FDI net inflows (US$ billion)   *Share of GDP, %*

Source: World Bank.

1.5 percent of their GDP in 2001 to almost 7 percent in 2007, largely supported by the rise in resource-related FDI.

Across regions, the relative importance of different types of capital flows varied somewhat. In most regions equity (especially FDI) accounted for both the bulk of capital inflows in 2007 and most of the increase in inflows over 2001–07 (table 2.3). In developing Europe and Central Asia, however, net debt flows grew from almost nothing in 2001 to almost 10 percent of GDP. As such they represented about two-thirds of total inflows in 2007. Had Europe and Central Asia received the same increase in debt flows as other developing regions, its overall inflows would have been closer to 8 percent of GDP, similar to those received by East Asia, South Asia, and Sub-Saharan Africa. Although many factors underpin the strength of debt inflows to the region—including enthusiasm for the region's long-term prospects within the European Union and the high share of foreign banks in the overall banking sector—the population's willingness to take on exchange rate risk by borrowing in foreign currencies helps to explain why bank lending—including to private individuals—played such a prominent role.

At the country level, absolute flows are extremely concentrated, with China, India, the Russian Federation, and Brazil accounting for about 50 percent of net inflows both in 2007 and, on average, over 2001–07; the four also account for 73 percent of all flows

less pronounced—both in 2001, and in 2007 when flows peaked. Flows to East Asia and the Pacific, relative to GDP, were only slightly above the developing-country average in 2001 and were actually below average in 2007. In contrast, while flows to developing Europe and Central Asia as a share of GDP were below average in 2001, they grew about fivefold by 2007. South Asia also saw inflows increase very rapidly, from only about 1 percent of GDP in 2001 to more than 8 percent in 2007. Contrary to accepted wisdom, Sub-Saharan Africa actually received close to average flows (relative to GDP) both in the pre-boom and end-of-boom periods. Both middle-income and low-income countries benefited from the surge in capital flows. The flows to low-income countries more than quadrupled, from

Table 2.3 Net capital inflows by region

	2001	2007	Avg. 2001–2007	2001	2007	2001	2007
	(US$ billion)			(% of total flows to developing countries)		(% of region's GDP)	
Developing countries	223	1,143	470			4	9
East Asia and Pacific	83	277	141	37	24	5	7
Europe and Central Asia	29	454	164	13	40	3	15
Latin America and the Carribean	87	215	87	39	19	4	6
Middle East and North Africa	5	21	12	2	2	1	3
South Asia	8	116	39	4	10	1	8
Sub-Saharan Africa	11	60	27	5	5	3	7

Source: World Bank.

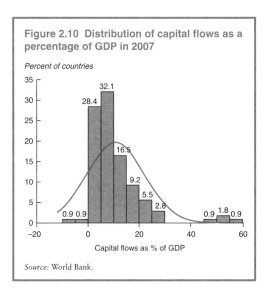

Figure 2.10 Distribution of capital flows as a percentage of GDP in 2007

Percent of countries

Source: World Bank.

(figure 2.10). However, relative to GDP, both the flows and the change in flows are more evenly distributed, with about 60 percent of countries receiving flows of between 0 and 10 percent of GDP in 2007 (figure 2.10).

Real-side consequences of the surge in global finance

The extent to which a given developing country benefited from the surge in global liquidity depended on a wide variety of factors, many of which are impossible or at best very difficult to measure in a consistent manner across countries.

Figure 2.11 reports simple correlations between private finance (as represented by domestic intermediation in the first column and foreign capital inflows in the second column) and borrowing costs, the quality of institutions, and the extent of real-side openness (all data are expressed in terms of the average from 2001 through 2007). Unsurprisingly, the levels of both domestic intermediation and private capital inflows are negatively correlated with borrowing costs—although the simple bivariate correlation illustrated here is not very strong, mainly because of the interaction of other factors (see below).

The quality of domestic institutions (proxied here by the Kaufmann–Kraay–Zoido-Lobaton index) is also correlated with both domestic and external finance. Demand for capital will depend on the potential revenues from a physical investment. Both domestic and international investors operating in countries with strong institutions and a well-functioning regulatory environment, including reasonable protection of property rights, will likely earn higher real-side returns and therefore, all else equal, be willing to take on more debt. Similarly, lenders providing finance to borrowers in countries with strong institutions and protection of property rights would be more likely to be able to enforce their claims for repayment and hence would be willing to lend more.

Finally, the extent of real-side integration of an economy is also a good predictor of the extent of financial intermediation and private capital inflows that a country receives (Figure 2.11 panel C. In the recent boom period, external factors such as the high price of commodities were also at play. Interestingly, while per capita income levels are highly correlated with the level of domestic intermediation (figure 2.12), the size of capital flows is only weakly related to income.

Although these correlations provide some insight into the differences in intermediation levels at a given point in time, they do not speak to what drove the changes observed during the boom (table 2.4).

By far the biggest drivers of the observed changes in the availability of domestic and international finance were changes in the cost of capital, here operating through the reduction of interest rates in high-income countries and interest rate spreads in developing countries. Cross-country regressions (box 2.6) suggest that for the average developing country a 500 basis point decline (roughly the mean decline observed over the estimation period—as well as a standard deviation across the sample of countries for which comparable data are available) in borrowing costs resulted in an increase in the level of domestic intermediation equal to 4.5 percent of GDP and an increase in

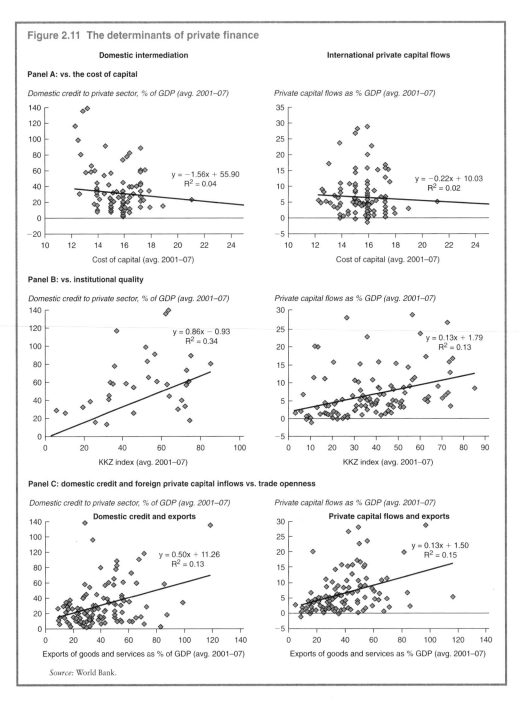

Figure 2.11 The determinants of private finance

Source: World Bank.

foreign capital inflows of 0.5 percent of GDP. Likewise, panel estimates suggest that financial conditions in developing countries were even more sensitive to international financial conditions. According to these estimates, a 1 point decline in the price of global risk (about the decline observed between 2003 and 2007) could result in an increase of 3.5 percent of GDP in foreign capital flows and an increase of 7.5 percent of GDP in domestic intermediation

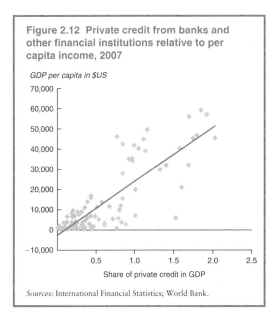

Figure 2.12 Private credit from banks and other financial institutions relative to per capita income, 2007

GDP per capita in $US

Share of private credit in GDP

Sources: International Financial Statistics; World Bank.

of capital. As a result, changes in the cost of capital (broadly understood to include the international price of risk) on average accounted for almost one-half of the observed fluctuation in capital inflows and about 60 percent of the increase in domestic intermediation (see table 2.4), with domestic intermediation being the only other quantitatively important factor in the determination of net capital inflows.

However, other factors, including institutional quality, overall economic openness, and the extent of domestic financial sector intermediation (in the case of the capital flows equation), were critical in explaining the wide differences in the levels of intermediation and inflows across countries both before and during the boom (lower panel of table 2.4). Cross-country differences in institutional quality (as measured by the Kaufmann–Kraay–Zoido-Lobaton Index) explained almost six-tenths of the variance in the level of domestic intermediation across countries and about one-third of the difference in net capital inflows. Indeed, a one-standard-deviation improvement in institutional quality (roughly equivalent to the average difference in institutional quality between Sub-Saharan Africa and Latin America) could generate a 12 percentage point increase in the ratio of private sector domestic credit to GDP, and an

(amounting to, respectively, more than two-thirds and more than three-fourths of the mean increase observed over the estimation period). The association is especially strong for debt inflows, and, not surprisingly, it does not hold for official aid.

Changes over time in other important determinants of domestic and international financial intermediation were not as large as the changes in international capital conditions and the cost

Table 2.4 Intertemporal changes in financial variables mainly reflected the cost of capital, but across countries institutional quality was most important

Financial variables	Net capital flows	Domestic intermediation
	(As a percent of GDP)	
Change over 2001–07 in sample mean of dependent variable	4.9	8.6
Contributions of changes in (sample mean of):		
Global cost of risk	2.2	5.1
Institutional quality	. . .	−0.08
Domestic intermediation	1.8	. . .
Difference in 2007 between top and bottom quartile in dependent variable		
Contribution of differences in:	1.61	34.5
Cost of capital	. . .	2.1
Institutional quality	3.7	19
Exports of GNFS	5.2	12.8

Source: World Bank.
Notes: Calculations based on estimates reported in box 2.6.
. . . Not estimated.

Box 2.6   Determinants of cross–country differences in domestic and international financial intermediation

Data limitations among other constraints prevent a comprehensive modeling of the factors that explain the extent of the expansion of domestic and international finance in developing countries in response to the global loosening of monetary conditions. However, cross-country regressions that seek to explain the average change in domestic intermediation (credit to the private sector) and international capital flows as a percentage of GDP provide important insights into the role of the country-specific potential explanatory variables (including changes in the cost of capital, institutional quality, financial development, exports, the budget surplus, and inflation).

These regressions confirm a statistically significant association between the level of domestic intermediation in developing countries and institutional quality, the share of exports in GDP, and their rate of growth (box table 2.6.1, column 2). The results also indicate a significant association between the level of international capital flows and institutional quality and exports (box table 2.6.1, column 3).

Both as a robustness check and to explore the role of the country-invariant risk-premium variable (discussed in chapter 3), panel regressions were also run for the period 2001–07, with net capital inflows and domestic intermediation as the dependent variables, and the risk premium plus the full set of regressors from the cross-sectional analysis as the independent variables. All independent variables were lagged, to diminish endogeneity concerns. These regressions confirm a statistically significant association between both domestic intermediation and capital inflows on the one hand and the international price of risk and financial development on the other (box table 2.6.2, columns 2 and 3). While the variation in the level of domestic financial intermediation was significantly associated with institutional quality, the variation in international capital flows was not. Nor did the cost of capital have an independent influence on either domestic or international intermediation beyond that of the price of international risk, likely reflecting the strong link between variations in the two variables (see chapter 3).

Box table 2.6.1   Cross-sectional regressions results

Dependent variable	Domestic intermediation (Private sector credit, % of GDP, Average 2001–07)	Net capital inflows (% of GDP, Average 2001–07)
Explanatory variables	Coefficient	Coefficient
Cost of capital[a]	−0.56*	−0.02
Institutional quality (Kaufmann–Kraay–Zoido-Lobaton index)[b]	0.69***	0.13***
Financial development (private sector credit, % of GDP)	—	−0.05
Export of goods and nonfactor services (% of GDP)	0.28**	0.13***
Export growth	0.53**	−0.244***
Budget surplus (% of GDP)	1.23***	0.12
Inflation (logs, percent)	−2.38	−0.52
R^2	0.46	0.36

Source: World Bank.
Note: All regressions estimated using average values over the period 2001–07 for the dependent variables, and initial values for the independent variables; number of countries = 103. Other controls include export growth, 1990–97 (percent, average annual rate); and indicators for countries in the upper quartile of both the fuel exports/GDP and the metals exports/GDP distribution.

*, **, and *** denote significance at, respectively, the 10 percent, 5 percent, and 1 percent level. Significance is evaluated using robust standard errors.
a. Measured as the U.S. T-bill rate, plus the country-specific spread, plus depreciation.
b. Measured on a scale of 0 to 100, with a cross-sectional standard deviation of 19.
— Not applicable.

Box table 2.6.2   Panel regression results

Dependent variable	Domestic intermediation (private sector credit, % of GDP)	Net capital inflows (% of GDP)
Explanatory variables	Coefficient	Coefficient
Global cost of risk[a]	−3.49***	−1.47*
Cost of capital[b]	−0.03	−0.03
Institutional quality (Kaufmann–Kraay–Zoido-Lobaton index)[c]	0.30**	−0.01
Financial development (private sector credit, % of GDP)	—	0.27***
Exports of goods and non-factor services (% of GDP)	−0.08	0.02
Budget surplus (% of GDP)	0.07	−0.03
Inflation (logs, %)	0.12	0.13
R^2	0.16	0.10

Source: World Bank.
Note: All regressions estimated using annual data over the period 2001–07, with all independent variables lagged once; number of observations = 498, 493. Other controls include indicators for countries in the upper quartile of both the (fuel exports/GDP and the metals exports/GDP distribution; and a full set of country-specific fixed effects.
*, **, and *** denote significance at, respectively, the 10 percent, 5 percent, and 1 percent level. Significance is evaluated using robust standard errors.
a. See above for details.
b. Measured as the U.S. T-bill rate, plus the country-specific spread, plus depreciation.
c. Measured on a scale of 0 to 100.
— Not applicable.

increase of 2 percent of GDP in private capital flows after controlling for all other factors. Countries with large export sectors and therefore a proven track record with foreign partners also tend to receive more foreign financing than those with weaker external ties. A country whose export sector was 5 percentage points larger than another's received, on average over 2001–07, an extra 0.5 percent of GDP in foreign capital inflows, and its total domestic intermediation amounted to an extra 1.5 percent of GDP. Cross-country differences in the extent of real-side openness were associated with about one-third of the differences in net capital flows and in domestic intermediation.

Table 2.5   Regional distribution of changes in financing conditions, 2000–07

	Change between 2007 and 2000 in:				
	Cost of capital	Capital inflows	Stock market capitalization	Private credit by deposits money banks	Investment
	(Basis points)		(% of GDP)		
Developing countries	−400	5.0	78.6	5.5	5.5
Low-income countries					2.3
Middle-income countries					5.6
East Asia and Pacific	−134	2.0	118.0	−10.7	5.5
Europe and Central Asia	−866	12.0	59.8	15.7	4.9
Latin America and the Caribbean	−471	2.0	39.8	2.2	1.4
Middle East and North Africa	269	2.0	36.2	6.2	5.0
South Asia	−142	7.0	107.3	14.8	8.1
Sub-Saharan Africa	−685	4.0	59.1	6.8	3.6

Sources: World Bank; Beck and Demirgüç-Kunt 2009; World Bank 2009.
Note: Regional values are simple averages of countries, except for investment rates which are weighted averages.

The association between capital inflows and macroeconomic stability (as represented by the budget surplus and inflation) was in general not statistically significant, after controlling for the cost of capital, institutional quality, export intensity, and the extent of financial sector intermediation. Although one would expect that macroeconomic stability would be an important determinant of credit worthiness and as a result the size of capital flows, the data suggest that the relationship is relatively weak.

Overall, ample global liquidity was a determining factor in the surge in global capital flows to developing countries, but where those flows went and in which form depended importantly on the characteristics of individual developing countries. Country-specific "pull" factors, such as the quality of the institutional environment and overall economic openness, shaped the direction of capital flows and the extent to which the domestic intermediation responded by increasing the availability of credit.

It follows that even in an international environment in which capital may become scarcer and more expensive, countries can take steps that can deepen their domestic capital markets and increase their access to international capital. In particular, the evidence suggests that improvements in the regulatory environment, increased market openness, and more generally reforms that improve the business environment and reduce the cost of capital can substantially influence the level of capital inflows and financial intermediation in a given country, especially in Africa where the quality of institutions remains well below the average elsewhere. Indeed, in the expected tougher global environment, such factors are likely to be even more critical in determining the direction of future flows—placing even more value on forging ahead with further reforms. Sufficient progress in these areas across enough countries could well mitigate to a large degree the expected increase in risk aversion, potentially allowing capital flows in the longer run to regain more recent levels (see discussion in chapter 3).

The liquidity boom and macroeconomic performance

The sharp increase in capital inflows to developing countries and the rapid expansion of domestic finance were associated with a generalized investment boom, although some countries were more or less successful in transforming additional finance into productive investments.[9] On average, between 2000 and 2007 investment-to-GDP ratios in developing countries increased by 5.2 percentage points, or 23 percent, compared with their 2000 levels (table 2.6).

Investment rates rose in all regions, most markedly in South Asia, the Middle East, and Sub-Saharan Africa. The very marked increase in investment rates in South Asia (up by more than 10 percentage points) partly reflects deep structural reforms that were undertaken during the 1990s, the influence of which on investment was redoubled by falling borrowing costs. In the rest of the developing world the rise in investment rates was more modest. Rates in low-income countries rose by 6 percentage points versus 5.2 percentage points in middle-income countries (inclusive of India). Despite the very strong capital inflows received by countries in Europe and Central Asia, investment rates in that region rose by only 3.5 percentage points—much less than the overall average for middle-income countries. By 2007, just before the onset of the crisis, investment rates in East Asia and

Table 2.6 Rising investment rates by region

	Investment rate		
	2000 (%)	2007 (%)	Change (% points)
Developing countries	22.7	28	5.2
Middle-income countries	22.8	28	5.2
Low-income countries	21.1	27.1	6.0
East Asia and Pacific (excluding China)	22.1	26	3.9
China	34.1	38.8	4.7
Europe and Central Asia	19.9	23.4	3.5
Latin America and the Caribbean	18.6	22.1	3.5
Middle East and North Africa	22.4	27.0	4.6
South Asia	22.0	32.8	10.8
Sub-Saharan Africa	16.9	20.9	3.9

Source: World Bank.

Table 2.7 Intertemporal and cross-country influences on investment

Change over 2001–07 in investment/GDP (sample mean)[a]	5.4
Contributions of changes in:	
Global cost of risk	1.9
Domestic intermediation	0.6
Terms of trade	1.4
Difference in 2007 between top and bottom quartile in investment/GDP[b]	11.5
Contributions of differences:	
Cost of capital	3.3
Net capital inflows/GDP	3.0

Source: World Bank.
a. Based on panel regressions.
b. Based on cross-sectional regressions.

the Pacific exceeded 26 percent of GDP. Those in Sub-Saharan Africa were much more modest (about 21 percent of GDP) but were nevertheless 3.9 percentage points higher than in 2000.

Many factors help explain the extent to which investment rates differ across countries and rise in some countries but not others (table 2.7; box 2.7). On average, about one-third of the increase in investment rates observed between 2001 and 2007 is accounted for by the reduction in the global cost of risk, a further 11 percent by increased domestic intermediation, and about one-fourth by improvements in the terms of trade in some countries.

Cross-country differences were more than twice as large as the changes over time, with about 30 percent of the variation accounted for by differences in the cost of capital and a further 30 percent by the level of capital inflows a country attracts. The impact of domestic intermediation and institutional quality was not statistically significant here, possibly reflecting difficulties in disentangling their effect from that of the cost of capital. Concretely, these results suggest that a reduction in the cost of capital from the average level found in Sub-Saharan Africa to that prevailing in Latin America would be associated with an increase in investment equal to almost 2 percent of GDP. This reinforces the importance of continuing with structural reforms aimed at expanding still-underdeveloped financial sectors (a point confirmed by the simulations discussed in chapter 3).

Investment does not, of course, mechanically translate into greater output and living standards: its efficiency must also be taken into account. In this context, additional econometrics suggest that increased financing was most likely to lead to increases in growth in those countries where the quality of institutions was high, a result that is consistent with the recent literature (Frankel 2009).[10]

Impact of the investment boom on growth and potential output

The prolonged reduction in interest rates during the liquidity boom was associated with a rise in potential output. Normally, the increase in investment from a fall in interest rates would be relatively short-lived (as would be the period of low interest rates). During this most recent bubble, however, interest rates remained low for a very long time, and as a result investors and economists alike began to talk of a new regime likely to be characterized by low interest rates. If investors' expected interest rates (and with them the cost of capital) had decreased on a permanent basis,[11] then economic theory suggests that investors would have sought to increase the amount of capital they employed to produce a given level of output. As predicted by theory, during this transition period to a higher capital output ratio, investment grew faster than usual and the ratio of the stock of capital to GDP rose (figure 2.13). As a result, the rate of growth of potential output increased—see box 2.8 for a brief description of the model of potential output employed here; the online technical annex (available at www.worldbank.org/GEP2010) to this chapter provides further details—more rapidly than normal during this period.

Overall, the rate of growth of potential output among developing countries increased by an average of 1.5 percentage points between 2003 and 2007 as compared with the pre-boom period 1995–2002, with 40 percent of that increase attributable to increased capital services as a result of higher investment rates.[12] Table 2.8 breaks down this aggregate result across different regions. Although both

Box 2.7   Understanding the increase in investment rates

Box table 2.7.1 reports cross-sectional regression results that seek to describe differences in investment across developing countries in terms of differences in the cost of capital, institutional quality, domestic intermediation, and international capital inflows, among other explanatory variables. These regressions confirm a statistically significant association between investment ratios on the one hand and initial values of the cost of capital and international capital inflows on the other. Both as a robustness check and to explore further the changes in investments observed over time, including the role of the country-invariant global risk premium, panel regressions were also run for the period 2001–07, with investment ratios as the dependent variables, and the risk premium, plus the full set of regressors from the cross-sectional analysis, as the independent variables. Also included as possible explanatory variables were interactions between capital inflows, financial

development, and institutional quality, to capture the notion that domestic conditions may affect the efficiency of investment. All independent variables were lagged, to diminish endogeneity concerns.

The results (box table 2.7.2) confirm a statistically significant association between investment on the one hand and both the global price of risk and domestic intermediation on the other. Even after controlling for the latter factors, the terms of trade have a significant impact on investment. In contrast, the impact of the cost of capital, institutional quality, and international capital flows is not statistically significant, possibly reflecting difficulties in disentangling their effect from that of other variables. Additional regression analysis, not reported here, indicates that equity capital inflows, notably FDI flows, have a stronger effect on investment rates than on international debt flows (bonds and bank lending).

Box table 2.7.1   Investment-to-GDP ratio, cross-sectional regression results

	Coefficient
Cost of capital	−0.59***
Institutional quality[a]	0.00
Financial development	−0.04
Net capital inflows	0.45*
Change in terms of trade	−0.01
R^2	0.22

Source: World Bank.
Note: All regressions estimated using average values over the period 2001–07 for the dependent variable, and initial values for the independent variables; number of countries = 106. Other controls include trade-weighted export market growth (percent) and indicators for countries in the upper quartile of both the fuel exports / GDP and the metals exports / GDP distribution. *, **, and *** denote significance at, respectively, the 10, 5, and 1 percent level. Significance is evaluated using robust standard errors.
[a] Measured on a scale of 0 to 100.

Box table 2.7.2   Investment to GDP ratio, panel regression results

	Coefficient
Global cost of risk	1.33*
Cost of capital	0.10
Institutional quality (Kaufmann–Kraay–Zoido-Lobaton index)[a]	0.08
Financial development (private sector credit, percent of GDP)	0.08*
Net capital inflows/GDP (percentage points)	0.34
Terms-of-trade index, weighted by trade ratio	0.06**
R^2	0.24

Source: World Bank.
Note: All regressions estimated using annual data over the period 2001–07, with all independent variables lagged once; number of observations = 430. Other controls include trade-weighted export market growth (percent); indicators for countries in the upper quartile of both the fuel exports/GDP and the metals exports/GDP distribution; and a full set of country-specific fixed effects. *, **, and *** denote significance at, respectively, the 10, 5, and 1 percent level. Significance is evaluated using robust standard errors.
[a] Measured on a scale of 0 to 100.

Box 2.8   Estimating potential output in developing countries

This *Global Economic Prospects* introduces new estimates of potential output based on a hybrid production-function model of potential output similar to that used by the Congressional Budget Office (CBO) in the United States, the OECD, the European Commission and the Federal Reserve Board (CBO 2001; OECD 2008; Cournède forthcoming; Denis and others 2006). In this model, which is described in more detail in the online annex to this publication, the supply side of GDP is described by a simple Cobb-Douglas function of the form

$$GDP = AK^{\alpha}L^{1-\alpha},$$

where *GDP* is gross domestic product, *K* is the capital stock, and *L* is labor employed. Potential output is the level of output attained when the entirety of the capital stock and effective labor supply is employed. Replacing *L* with the working-age population (P_{1565}), the labor force participation rate (*Pr*), and the unemployment rate (*UNR*) gives

$$GDP = AK^{\alpha}(P_{1565} * Pr * (1 - UNR))^{1-\alpha}.$$

And stating everything in growth terms gives

$$\dot{y} = T\dot{F}P + \alpha \dot{K} + (1-\alpha) * (\dot{P}_{1565} + \dot{Pr} + (1-\dot{UNR}))$$

Assuming that all of the capital stock and all of the labor force are fully employed (*UNR* and *Pr* equal their equilibrium values), that all of the services of the available capital stock are used, and that total factor productivity (*TFP*) is growing at its trend rate gives an expression for the rate of growth of potential. For most developing countries, we do not have reliable economy-wide data for *Pr* and *UNR*, so for the purposes of calculating the rate of growth of potential, it suffices to assume that the equilibrium unemployment and participation rates are constant, which leaves us with

$$\dot{y} = T\dot{F}P + \alpha \dot{K} + (1-\alpha) * (\dot{P}_{1565})$$

as an expression for the rate of growth of potential output.

For the purposes of this study, the capital stock was estimated using the perpetual inventory method from investment data (running from 1960 in the case of most countries) and assuming a depreciation rate of 7 percent (IMF 2005). Trend TFP was calculated using an Hodrik-Prescott filter through spot estimates of TFP calculated by inverting the above equation in level terms. The end-point problem was resolved by assuming that TFP growth from 2008 through 2009 was equal to the average rate of growth of TFP during the period 1996–2006. The share of capital income in total output (alpha) was assumed to be a uniform 40 percent in all developing countries.

An alternative approach used until recently by the OECD (it was recently abandoned in favor of one similar to that described here) calculates the capital stock on the basis of a smoothed investment rate series. This results in an estimate of potential that is less sensitive to cyclical changes in investment behavior but has the disadvantage that full employment capital services are disconnected from the actual observable capital stock. In the words of the U.S. Congressional Budget Office, which also eschews using the smoothed investment method, "unlike the labor input, the capital input does not need to be cyclically adjusted to create a 'potential' level—the unadjusted capital input already represents its potential contribution to output. Although use of the capital stock varies greatly during the business cycle, the potential flow of capital services will always be related to the total size of the capital stock, not to the amount currently being used" (CBO 2001).

The use of actual rather than a smoothed capital stock means that the output gap fluctuates less over the cycle.

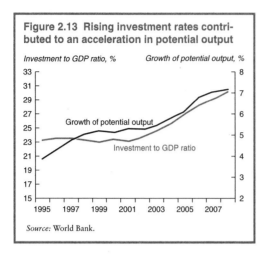

Figure 2.13 Rising investment rates contributed to an acceleration in potential output

Source: World Bank.

results are sensitive to the level of investment rate used in the counterfactual exercise, the broad result that capital deepening accounted for almost half of the acceleration in potential output observed during this period is robust to different specifications.[13]

Concluding remarks

Finance, whether it is delivered through the domestic banking system or originates from abroad, is an important enabler of economic development. At its best, it improves efficiency by funding potential-enhancing investment projects that would otherwise not have been funded and by promoting and facilitating the transfer of technologies and the spread of best practices within an economy. However, the extent to which an increase in intermediation is able to achieve these results depends importantly on the quality of domestic institutions, regulations, and overall absorptive capacity of an economy. Where the supply of credit, whether domestic or foreign in origin, exceeds the absorptive capacity of an economy, it can lead to macroeconomic instability and thus make a negative contribution to long-term growth and potential output.

For the vast majority of developing countries, the period of 2000–07 was one of very liquid financial conditions. Both domestic and international finance expanded rapidly, with those countries most open to world trade and finance receiving the largest shares of the increase in credit. For most countries this expansion fueled an investment boom that contributed to faster productivity growth and increased potential output through capital deepening—without generating domestic inflation or serious external imbalances. That in turn suggests that for these countries a preexisting capital constraint was at least temporarily relieved, ushering in a golden age of rapid and, at least at the country level, sustainable growth. For a few countries, most notably a number in the Europe and Central Asia region, inflows and domestic credit creation either

middle- and low-income countries saw their potential growth rates increase by about the same amount, with capital deepening accounting for a larger share of the total among low-income countries, with the remaining 60 percent increase attributable to growth in population and in total factor productivity. In the case of China, almost all of the increase in output during this period can be ascribed to increases in the capital stock. While these

Table 2.8 Decomposition of increase in potential output growth directly attributable to capital deepening

	Total	Due to capital deepening	Share due to capital deepening
	Change in growth rate of potential output (2003–2007 vs 1995–2003)		
Developing countries	1.5	0.6	40.3
Middle-income countries	1.5	0.6	39.8
Low-income countries	1.3	0.8	63.7
East Asia and Pacific (excluding China)	0.4	−0.1	−19.8
China	0.3	0.9	283.5
Europe and Central Asia	3.1	0.6	18.7
Latin America and the Caribbean	0.3	0.1	46.6
Middle East and North Africa	0.8	0.5	66.7
South Asia	1.4	1.1	78.5
Sub-Saharan Africa	1.9	1.5	79.5

Source: World Bank.

exceeded the domestic economy's absorptive capacity or found its way into nonproductive hands, helping to feed an unsustainable increase in consumer demand that generated large and ultimately unsustainable internal and external imbalances.

The financial crisis has brought an end to these favorable conditions for both groups of developing countries. For the moment, the most serious impacts have been felt in those countries where the largest imbalances accrued. Going forward as financial conditions improve, conditions in developing countries should also improve. But growth rates are unlikely to regain their boom-period levels, if global liquidity is both more expensive and less abundant in coming years, particularly over the next several years as countries adjust to tighter international conditions. International capital flows to developing countries are not expected to reach their pre-crisis levels in the medium term. Competition among developing countries to attract investment flows (such as FDI) will be tougher than in previous years. Factors such as institutional quality, trade openness, and regulatory framework will play an increasingly important role in attracting these cross-border investments and financial intermediation. To what extent financial conditions and developing-country growth potential will be affected will depend importantly on the nature of the changes to come in the international financial architecture, the extent that these changes impinge on financing conditions for developing countries, and the success with which developing countries are able to offset the less propitious external conditions by improving domestic financial conditions. The nature of these changes and their expected impact on growth and the growth potential of developing countries are explored in more detail in chapter 3.

Notes

1. Total claims on BIS-reporting banks increased by 21 percent a year on average between 2002 and 2007, compared with a 10 percent annual increase in nominal world GDP.

2. The lack of information available to buyers of these instruments also should reduce their price. However, sustained low interest rates during the 2002–07 boom appear to have eroded concerns over risk taking on the part of many investors. Information asymmetries may also be mitigated by more stringent covenants on loans sold on secondary markets than on loans held by the originating bank, although it is difficult for covenants to anticipate all potential repayment issues.

3. Data on reported CDS spreads are taken from Datastream.

4. Over-the-counter derivatives played an important role in the excessive volatility affecting foreign currency and asset markets during the East Asian crisis of 1997–98 (Kregel 1998).

5. Firms operating in countries at low levels of financial development are constrained from making the investments required to assimilate new technologies (Aghion and others 2004). Moreover, the intermediation services of a healthy financial sector also contribute to development, efficiency, and economic growth by enabling arms-length transactions that increase competition and the range of options available for both suppliers and buyers. Financial intermediation also helps to move resources from less productive uses to more productive ones, and to reduce information and transactions costs, such as the cost of acquiring information on investments, monitoring of firms' managers, and enforcing contracts (Levine 1997).

6. Rothenberg and Warnock (2006) find that nearly half the "sudden stop" crises in emerging markets can best be attributed to capital flight by local investors, while Cowan and others (2008) find that one in five episodes are driven by surges in outflows rather than stops in inflows.

7. During the recent boom, the biggest expansion in finance (both domestic and external) among the developing regions was in Europe and Central Asia, largely reflecting optimism about long-term prospects for the region given its quality labor force and its increasing political and economic integration with high-income EU economies. Unlike other regions, the expansion in finance (increases of 12 percent of GDP in external flows and 15.6 percent in domestic intermediation) exceeded the absorptive capacity of many countries, spilling over into increased consumption, inflation, and rising current account deficits.

8. Bond markets also increased significantly in some of the middle-income countries, as discussed in World Bank 2009.

9. At first blush, this appears to contradict some of the evidence outlined in box 2.3 suggesting that increased intermediation increases GDP and investment mainly by contributing to increased total factor

productivity. However, they are consistent but here the expansion in potential output that drives an increase in investment derives (principally) not from increased TFP but from a fall in the cost of capital. Although TFP growth did increase during the 2000s, the sharpest change observed was the decline in borrowing costs and with them the cost of capital. As a result, the quantity of capital that could be supported by a given level of productivity and labor increased, inducing an increase in investment, an acceleration in GDP growth, and an increase in potential output.

10. These regressions also suggested a negative relationship between growth and the global price of risk and the cost of capital. However, this link may be spurious: the estimated negative relationship between growth and domestic credit expansion suggests that the data may be finding it hard to disentangle the impact of the domestic credit expansion from that of some of its underlying determinants.

11. Indeed, some argue that long-term forces will yet force interest rates back down to the levels observed during the first half of the 2000s.

12. Calculations based on the results of counterfactual simulations were conducted by assuming investment-to-GDP ratios between the period 2002 and 2007 held constant, instead of increasing significantly, as they did in many countries. This has the effect of reducing the level of the capital stock and therefore the services of capital in the calculation of potential output. See box 2.8 for more on the model of potential output employed here.

13. The share attributable to capital deepening ranges from a high of 57 percent when assuming a base year of 2000 to a low of 42 percent when assuming a base year of 2003.

References

Aghion, Philippe, Peter Howitt, and David Mayer-Foulkes. 2004. "The Effect of Financial Development on Convergence: Theory and Evidence." Working Paper 10358, National Bureau of Economic Research, Cambridge, MA.

Al-Taimimi, Hussein A. Hassan, Mouawiya Al-Awad, and Husni Charif. 2001. "Finance and Growth: Evidence from Some Arab Countries." http://www.fmpm.ch/docs/5th/Al_Tamini.pdf.

Al-Yousif, Khalifa Yousif. 2002. "Financial Development and Economic Growth: Another Look at the Evidence from Developing Countries." *Review of Financial Economics* 11 (2): 131–50.

Arestis, Philip, and Panicos Demetriades. 1997. "Financial Development and Economic Growth: Assessing the Evidence." *Economic Journal* 107(442):783–799.

Beck, Thortsen and Asli Demirgüç-Kunt. 2009. "Financial Institutions and Markets across Countries and over Time: Data and Analysis." Policy Research Working Paper 4943, World Bank, Washington, DC.

Beck, Thorsten, Asli Demirgüç-Kunt, and Ross Levine. 2007. "Finance, Inequality and the Poor." World Bank, Washington, DC.

Beck, Thorsten, Ross Levine, and Norman Loayza. 1999. "Finance and the Sources of Growth." Policy Research Working Paper 2057, World Bank, Washington, DC.

Bernanke, Ben. 2005. "The Global Savings Glut and the U.S. Current Account Deficit." Sandridge Lecture, Virginia Association of Economics, Richmond, Virginia. April 14. http://www.federalreserve.gov/boarddocs/speeches/2005/200503102//

BIS (Bank for International Settlements). 2006. 76th *Annual Report*. Basel.

Calvo, Guillermo A. 2009. "Financial Crises and Liquidity Shocks: A Bank-run Perspective." NBER Working Papers 15425, National Bureau of Economic Research, Cambridge, MA.

CBO. 2001. "CBO's Method for Estimating Potential Output: An Update." *CBO Paper*, Congressional Budget Office, Washington, DC.

Clarke, George, Robert Cull, and Maria Soledad Martinez Peria. 2001. "Does Foreign Bank Penetration Reduce Access to Credit in Developing Countries? Evidence from Asking Borrowers." Policy Research Working Paper 2716, World Bank, Washington, DC.

Cournède, Boris. Forthcoming. "Revised Estimates of Potential Output in the OECD." OECD Working Papers, Organisation for Economic Co-operation and Development, Paris.

Cowan, Kevin, Jose De Gregorio, Alejandro Micco, and Christopher Neilson. 2008. "Financial Diverisification, Sudden Stops and Sudden Starts." In *Current Account and External Financing*, ed. Kevin Cowan, Sebastián Edwards, and Rodrigo O. Valdés. Santiago: Central Bank of Chile.

Crotty, James. 2009. "Structural Causes of the Global Financial Crisis: A Critical Assessment of the 'New Financial Architecture.'" *Cambridge Journal of Economics* 33: 563–80.

De Haas, Ralph, and Ilko Naaborg. 2006. "Foreign Banks in Transition Countries: To Whom Do They Lend and How Are They Financed?" Munich Personal RePec Archive Paper. 6320, http://mpra.ub.uni-muenchen.de.

Demetriades, Panicos O., and Khaled A. Hussein. 1999. "Does Financial Development Cause Economic Growth? Time Series Evidence from 16

Countries." *Journal of Development Economics* 51 (2): 387–411.

Denis, Cécile, Daniel Grenouilleau, Kieran McMorrow, and Werner Röger. 2006. "Calculating Potential Growth Rates and Output Gaps: A Revised Production Function Approach." Economics Working Papers 247, European Commission, Directorate-General for Economic and Financial Affairs, Brussels.

Detragiache, Enrica, Thierry Tressel, and Poonam Gupta. 2006. "Foreign Banks in Poor Countries: Theory and Evidence." Working Paper 06/18, International Monetary Fund, Washington, DC.

Duffie, Darrell. 2007. "Innovations in Risk Transfer: Implications for Financial Stability." Working Paper 225, Bank for International Settlements, Basel.

Farhi, Maryse, and Marcos Antonio Macedo Cintra. 2009. "The Financial Crisis and the Global Shadow Banking System." *Revue de la regulation* 5 (1). http://regulation.revues.org/index7473.html.

Frankel, Jeffrey. 2009. "The Global Financial Crisis: A Selective Review of Recent Research in the International Finance and Macroeconomics Program." *NBER Reporter*, No. 2. http://www.nber.org/programs/ifm/ifm.html.

Frankel, Jeffrey, and Sergio Schmukler. 1996. "Country Fund Discounts and the Mexican Crisis of December 1994." *Open Economies Review* 7.

Gormley, Todd A. 2005. "Costly Information, Foreign Entry and Credit Access." Mimeo. Washington University in St. Louis. Olin School of Business. http://ssrn.com/abstract=896000.

Griffith-Jones, Stephany, and Jonathan Leape. 2002. "Capital Flows to Developing Countries: Does the Emperor Have Clothes?" QEH Woking Paper Series 89, Queen Elizabeth House, Oxford University, Oxford, U.K.

Guttmann. 2009. "Asset Bubbles, Debt Deflation and Global Imbalances." *International Journal of Political Economy* 38(2): 46–69.

Hurlin, Christophe, and Baptiste Venet. 2008. "Financial Development and Growth: A Re-examination Using a Panel Granger Causality Test." Laboratoire d'economie d'orleans, Orleans, France.

IMF. 2005. *World Economic Outlook*. Appendix 2.1. International Monetary Fund, Washington, DC. September.

Jalilian, Hossein, and Colin Kirkpatrick. 2002. "Financial Development and Poverty Reduction in Developing Countries." *International Journal of Finance and Economics* 7 (2): 97–108.

Jenkins, Hatice. 2000. "Commercial Bank Behavior in Micro and Small Enterprise Finance." Develop-ment Discussion Paper 741, Harvard Institute for International Development, Harvard University, Boston, MA.

Kawai, Masahiro, Richard Newfarmer, and Sergio Schmukler. 2001. "Crisis and Contagion in East Asia: Nine Lessons." Policy Research Working Paper 2610, World Bank, Washington, DC.

King, Robert G., and Ross Levine. 1993. "Finance and Growth: Schumpeter Might Be Right." *Quarterly Journal of Economics* 108 (3): 717–38.

Kregel, J. A. 1998. "Derivatives and Global Capital Flows: Application to Asia." *Cambridge Journal of Economics* 22: 677–92.

Levine, Ross. 1997. "Financial Development and Economic Growth: Views and Agenda." *Journal of Economic Literature* 35 (2): 688–726.

Levine, Ross, Norman Loayza, and Thorsten Beck. 2000. "Financial Intermediation and Growth: Causality and Causes." *Journal of Monetary Economics* 46: 31–77.

Levine, Ross, and Sara Zervos. 1998. "Stock Markets, Banks, and Economic Growth." *American Economic Review* 88 (3): 53758.

Luintel, Kul. B., and Mosahid Kahn. 1999. "A Quantitative Reassessment of the Finance-Growth Nexus: Evidence from a Multivariate VAR." *Journal of Development Economics* 60 (2): 381–405.

Neusser, Klaus, and Maurice Kugler. 1998. "Manufacturing Growth and Financial Development: Evidence from OECD Countries." *Review of Economics and Statistics* 80 (4): 638–46.

Nourzad, Farrokh. 2002. "Financial Development and Productive Efficiency: A Panel Study of Developed and Developing Countries." *Journal of Economics and Finance* 26 (2): 138–49.

OECD. 2008. "Beyond the Crisis: Medium-Term Challenges Relating to Potential Output Unemployment and Fiscal Positions." Chapter 4 in *Economic Outlook*, No. 85. Paris.

Rothenberg, Alexander D., and Francis E. Warnock. 2006. "Sudden Flight and True Sudden Stops." Working Paper 12726, National Bureau of Economic Research, Cambridge, MA.

Rousseau, Peter L., and Paul Wachtel. 1998. "Financial Intermediation and Economic Performance: Historical Evidence from Five Industrial Countries." *Journal of Money, Credit, and Banking* 30: 657–78.

Saxena, Sweta and Agustin Villar. 2008. "Hedging Instruments in Emerging Market Economies." In *Financial Globalisation and Emerging Market Capital Flows*. BIS Paper 44, Bank for International Settlements, Basel.

Shan, Jordan. 2005. "Does Financial Development 'Lead' Economic Growth? A Vector Auto-regression Appraisal." *Applied Economics* 37: 1353–67.

Shan, Jordan, and Alan Morris. 2002. "Does Financial Development 'Lead' Economic Growth?" *International Review of Applied Economics* 16 (2): 153–68.

World Bank. 1998. *Global Development Finance.* World Bank. Washington DC.

———. 2006. *Global Development Finance.* Washington, DC.

———. 2007. *Global Development Finance.* Washington, DC.

———. 2009. *Global Development Finance.* Washington, DC.

3

Medium-Term Impacts of the Crisis on Finance and Growth in Developing Countries

The lessons of the financial crisis are likely to shape financial policies and market reactions for some time to come. Beyond the immediate and unprecedented global recession that it has provoked the crisis can be expected to alter the global financial landscape significantly over the next 5 to 15 years in at least three important ways.

First, authorities in high-income countries will almost certainly strengthen financial regulation to reduce excessive risk-taking by financial intermediaries, which will involve broadening the coverage of regulation and the imposition of higher capital requirements and other limits on excessive and risky lending.

Second, authorities in developing countries are likely to introduce rules and policies that insulate them from excessive financial volatility, by placing greater emphasis on domestically managed risk management strategies such as capital controls and reserve accumulation.

Third, market participants will likely be more risk averse than they have been over the past decade, and the extent to which today's risk management instruments are used to increase leverage and global liquidity is likely to shrink.

Stronger regulation in high-income countries is likely to reduce volatility in financial markets, which should contribute to more stable and sustained growth over the longer term. At the same time, better regulation and higher risk aversion also imply that firms and governments in developing countries will face higher borrowing costs, less abundant domestic finance, reduced availability of external finance, and a more constrained environment for domestic financial intermediation than during the boom. Efforts by developing-country governments to reduce dependence on foreign capital may also reduce firms' access to finance and perhaps the efficiency of domestic intermediation.

As businesses adapt to higher capital costs, the rate of growth potential output in developing countries can be expected to slow by between 0.2 and 0.7 percentage points for between five and seven years. And, unless offset by policy reforms to reduce domestic borrowing costs, these constraints could result in as much as an 8 percent decline in long-term potential output (the level of output if the available labor and capital were fully employed). This chapter outlines these expected changes and their consequences for finance, investment, and economic activity over the medium term. The main conclusions are:

Necessary and desirable steps to rein in excessive risk taking by financial intermediaries, together with increased risk aversion as a result of the financial crisis, will constrain global liquidity going forward. Tighter regulations, an increase in the range of financial activities and firms that come under regulatory scrutiny, increased cross-border supervision, the necessity of banks to rebuild their balance sheets, and increased risk aversion on the part of investors will contribute to a more stable global financial environment but also result in less abundant and more expensive capital. Although developing-country borrowing costs have declined from their immediate post-crisis highs, spreads appear to have stabilized at levels that are about 150 basis points higher than during the boom period. Currently, the price of risk in both high-income and developing countries is being held down by very low policy rates and quantitative easing. As monetary easing is withdrawn, base interest rates in high-income countries are expected to rise and with them the risk premiums and interest rates paid by developing-country borrowers. Interest rates charged developing-country borrowers could rise 70 to 270 basis points above boom-period levels.

As a result of the crisis, external capital flows will decline over the medium term, with the extent of the decline dependent on the type of capital flow. Unsecured bond and bank lending, as well as portfolio equity flows, are likely to be severely constrained by the new global financial environment. Trade finance, which often carries lower risk than other forms of bank lending because it is directly tied to collateral, should be less affected. The rise in risk aversion and more stringent regulation is not expected to hit foreign direct investment (FDI) to the same degree as debt flows, partly because in the future, investors can be expected to privilege less risky investment forms such as FDI. Nevertheless, FDI inflows are projected to decline from recent peaks of 3.9 percent of developing-country GDP to 2.8–3.0 percent of GDP. And foreign bank participation in developing countries' domestic financial systems may decline (or rise less quickly) because both recent losses and tighter regulation will force parent banks to build up their capital. How quickly and how durably these impacts will be felt depends critically on how long it takes to achieve sound, well-functioning financial systems in high-income countries and on the policy reactions to the crisis in developing countries.

Higher borrowing costs and tighter rationing of credit will reduce potential output and growth in developing countries. Higher borrowing costs will reduce firms' desired capital-to-output ratios, as firms economize on capital relative to labor and natural resources. Because entrepreneurs will be working with less capital than they would have had interest rates remained stable, the level of output that developing economies will be able to sustain could fall by between 2 and 8 percent of GDP. Moreover, during the transition period to the new, lower capital-output ratio, the rate of growth of potential output could decline by between 0.2 and 0.7 percentage points annually for about seven years.

Despite higher borrowing costs than during the boom period, borrowing costs will remain as much as 500 basis points lower than they were in the 1990s (depending on the region), reflecting years of policy reform and improved economic fundamentals. Better debt management, more flexible exchange rates, and more stable political regimes are among the factors that mean borrowing costs will not return to pre-boom levels. The biggest projected improvements in borrowing costs compared with the 1990s are in Latin America and the Caribbean, Europe and Central Asia, and Sub-Saharan Africa.

Developing countries are likely to rely more on domestic financial intermediation. Given the severity of the crisis in high-income countries, the global financial system's ability to provide ample credit is likely to be impaired for an extended period of time. Moreover, authorities in developing countries may take a more skeptical view toward globalization and seek to promote domestic financial intermediation as an alternative to reliance on foreign capital. This strategy could ultimately benefit some of the middle-income countries that have a strong framework for financial intermediation, by increasing the efficiency of domestic financial intermediaries through learning by doing and economies of scale. However, a weaker international system may have undesirable effects in many low-income countries, where deficiencies in domestic intermediation systems are likely to prevent them from compensating for a reduced foreign presence.

The traumatic impact of the financial crisis will encourage developing countries to take steps to insulate their economies from external shocks. Further efforts to raise international reserves are understandable in this context, partly because high reserve levels may be useful in deterring speculators and reducing the amplitude of smaller shocks. However, the benefits from holding reserves are subject to diminishing returns. This, combined with low returns and risks from the concentration of reserves in dollars will make increasing reserves and holding high reserve levels costly. And even substantial reserves cannot prevent a country from feeling the effects of a massive shock. Similarly, some countries may be tempted to pursue slower capital account liberalization or even to reverse past reforms, which could have heavy long-term consequences.

The financial crisis is likely to encourage moves toward greater regional cooperation. Such cooperation holds some potential to help strengthen financial services by capturing economies of scale and facilitating risk sharing through pooled reserves. It may also help strengthen South-South financial flows, such as FDI, which are likely to be of increased importance for low-income countries. However, progress in regional financial cooperation has been slow in developing countries. Further, such arrangements are likely to be of greatest benefit to regions that already have relatively robust domestic financial systems, such as East Asia and the Pacific. Poor countries with weak institutions are unlikely to strengthen their financial systems by promoting integration with other poor countries with weak institutions.

Developing countries can mitigate the costs of tighter global financial conditions by reducing the cost of intermediation domestically. Inefficiency of domestic financial sectors, corruption, weak regulatory institutions, poor protection of property rights, and excessive limits on competition can push borrowing costs in developing countries as much as 1,000 basis points higher than in high-income countries. Improvements in the policies and institutions governing countries' domestic financial sectors

may significantly boost domestic financial intermediation, potentially more than offsetting any potential negative impact of higher global risk premiums. For example, if the poor institutional framework in many Sub-Saharan African countries could be improved to the level of South Asia, borrowing costs would fall by an estimated 275 basis points, more than the most pessimistic estimate of the increase in developing-country borrowing costs coming from tighter global financial conditions. Were countries in Europe and Central Asia, Latin America, and Sub-Saharan Africa to reduce intermediation costs to the levels observed in Asia, they could see increases in potential output of 8 percent or more.

The remainder of this chapter analyzes in more detail the qualitative and quantitative impact of the expected changes in global regulations, risk aversion, and developing-country attitudes toward financial volatility on intermediation, international capital flows, investment, and growth.

The impact of post-crisis regulatory and structural changes

The financial crisis exposed a wide range of weaknesses in financial markets in high-income and some developing countries. A laissez-faire implementation of the revised Basel II prudential guidelines that relied upon large banks in some high-income countries to use internal risk assessments to help determine the necessary level of loan provisioning, combined with very strong incentives to maximize short-term profits, resulted in many of these institutions taking on far too much risk. They may also have placed excessive confidence in the capacity of their hedging and risk-management strategies to deal with their highly leveraged portfolios.

In addition, banks reduced their capital requirements by selling loans to subsidiaries, thus moving the loans off the banks' balance sheets. While some of these loans were sold

Box 3.1   Likely directions of financial sector reforms

The precise nature of the reforms that eventually will be instituted are as yet unclear. However, there is broad agreement on the directions that reform should take. Any eventual reform should:

- Expand the perimeter of financial sector surveillance to ensure that the systemic risks posed by unregulated or less regulated financial sector segments are addressed and introduce mechanisms to discourage regulatory arbitrage and ensure effective enforcement of regulation.
- Bring on-book the off-balance-sheet transactions of major banks.
- Recognize that a more systemwide approach to financial sector regulation is needed, notably one that extends beyond the health of individual banks and firms and that encompasses the interdependencies among them.
- Ensure that existing regulations are effectively enforced.
- Eliminate the pro-cyclicality of existing capital requirements and prudential norms, possibly even making these rules countercyclical.
- Recognize the central role played by private sector ratings agencies and bring them into the regulated sphere.
- Resolve the political and legal impediments to the effective regulation of cross-border institutions, develop special insolvency regimes for large cross-border financial firms, and harmonize remedial action frameworks.

Source: This box draws heavily on Cortavarria and others (2009) and Brunnermeier and others (2009).

to outside investors, banks often retained at least a portion of the risk through such mechanisms as "implicit recourse," whereby banks essentially reduced potential investors' losses in securitized issues to preserve the banks' reputation and retain access to the market. The exposure inherent in implicit recourse was not subject to capital requirements.[1] The combination of securitization and implicit recourse increased banks' leverage (implicit loan to risk-weighted capital ratios) and short-term profits (because investors would pay a higher price to buy loans where banks were willing to make good a portion of subsequent losses), but it also increased their vulnerability to a downturn by effectively eroding capital adequacy.[2]

Finally, neither public nor private sector quasi-regulators such as security exchange commissions and ratings agencies foresaw the fragility of the overall global financial system. This failure arose in part because these agencies' regulatory remit failed to provide adequately for the interdependencies that had crept into the system. As a result, the failure of one financial institution could, and did, lead to a rapid deterioration in the balance sheets of other seemingly healthy companies.[3] Essentially, no regulator had the responsibility for overseeing all systemically important financial institutions (Jickling 2009), and therefore none had the responsibility to focus on how failures in one institution could affect the system as a whole.

The broad outline of measures to be adopted can already be seen in the changes to financial sector regulation proposed by authorities in the United States and Europe.[4] Both a tightening of regulatory requirements (box 3.1) and the more effective enforcement of existing regulations will be required. Regulators can be expected to increase capital requirements for deposit-taking institutions, in particular requiring higher capital levels during booms to reduce the degree of procyclical lending. Regulators may also set maximum leverage ratios and minimum levels of liquidity, undertake more vigorous review of risk assessment procedures, and tighten requirements governing off-balance-sheet transactions and nonbank subsidiaries. Authorities also are likely to increase scrutiny and prudential requirements for nonbank financial institutions, particularly those that are large enough to pose a systemic risk, and ensure that supervision takes into account the interdependencies among financial institutions.

Supervisors may devote more scrutiny to how the structure of compensation affects risk taking and accountability and may establish stronger firewalls within institutions where the potential for conflicts of interest is high. More attention is likely to be placed on whether authorities have the appropriate tools and contingency plans for taking over insolvent institutions and responding to a financial crisis. Markets for derivatives and other innovative financial products will be subject to greater transparency requirements, and efforts to protect consumers of financial products from fraud and excessive risk will be redoubled. Finally it is likely that any new regime will include enhanced cross-border monitoring, regulation, and coordination mechanisms.

In addition, regulators are likely to take a much closer look at industry self-regulation mechanisms such as securities exchanges and private ratings agencies, which are rightly or wrongly blamed by many for failing to identify the elevated and dangerously unsustainable level of risk that was being undertaken. For example, some observers claim that the scandals earlier in this decade surrounding Enron, WorldCom, and some mutual funds, as well as failures of oversight tied to the current banking crisis, have undermined public confidence in self-regulation by stock exchanges (Ellis, Fairchild, and Flether 2008). Some ratings agencies failed to implement required procedures (for example, the rule that analysts should not participate in discussions of fees with issuers) to limit the conflict of interest involved in relying on fees from the institutions that issued the rated financial instruments (SEC 2008). Any erosion of the accuracy of ratings because of these conflicts had systemic implications, because many laws and regulations mandate the use of ratings to determine permissible investments (for example, by insurance and pension companies) and bank capital requirements (Jickling 2009).

The financial crisis has brought on large, endogenous structural changes, including a significant further consolidation in the banking sector in high-income countries, and the transformation of leading investment banks from loosely regulated institutions to more traditional banks. The first change may increase monopolistic tendencies within the sector, raising costs for borrowers and reducing returns for savers, while the second may reduce the supply of funds to developing-country firms seeking additional equity financing.

In addition, the financial crisis demonstrated that the ability of securitization and other exotic financial transactions to manage and reduce the cost of risk had been grossly overstated. The complexity of these products and the intricate interdependencies between financial agents made individual risk exposures very difficult to evaluate correctly—particularly because these exposures depended to a large degree on the even-less-well-understood risk exposure of counterparties. As a result, these products can be expected to play a much more modest role in the evolution of global finance in the years to come.

The following subsections attempt to assess how these changes are likely to affect financial conditions, investment, and growth prospects for developing countries in the years ahead.

Impact on developing countries of tighter financial sector regulations in high-income countries

Although the financial crisis was centered in the banking sectors of high-income countries, it has affected near-term real-side prospects throughout the world, including countries that have followed very prudent micro- and macroeconomic policies. The banking sectors of most developing countries have not come under the same kind of stress, nor required the extensive national and international assistance, as have those of the high-income countries—with the notable exception of those in the Europe and Central Asia region.

Several features of the expected tightening of regulation in high-inome countries is expected to benefit developing countries. Improved transparency requirements (for over-the-counter derivatives and commercial bank off-balance-sheet liabilities, for example) could ease investors' concerns over the risks involved, thus moderating the decline in flows. Regulatory changes intended to control the market segments that loomed large in the boom-and-bust cycle, such as subprime mortgages in the United States, could encourage greater investment in markets where such problems were much less important, such as developing countries. Tougher disclosure rules that reduce the attractiveness of using offshore centers for tax evasion could shift flows to developing countries. Higher capital requirements in high-income countries may increase the relative attractiveness of setting up subsidiaries in developing countries, where there is likely to be less pressure to raise capital requirements (because most developing-country banking systems did not suffer from the same weaknesses as banks in the high-income countries that were the source of the crisis). Developing countries may also benefit from a perception of increased risk in high-income countries, both because they were the center of the crisis and because of the rise in public debt from efforts to support demand (see below).

However, the tightening of financial regulations in high-income countries will also have negative consequences for finance in developing countries. Tighter rules will also increase borrowing costs and reduce liquidity in developing countries as compared with the boom period. New regulations may affect the conditions under which foreign banks establish branch-bank activities in developing countries and may change the nature and basis upon which trade finance is arranged. Finally, the structural changes in the high-income financial world may have implications for equity markets in developing countries and the ability of companies in the developing world to raise equity in the high-income world.

On balance, while tighter regulation will contribute to a more stable international environment and promote sustainable growth, tighter regulation also is likely to reduce loans to all high-risk borrowers, including governments and firms in developing countries.

Consequences for the role of foreign banks in developing-world intermediation

The financial crisis could lead to lower foreign bank participation over the medium term because stricter cross-country regulation and higher capital requirements (or the need to build up capital after the huge losses during the crisis) will reduce not only banks' ability and willingness to lend but also the attractiveness of foreign operations. The implications for financial conditions, investment, and output in developing countries extend beyond the direct impact that reduced activity might have on international capital flows. The reliance by foreign banks on home-country deposits to fund lending implies a net inflow of capital. However, loans by foreign banks are also funded from domestic deposits that do not involve net capital inflows. Moreover, the benefits of foreign bank participation extend beyond the impact it might have on credit creation and may include improved stability and economic efficiency.

A reduced presence of foreign banks could impair growth and efficiency in developing countries' banking systems. In an appropriate institutional environment, foreign banks tend to generate additional competitive pressures, which induce cost reductions and quality improvements in domestic banks; improve accounting, auditing, and rating institutions; and increase pressures on governments to improve the overall legal framework governing the financial system (Levine 1996). Except for Latin America, where results are mixed, foreign banks in developing countries generally tend to be more efficient than domestic banks, and competition from foreign banks helps to improve the efficiency of domestically owned banks, as measured by reduced costs and spreads (Cull and Martinez Peria 2007).[5] As a result, a reduced foreign bank presence can be expected to raise the cost of borrowing and lower the supply of financial intermediation, thereby reducing firms' access to resources for investment.

A decline in foreign bank participation could be less important for countries where

Box 3.2   The impact of foreign bank participation on stability

In general foreign bank participation tends to reduce volatility in developing economies, depending on individual country (or bank) circumstances. Foreign banks are likely to be more diversified than domestic banks. Partly reflecting the internal resources of international banking organizations and their greater access to capital markets, they tend to fund more of their lending operations from deposits held abroad, and their lending operations tend to be less procyclical than domestic banks (Cetorelli and Goldberg 2009). At the same time, foreign banks may import instability as they reduce lending in response to shocks in their home countries. And foreign banks may reduce the franchise value of domestic banks by cherry-picking the top clients, thus forcing domestic banks into lower-return and riskier market segments (Hellman, Murdock, and Stiglitz 2000). Thus the impact of foreign banks on stability is an empirical question.

The weight of evidence indicates that foreign banks tend to be more stable lenders than domestic banks (Cull and Martinez Peria 2007). Demirgüç-Kunt, Huizinga, and Claessens (1998) find that foreign bank participation reduces the likelihood of a banking crisis. Martinez Peria, Powell, and Vladkova-Hollar (2002) find that foreign bank lending is not significantly curtailed during crises, a view supported by case studies for Malaysia (Detragiache and Gupta 2004), Argentina and Mexico (Goldberg, Dages, and Kinney 2000), Latin America (Peek and Rosengreen 2000), and 10 Central and Eastern European countries (De Haas and van Lelyveld 2006). In studies of selected Latin American countries, Goldberg, Dages, and Kinney (2000) and Crystal, Dages, and Goldberg (2002) show that credit growth in foreign banks that had a long history in the host country was less volatile than in domestic banks. Arena, Reinhart, and Vazquez (2007) find weak evidence that foreign banks in 20 developing countries were less sensitive to monetary conditions than domestically owned banks.

---

barriers to competition—high bank concentration, rules that strictly limit banks' activities, or excessive regulatory barriers to entry and exit—are significant. In such circumstances, foreign bank entry may fail to exert competitive pressures on domestic banks. Indeed, research suggests that, faced with barriers to competition, high bank concentration, and profitability, foreign banks may invest expressly to reap the rents available from the distorted environment for financial intermediation. In these environments, reduced foreign bank participation would have limited implications for efficiency.

However, a lower foreign bank presence could increase instability in developing-country financial systems. Foreign banks tend to be less dependent on domestic deposits and therefore less affected by domestic economic instability than domestically owned banks (box 3.2). That said, the effect of foreign banks on stability depends on the source of the shock: foreign banks may increase instability if they are

constrained by adverse conditions in their home countries. This appears to be happening in the current context, where huge bank losses in industrial countries are reducing lending from parent and other overseas affiliates of foreign-owned banks in developing countries (Cetorelli and Goldberg 2009).

Preliminary data indicate that between June and December 2008 lending by foreign-owned banks (at least those reporting to the Bank of International Settlements, or BIS) fell by 13.6 percent, much more than the 4 percent decline in total bank lending in developing economies (table 3.1).[6] In some regions, however, foreign banks have been a source of stability. In Latin America and the Caribbean lending by foreign banks declined by less than total lending, and in the Middle East and North Africa (where foreign banks have a small share of total claims) foreign bank claims rose more rapidly than total bank claims. In the other four regions, however, claims by foreign-owned banks fell considerably faster than did

Table 3.1 Credit growth by foreign banks versus total credit growth, developing countries
(Percent)

Region	Foreign bank claims as a % of total claims, June 2008	Growth rate of foreign bank claims, June– December 2008	Growth rate of total bank claims, June– December 2008
East Asia and Pacific	3.8	−3.6	4.2
Europe and Central Asia	30.6	−12.2	−8.8
Latin America and the Caribbean	27.3	−19.9	−21.4
Middle East and North Africa	9.7	11.7	5.0
South Asia	10.2	−7.7	−2.4
Sub-Saharan Africa	26.1	−15.1	−6.5
All developing countries	14.4	−13.6	−4.0

Source: Bank for International Settlements and International Financial Statistics.

total bank claims (or total bank claims actually rose, as in East Asia and the Pacific). The more rapid decline in lending by foreign banks is attributable not to just a few large countries with substantial weight in the total. Of the 89 developing countries with complete data on both foreign bank claims and total claims, foreign bank claims fell by more (or rose by less) than total claims in 59. Despite these declines, as of December 2008 foreign bank claims remained 40 percent above the level in December 2006, so although foreign bank presence has declined, that decline has yet to undo the substantial increase that preceded it during the boom period.

Trade credit is critical to sustaining the international trading system.[7] In the acute phase of the financial crisis, a sharp decline in the access of developing-country firms to trade finance exacerbated the decline in exports that reflected the fall in global demand (box 3.3). As the crisis intensified, the availability of trade finance tightened and its cost rose for four main reasons: growing liquidity pressure in mature markets; a perception of heightened country and counterparty risks, resulting in increased demand for letters of credit, insurance, and guarantees because exporters needed

greater assurance that importers would pay on schedule; market disruption caused when critical market participants either collapsed (Lehman Brothers and others) or encountered severe difficulties (many commercial banks); and a drying up of the secondary market for short-term exposure because of deleveraging by banks and other financial institutions.

Insofar as the decline in trade finance represented a typical short-term crisis response, exacerbated (compared to previous developing-country crises) by the breakdown of financial systems in high-income countries, trade finance should recover over the medium term. However, the exact terms under which it will recover and at what cost remain to be determined (see the following section on borrowing costs). The extent of the recovery will depend on the precise rules adopted for banking regulation. In particular, the Basel II Accord on banking laws and regulations does not discriminate among different forms of short-term credits (maturities of a year or less) with respect to maturity or risk profile. Thus a rigid application of the Basel II rules would imply that banks would have to allocate as much capital for trade finance as for other short-term loans, even though trade finance often has a relatively short maturity (perhaps a few weeks) and is lower risk (because the goods being financed serve as collateral) than many other forms of short-term exposure.

Going forward, policy makers will need to take care that regulatory changes are sensitive to the importance of credit to trade, and that restrictions on the use of secondary markets for securitized loans do not combine with blunt restrictions on country-specific loan exposure limits to restrict trade in a permanent manner. To overcome this possibility, capital requirements for secured trade transactions should be made less onerous than those on unsecured loans. Until such time as Basel II regulations are revised, national authorities should take advantage of existing flexibility that allows them to establish different categories of short-term credit with different reserve requirements.

Box 3.3   Survey evidence on the decline in trade finance during the crisis

Survey data clearly indicate the deterioration in developing-country firms' access to trade finance during the financial crisis. In a World Bank survey of 60 global buyers and suppliers in early 2009, 30 percent attributed the postponement or cancellation of foreign sales to difficulties in obtaining trade finance (Shakya 2009). Another set of firm-level surveys undertaken in 2009 found that most firms, in particular small and medium-size enterprises and new firms, have been affected by increased costs of trade finance and more stringent requirements, including guarantees, to obtain more trade finance (Malouche 2009).[a] Higher down payments, more stringent collateral requirements, and higher interest rates have reduced access to preexport financing and become a particularly important obstacle for exporters.

Banks have tightened counterparty bank criteria, excluded certain banks and countries from lending portfolios; demanded additional insurance and confirmation from banks; carried out more detailed due diligence to preselect counterparties; adopted additional safeguards to loans through guarantees and higher confirmation fees; and taken more restrictive attitudes toward new markets, new clients, and new products.

As a result, the cost of letters of credit was reported to have doubled or tripled for buyers in emerging countries, including Argentina, Brazil, Bangladesh, China, Pakistan, and Turkey (IMF/BAFT 2009).

By the end of 2008, trade finance deals were offered at 300–400 basis points over interbank refinance rates—two to three times more than the rate a year earlier. More than 70 percent of respondents indicated that the price of various types of letters of credit increased because of an increase in their own institution's cost of funds (80 percent of respondents), an increase in capital requirements (60 percent of respondents), or both. In the IMF/BAFT survey of global banks (IMF/BAFT 2009) 71 percent of banks reported a decline in the value of their letter-of-credit business, with an overall 8 percent decline in the first nine months of 2008 (compared with the same period in 2007), accelerating to 11 percent during the period October 2008 to January 2009. While 73 percent of banks recognized the role falling trade demand played in the decline in trade finance lines, more than half also attributed the trade finance decline to a decline in available credit (that is, a decline in supply).

a. This survey covered 425 firms and 78 banks in 14 developing countries across Asia, Europe, Latin America, and Africa.

Higher cost and reduced access to trade finance have particularly affected firms that are highly dependent on external finance, notably in several upper-middle-income countries such as Brazil that have enjoyed relatively easy access to international credit markets. Also affected have been firms that are highly integrated in global supply chains and marginally creditworthy firms such as small and medium-size enterprises. By contrast, less affected firms may include those that are less reliant on the banking system for trade finance (firms in a few low-income African countries, for example, that primarily rely on self-financing or cash in advance) and firms in a few middle-income countries (such as South

Africa) where the banking system is comparatively insulated from the international financial market.

Impact of re-regulation on developing-country equity markets

Tighter financial market regulation and the restructuring of investment banking activity in high-income countries, while reducing the likelihood that these firms contribute to financial instability, also may reduce the supply of equity investment to firms in developing countries. This could directly affect the capacity of innovative firms to expand or start up new product lines. Weighted by value,

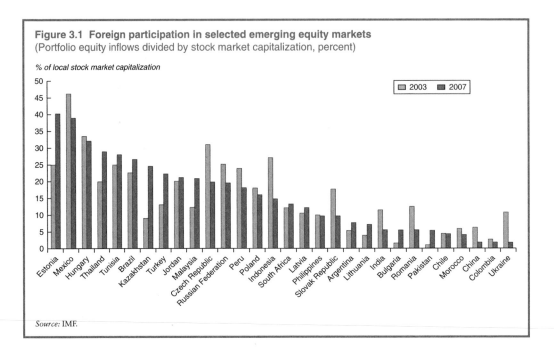

Figure 3.1 Foreign participation in selected emerging equity markets
(Portfolio equity inflows divided by stock market capitalization, percent)

Source: IMF.

approximately 86 percent of all developing-country initial public offerings (IPOs) over the past 10 years have been at least partially intermediated by American investment banks (accounting for 32 percent of the total number of deals).[8] Moreover, investment banks have been instrumental in the creation of mutual funds[9] and other instruments that have allowed individuals and regulated institutional investors in high-income countries to include firms in developing countries in their overall portfolio of assets.

Comprehensive data on the contribution of foreigners to developing-country equity markets are not available. However, portfolio investment inflows as recorded in the balance of payments accounted for as much as 40 percent of the market capitalization in some developing countries in 2007 (figure 3.1). Of course, inflows of funds to purchase stocks may be balanced by outflows from the sale of stocks, so the figure on inflows certainly overstates the net new purchases of stocks by foreigners on these markets. At the same time, the share of stocks traded in any one year in many emerging equity markets is low, so high levels of inflows relative to total market capitalization may represent very high levels of inflows relative to the market value of traded stocks. Despite these weaknesses, the data in figure 3.1 do suggest that in many markets foreign equity has played an important role in financing firms' activities.

The developmental impact of portfolio equity inflows goes beyond the purely financial aspect of the transactions. Empirical studies tend to find a positive impact of net portfolio equity flows on growth, both in macroeconomic terms[10] and in industry- and firm-level data (Kose and others 2006).[11] Foreign participation in equity markets increases their overall liquidity, which improves their attractiveness to other investors (because liquidity increases an investor's ability to divest in a timely manner) and encourages greater investment in projects with a long time horizon, because individual investors can easily sell their holdings before the benefits are realized.[12] Moreover, well-developed equity markets contribute to transparency, because firms release information to attract capital, a process that ultimately improves the efficiency with which investment is allocated.[13]

The participation of globally savvy investors can also improve the identification of projects with global potential and lead to demonstration effects that might otherwise be missed. Openness to external financial flows can spur equity market development by increasing liquidity and pressures for improvements in essential infrastructure.[14]

Impact on FDI

The sharp increase in global FDI flows before the financial crisis partly reflected a surge in inexpensive debt financing: the value of cross-border syndicated bank borrowing and international bond issuance for the purpose of acquisition (including both domestic and cross-border) rose to almost $1 trillion in 2007, from $131 billion in 2003 (figure 3.2).[15] In addition, almost 30 percent of global merger and acquisition (M&A) deals between 2003 and 2008 were carried out by high-income investment banks, hedge funds, and other private equity firms (UNCTAD 2009).

The tightening of financial conditions may thus affect firms' ability to finance FDI. Similarly, changes in the legal status of these institutions and the expected expansion of regulation to encompass more of their activities could further depress developing-country M&A deals. However, crises tend to affect FDI to developing countries less than they affect debt flows (box 3.4), and the anticipated 30 percent fall in FDI flows in 2009 is well below the 90 percent decline projected for net private debt flows.

The 1990s offer some insight into how the tighter financial environment could affect FDI. For example, during that period, banking sector difficulties in Japan translated into a sharp decline in Japanese investments in the United States. A single downgrade in credit ratings of Japanese banks resulted in a 30 percent decline in the number of projects initiated by Japanese investors in the United States (Klein and others 2002). And domestic financial markets and the availability of credit were found to be important factors in explaining investment outflows through cross-border M&As during the late 1990s (Di Giovanni 2005).

Despite their sensitivity to financial conditions, FDI inflows to developing countries are unlikely to be as constrained as debt flows over the medium term. South-South FDI flows may be more resilient than flows from high-income to developing countries, owing to the significant role of state-owned enterprises with softer budget constraints, limited reliance of Southern multinationals on international debt markets, and continued efforts (particularly by China) to gain access to energy and minerals.[16] In addition, tighter access to equity and debt-creating credit for firms in marginally creditworthy developing countries may increase their willingness to enter into FDI-based mergers and acquisitions. Overall, FDI inflows to developing countries are expected to be sharply lower than they were during the boom period when they reached just under 4 percent of developing-country GDP, although they should recover to levels around 3 percent of GDP, around the same levels observed during the preboom period.

The effect of lower FDI inflows on growth prospects for individual developing countries will depend partly on the share of FDI in total investment. While FDI represents less than 5 percent of total investment in some regions, in others, notably Europe and Central Asia, Latin America, and Sub-Saharan Africa, it can account for as much as 20 percent of all

Figure 3.2 Debt financing of M&A transactions, 1995–2008

US$, billions

Source: World Bank.

Box 3.4 FDI and debt flows during crises

FDI inflows tend to be less subject to sharp up-swings and downswings during crises than debt flows. For example, net private-source debt flows to Latin America and the Caribbean fell from 5.7 percent of GDP the year before the onset of the 1980s crisis to −1.6 percent the year after (and would have fallen by more if not for concerted lending), while FDI flows only fell from 1 percent of GDP to 0.8

percent of GDP (box table 3.4.1). Net private debt flows continued to be negative four years after the crisis, while FDI remained stable. Similarly, during the East Asian crisis net private debt flows to the most affected countries plummeted the year of the crisis while FDI was little affected, in part because of the buying opportunities generated by the steep exchange rate depreciations.

Box table 3.4.1 Net private-source debt flows versus FDI before and after crisis episodes
(Percent of GDP)

	Crisis − 4	Crisis − 3	Crisis − 2	Crisis − 1	Crisis	Crisis + 1	Crisis + 2	Crisis + 3	Crisis + 4
Latin American 1980s crisis									
Net private-source debt flows	4.50	5.39	5.57	5.67	3.88	−1.63	−0.24	−0.38	−0.57
FDI	0.75	0.89	0.87	1.01	0.85	0.76	0.60	0.79	0.61
East Asian crisis countries[a]									
Net private-source debt flows	1.91	3.52	3.16	0.56	−4.23	−2.78	−1.99	−1.35	−0.70
FDI	1.05	1.27	1.49	1.68	2.34	2.22	1.33	0.72	0.94
Mexico pesos crisis									
Net private-source debt flows	2.79	0.59	3.54	1.98	1.09	1.43	0.79	2.61	2.55
FDI	1.51	1.21	1.09	2.60	3.32	2.76	3.20	2.95	2.85
Argentina									
Net private-source debt flows	5.89	3.57	1.07	1.11	−5.83	−10.26	0.42	−1.49	9.91
FDI	3.13	2.44	8.46	3.67	0.81	2.11	1.27	2.69	2.87

Source: World Bank.
a. Indonesia, Republic of Korea, Malaysia, and Thailand.

investment (figure 3.3). And in low-income countries, FDI represents an even larger share in total investment. In such countries, a 30 percent decline in FDI could represent as much as a 6 percent of GDP decline in investment unless domestic investment steps in to pick up the slack.

Of course not all FDI constitutes investment in the national accounting sense of an addition to the productive capacity of a country, because much of what is recorded as FDI in the balance of payments represents merger and acquisition of already existing firms. Nevertheless, a significant portion of FDI flows do represent both greenfield and brownfield extensions of productive capacity—a point that is supported by the regression

Figure 3.3 FDI as a share of investment in developing countries, 1995–2008

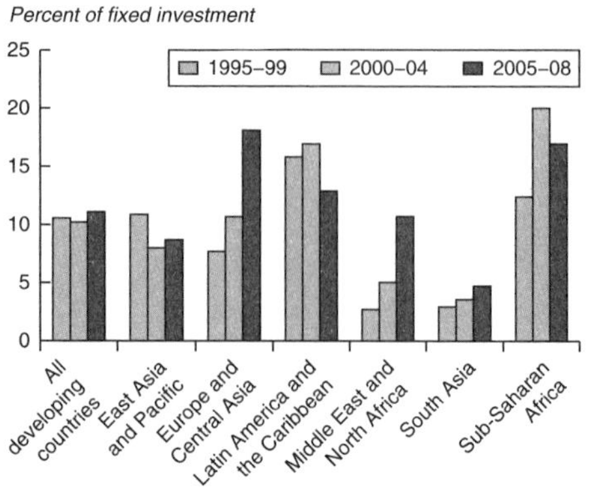

Source: World Bank.

analysis in chapter 2, which found that FDI tended to have a greater impact than other capital flows on investment rates in developing countries. Moreover, as described in the 2008 edition of *Global Economic Prospects* (World Bank 2008), FDI can be an important source of technology transfer in the form of capital goods but also in the form of business processes, which can have large spillover effects in developing countries.[17] Finally, FDI can provide the impetus for important regulatory and governance changes that can have spillover effects throughout the economy, reducing both the costs of doing business and the effective cost of capital—thereby spurring further investment (domestic and foreign).

Impact on private-source debt flows

The tighter financial environment expected in the post-crisis period, while reducing volatility in financial markets, is also likely to constrain developing countries' access to international debt markets over the longer term as well as in the short run (see chapter 1). The necessity to rebuild banks' capital and greater concern over risky loans will reduce both cross-border lending and foreign bank participation in developing countries. Restrictions on financial institutions' ability to assume risk may also limit developing-country borrowers' ability to issue bonds in international markets, as regulatory strictures are extended to many of the institutions (such as hedge funds) that participate in this market. Finally the elimination of some instruments may reduce the ability of some regulated institutional investors, notably public and private sector pension funds, from taking both direct and indirect positions in some forms of developing-country debt.

However, some aspects of the reaction to the crisis could moderate the decline in debt flows to developing countries. For example, if risk aversion among borrowers in high-income countries increases and they decide to repay rather than roll over debt (as happened during Japan's prolonged recession), room could be freed up for banks to lend to developing countries. Moreover, a more stable and transparent global financial system could encourage some lending to high-risk borrowers, which could limit the decline in flows.

The restructuring of high-income countries' financial systems and tighter constraints on risk taking may also reduce interest in project finance transactions, where the involvement of foreign institutions (such as syndicated commercial banks, bond underwriters, firms involved in leasing equipment, dedicated equity funds, and official export credit agencies) has helped to ensure access to international capital markets, to reduce financing costs through innovative financing techniques that tie debt service obligations to the timing of expected project proceeds, to tap extended debt maturities (consistent with the extended time required for construction of many projects) that may not be available in the domestic market, and to obtain expertise necessary to construct complex financial arrangements.[18] Because the lead arrangers of project finance transactions are largely financial institutions in industrial countries, a smaller profile of foreigners could make it more difficult to arrange these complex financial transactions. However, this constraint is unlikely to be too binding. Institutions in developing countries have begun to take a more significant role in arranging project finance transactions.[19] Moreover, even if regulatory constraints limit industrial-country firms' participation in project finance, they could still provide financial expertise on a fee-for-service basis.

Countries that have relied heavily (in relative terms) on debt financing to meet their current account obligations and finance investment may be most vulnerable to a change in the extent to which such financing is forthcoming. Notwithstanding that developing countries were net exporters of private capital during the boom period, among developing countries with current account deficits, net debt inflows on average financed about one-third of the overall deficit (table 3.2), a ratio that rose to 90 percent in the case of countries in Europe and Central Asia.

Table 3.2 Contribution of private-source debt inflows to external finance of developing countries with current account deficits, average 2003–07

Income category	Number of countries with current account deficits	Current account deficit (% of GDP)	Net debt inflows from private sources (% of GDP)
All countries	53	6.3	2.2
Low income	16	5.8	0.8
Lower-middle income	20	6.1	0.8
Upper-middle income	17	7.1	5.3
Of which: Europe and Central Asia	8	8.5	8.1

Source: World Bank.
Note: Data on current account deficits and debt inflows are simple averages of country numbers. Excludes small island economies.

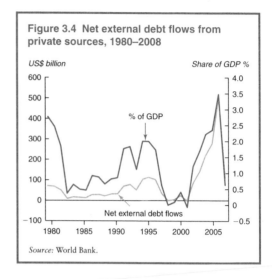

Figure 3.4 Net external debt flows from private sources, 1980–2008

Source: World Bank.

Unsurprisingly, it is the upper-middle-income countries (excluding minerals exporters) that relied most on debt inflows from private sources; such inflows financed three-quarters of their current account deficits, on average. Of these countries, those in the Europe and Central Asia region account for the largest private-source debt inflows (averaging 8 percent of GDP); private-source debt inflows for the other countries in this group averaged 2.5 percent of GDP.

Impact on macroeconomic stability

A more closely regulated international financial sector—especially if provisions to reduce the procyclical nature of prudential requirements are adopted—may help to reduce the volatility of private debt flows. In addition to the vertiginous drop in private debt flows during the current crisis, such flows also dropped from almost 3 percent of developing-country GDP just before the Latin American debt crisis in the 1980s to 1 percent of GDP in the depth of the crisis in 1983 (figure 3.4). Arguably their rapid increase during the recent boom period was a principle cause of the imbalances that arose in some countries, notably those in

developing Europe and Central Asia—where, at least in ex post terms, the inflow of capital exceeded these countries' capacity to absorb or manage it. More generally, debt-creating flows tend to contribute to volatility in developing-country consumption rather than facilitating consumption smoothing, as might be expected from a theoretical point of view (Kose, Prasad, and Terrones 2005; Kose and others 2006).[20]

Implications of a potential developing-country retreat from financial integration

Although the global liquidity expansion in the early 2000s ushered in a lengthy period of rapid and arguably sustainable expansion of the supply potential of most developing countries, the financial crisis brought that boom period to an end—generating a substantial, sharp, and painful deceleration in economic activity throughout the developing world. The speed of the global downturn and the costs that it has imposed on countries that otherwise had followed exemplary policies and whose own financial systems did not engage in unsustainable practices has quite naturally led many observers to question the relative benefits and costs of global financial integration.

Policy and behavioral changes following earlier crises suggest that this crisis may generate a number of important changes in the nature and behavior of financial markets in developing countries over the next 5 to 10 years. For example, countries and national authorities can be expected to be much more cautious in the management of their reserves. Following the Asian crisis of 1998, many Asian economies placed a greater emphasis on reserve accumulation as a self-insurance strategy against external instability. A more skeptical and slow approach to capital account liberalization, or even a reversal of reforms made to date, is also possible. Countries in both Latin America and East Asia took such steps following crises in their regions in the 1970s and 1990s. Finally, countries may seek to reduce their vulnerability to external finance by developing their own domestic financial sectors or seeking to establish regional financial mechanisms.

Reserves policies

Developing countries may decide to increase their reserves to provide themselves some insurance against future fluctuations in global financial conditions. An ample supply of international reserves can help countries compensate temporarily for a sudden reversal in external capital flows, thereby avoiding a sharper real-side adjustment than might otherwise be required. Large reserves can also dissuade speculators from provoking a capital crisis by demonstrating the authorities' capacity to prevent a disruptive adjustment. Following the East-Asian crisis, oil-importing countries in the region (excluding China) increased their reserves from an average of about 3 months worth of imports before the crisis to more than 9 months worth in 2007. In China the increase was even more marked, from about 7 months worth of import cover in the pre-crisis period to almost 18 months

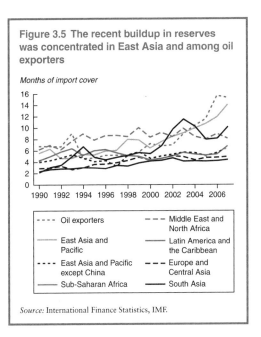

Figure 3.5 The recent buildup in reserves was concentrated in East Asia and among oil exporters

Months of import cover

Legend:
- - - - Oil exporters
——— East Asia and Pacific
- - - - East Asia and Pacific except China
——— Sub-Saharan Africa
– – – Middle East and North Africa
——— Latin America and the Caribbean
– – – Europe and Central Asia
——— South Asia

Source: International Finance Statistics, IMF.

in 2007. Other developing countries also increased reserves during this period but to a lesser extent (figure 3.5).

In some of these countries, a desire to have a larger cushion against a financial reversal was one motivation for increasing reserves (Jeanne 2007). Issues of sound macroeconomic management also played an important role in reserve increases in many countries. Sharp increases in capital inflows (see chapter 2) and very strong commodity revenues during the boom period may have exceeded the domestic economy's capacity to invest productively. In such cases, a sterilized accumulation of excess capital inflows may have been the main reason for reserve accumulation.

Although the existence of high reserves might prevent a run on a country's currency, the extent to which reserves actually helped lessen the real-side impact of this crisis is not clear. In fact, although accumulation of reserves stopped at the peak of the crisis, relatively few countries actually used their reserves to smooth adjustment. Thus, while developing-country reserves fell from $3.7 trillion in December 2007 to $2.2 trillion in

December 2008 (in part owing to the appreciation of the dollar), the precipitous fall in imports meant that import-cover ratios actually rose.

Moreover, countries with large reserves suffered downturns almost as severe as did countries with small reserves. The correlation of the slowdown in GDP growth in 2008 with ratios of reserves to imports in 2007 is only 0.15, which is not significantly different from zero at the 5 percent level.[21] Reserves levels also played no role in supporting exchange rates: the correlation between reserves to imports and the change in exchange rates during 2008 is −0.04 (the same result is obtained if one excludes countries in Europe and Central Asia, which suffered very large exchange rate changes). Finally, there is little relationship between reserves levels and output declines, even if one controls for other determinants of the impact of the crisis on growth, including trade and financial openness, exposure to falling commodity prices, initial current account imbalances, and other financial vulnerabilities (Blanchard, Faruqee, and Klyuev 2009). At least in the case of a generalized financial crisis, very high reserve levels appear to make little contribution to easing real-side adjustment.

Significant costs are associated with maintaining higher reserves. Most reserves are held in the form of low-yield securities that are issued by high-income-country governments. To accumulate foreign currency reserves, central banks must issue debt in local currencies—usually at much higher interest rates than can be earned on the foreign currency being purchased, with the difference between the two (after exchange rate movements) having to be paid by the treasury. The cost of holding reserves can be disaggregated into the forgone return from alternative uses, typically increasing public investment or reducing debt; minus the financial return on reserves and lower spreads on foreign debt if higher reserves improve creditworthiness; plus the current cost of past sterilizations.[22] During the 1990s when reserves averaged about 8 percent of GDP, most developing countries enjoyed a net benefit from reserves (Hauner 2005). By 2004, however, with reserves equal to 19 percent of GDP on average, most developing-country groups were losing money—as much as 0.2 percent of GDP in the Middle East and Central Asia, and 0.6 percent of GDP in Sub-Saharan Africa and emerging Europe. And the cost must have increased substantially by 2007, when reserves represented 26 percent of developing-country GDP.[23] Jeanne (2007) estimates the annual cost of reserves holdings for 20 emerging markets at about 1 percent of GDP over 2000–2005, and Rodrik (2006) obtains roughly the same result for developing countries.

Exchange rate movements represent a further potential cost for developing countries that react to the financial crisis by increasing their reserve holdings. As of the second quarter of 2009, the U.S. dollar accounted for 63 percent of the known composition of official international reserves,[24] with the euro representing 27 percent, and other smaller currencies and special drawing rights the remainder. Large currency swings in exchange rates can be extremely expensive for countries with extensive reserves. For example, if developing countries in East and South Asia hold the same proportion of reserves in dollars as the global average, a not unusual 20 percent decline in the dollar would reduce the value of their international reserves by approximately 10 percent of their GDP.

Capital account restrictions

The financial crisis may also cause countries to reconsider plans or recent moves to liberalize their capital accounts. As discussed in chapters 1 and 2, the abrupt reversal of international capital flows at the onset of the crisis caused not only local equity markets to crash (losing as much as 50 percent of their value in days) but also virtually every non-pegged currency in the world to depreciate by between 10 and 30 percent against the dollar. Imposing some sort of capital controls might have prevented or at least moderated the pace of the outflows, reducing the domestic disruption and wealth loss that ensued. Of course, tighter controls, had they been in place, might well have reduced the benefits that countries enjoyed from the boom period (see chapter 2).

The empirical evidence on the effectiveness of these controls is mixed. Controls have had little success in reducing capital outflows (except in Malaysia during the East Asian crisis), although controls on inflows have had some effect in increasing the independence of monetary policy (Magud and Reinhart 2006). Moreover, with the exception of a few countries with unsustainable current account positions, large capital outflows do not appear to have been a major cause of financial distress during the current crisis. Indeed, developing countries reduced their deposits in BIS-reporting banks by about $260 billion (adjusted for exchange rate changes) during the last quarter of 2008—suggesting a repatriation of capital rather than flight.[25] Nevertheless, developing-country policy makers may take a more skeptical stance toward large external debt inflows during booming economic conditions and toward allowing domestic banks and firms to take speculative positions in foreign currencies.

Indeed, one of the effects of the Asian crisis was to slow the pace of capital account liberalization. Following that crisis, some of the most affected countries tightened restrictions on capital account transactions. The Chinn-Ito index of capital account liberalization declined in Malaysia and Indonesia following the crisis, and the pace of improvement in Thailand and the Philippines slowed markedly. More generally, even countries not directly involved in that crisis slowed or reversed the pace of liberalization (figure 3.6). While the pace of liberalization eased for middle-income countries in the middle 2000s, it came to an almost standstill among low-income countries.[26]

How a tightening of restrictions on capital account transactions would affect growth and stability in individual developing countries will

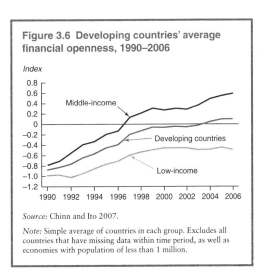

Figure 3.6 Developing countries' average financial openness, 1990–2006

Index

Source: Chinn and Ito 2007.

Note: Simple average of countries in each group. Excludes all countries that have missing data within time period, as well as economies with population of less than 1 million.

depend on the type of restrictions introduced, the international economic environment, investors' views on economic prospects for the country, and the quality of macroeconomic policy and institutions. In general, evidence tying economic growth or real-side investment to capital account openness is weak both because of technical reasons surrounding estimation methods and because of complex interactions that make generalizations difficult (box 3.5). Some studies point to beneficial effects from increased competition and better economic policies, while others focus on the increased instability that can accompany capital account openness, particularly with rapid liberalization in a context of weak domestic institutions.

Increased reliance on domestic and regional financial arrangements

A weaker international financial system will almost certainly result in a movement toward increased reliance on domestic and regional sources of capital. Indeed, a weaker international intermediation system will increase reliance on other sources of intermediation, even if the domestic or regional markets do not grow in size. However, the reduced competitive pressure from abroad can be expected to increase the potential private economic return

Box 3.5   The debate over capital account liberalization

Maintaining an open capital account can contribute to increasing financial depth, and hence spur development, but mostly in industrial countries and developing counties with high institutional quality (Klein and Olivei 2008). Open capital accounts can strengthen domestic financial systems by promoting competition and economic policies through market discipline (Kaminsky and Schmukler 2002), as well as improve returns and diversification for developing country residents' savings. Despite these theoretical benefits, empirical studies of the relationship between capital account openness and growth have shown decidedly weak results.[a]

Several reasons are offered for the limited empirical support for the theoretical benefits of capital account openness. The efficiency effects can be hard to measure and thus may not be detected by panel regressions (Kose and others 2006). It is difficult to define exactly how open economies are to capital account transactions, given the myriad forms of controls that are possible and their varied effectiveness. These benefits provide only a temporary, but not permanent, impact on growth, so the effect may not be found in cross-section analyses (Henry 2007). The endogeneity of financial integration with respect to growth also can complicate measurements of the relationship of the two. The benefits of capital account openness may be greater in environments with strong policies and institutions (for example, external competition may strengthen sound financial intermediaries, but destroy weaker ones). However, it is difficult

to define the quality of institutions, or how "strong" they would need to be to benefit from capital account liberalization.[b]

Capital account openness may also promote instability. The East Asian crisis of 1997–98 and subsequent episodes increased concerns over the potential for open capital accounts to raise instability. Calvo (1996) emphasizes the risk that investors' herd behavior leads to excessive volatility in cross-border capital flows, and Furman and Stiglitz (1998) emphasize the important role that contagion played in exacerbating capital flight from open financial systems during the East Asian crisis. Some cross-country empirical tests find little evidence that open capital accounts increase the incidence of crises (Glick and Hutchison 2001; Edwards 2005), while others find that capital controls help insulate countries from the negative impact of widespread financial instability on growth (Eichengreen and Leblang 2002) and that capital account liberalization increases output volatility in less financially developed economies, but not in more developed economies (Mukerji 2008).

Whatever the average relationship between capital account liberalization and crises, or between liberalization and long-term growth, crises are traumatic and costly, both in terms of welfare and politicians' careers. It is fair to say that the economic literature does not provide a convincing argument that the welfare benefits of liberalization are extremely large, or that the risks of crises are extremely small, in developing-country environments.

a. Kose and others (2006) summarize the results of 25 empirical studies, in which the majority find that international financial integration has either no effect on growth in developing countries or mixed effects depending on model specifications.

b. Kose, Prasad, and Taylor (2009) define threshold levels of financial development, openness to trade, institutional quality, and macroeconomic stability that make it possible to realize the benefits of financial openness, while recognizing that some of these threshold levels have relatively wide confidence intervals.

from these activities and from public incentives to strengthen the surrounding infrastructure—including the domestic and regional competitive environment. As a result, domestic and regional financial intermediation may well expand compared with a no-change scenario.

The severity of the financial crisis and its transmission through global capital markets is likely to turn policy makers' interest toward

regional cooperation in an effort to buffer shocks originating in high-income countries. Indeed, in the period following the financial crises in both Latin America and East Asia, there was a concerted effort to build regional and domestic institutions that could complement or even replace international financial institutions and thus reduce reliance on what was perceived to be an excessively volatile source of intermediation services. Among these efforts were the pooling of financial resources and reserves (for example, currency swaps under the Asian Chiang Mai Initiative and the Latin American Reserve Fund), initiatives to promote or create a new reserve currency, and the closer integration of local financial markets. The latter included the harmonization of bond market standards and conventions across ASEAN (Association of Southeast Asian Nations) countries (Miyachi 2007) and the Manila Framework to monitor domestic policies, to provide technical assistance for strengthening domestic financial sectors, and to establish cooperative arrangements to stabilize Asian currencies (Jeon 2002).

To the extent that efforts to promote regionally based intermediation solutions are successful—and assuming that regional investors understand better than international investors the differences across countries within regions—regional capital markets should help reduce domestic borrowing costs, both by reducing transaction costs[27] and by reducing risk, notably by lowering the likelihood of contagion (when investors withdraw from countries based on problems in other countries that are perceived to share similar features) affecting all countries in a region when one runs into fundamental difficulties. Regional financial integration could also support regional trade integration; help reap the benefits of scale economies achievable through the amalgamation of regional

exchanges, along with attendant standardization of requirements and regulatory cooperation; and improve coordination of fiscal and monetary policies among closely linked regional economies.

To what extent these potential benefits can be realized is uncertain. In countries or regions with strong domestic institutions and intermediation, greater reliance on domestic and regional intermediation may have long-run positive effects. In others, where local institutions are weak, the absence of a foreign option may reduce investors' overall access to savings and reduce competitive forces that serve to keep borrowing costs low.

Because of a poor legal and institutional framework for the financial sector or limited financial sector development, many domestic (and regional) financial systems are poorly prepared to substitute for foreign financial services. As discussed in chapter 2, domestic intermediation in much of the developing world remains low; equity markets, although growing, are thinly traded and dispersed; and significant domestic debt markets are restricted to just a few countries (World Bank 2006). Sub-Saharan Africa, for example, has the weakest domestic framework for financial intermediation—the worst levels of corruption, poorest legal framework, lowest regulatory quality, largest levels of capital flight, and smallest banking sectors of the developing regions (table 3.3). The development of regional equity markets in

Table 3.3   Indicators of the quality of domestic financial systems

Region	Control of corruption	Rule of law	Regulatory quality	Liquid liabilities as a % of GDP	Private credit as a % of GDP	Offshore deposits as a % of domestic bank deposits
East Asia and Pacific	−0.6	−0.4	−0.1	70.3	54.1	4.5
Europe and Central Asia	−0.3	−0.3	0.2	42.7	36.9	6.5
Latin America and Caribbean	−0.4	−0.6	−0.1	38.2	32.5	60.2
Middle East and North Africa	−0.3	−0.2	−0.2	76.3	45.5	13.7
South Asia	−0.6	−0.4	−0.5	56.9	36.0	4.7
Sub-Saharan Africa	−0.6	−0.6	−0.5	27.3	21.4	82.1
High-income countries	1.5	1.4	1.4	94.8	122.9	13.4

Source: World Bank databases: Governance Matters and Financial Institutions and Structure.
Note: Values for the first three indicators range from −2.5 to 2.5, with higher values indicating better performance.

Sub-Saharan Africa could boost liquidity and reap economies of scale in the provision of services and supervision, particularly if the weaker economies can integrate with more developed regional financial markets (such as South Africa). However, pursuing integration among the poorest African countries with weak institutions could simply create a large, illiquid, and poorly functioning market. Thus it is important for these countries to reach out beyond the region to the international investment community.

In any event, increasing regional cooperation and integration will require time. For example, progress on the pooling of international reserves in Asia has been slow, although in May 2008 the ASEAN + 3 ministers reached agreement to set up the pool with $120 billion in reserves by the end of this year.[28] Regional integration of Asian bond markets appears to have slowed since 2002, at least as shown by the correlation of returns across countries (Fung, Tam, and Woo 2008). Low levels of liquidity and insufficient administrative expertise have limited steps toward integration in Sub-Saharan Africa. The Caribbean Community has failed to implement its commitment to a monetary union (Ocampo 2006). While several regional financial institutions have emerged in the Arab world, these have largely been devoted to the provision of aid to low-income countries (Corm 2006). And even the creation of procedures to enhance macroeconomic dialogue in Latin America has made only limited progress (Machinea and Rozenwurcel 2006).

The impact of higher borrowing costs

The preceding discussion suggests that over the medium term the supply of both domestic and international finance could be significantly lower (relative to economic activity) than it was during the pre-crisis boom period. With a reduced supply of credit, borrowing costs and the premiums associated with a given level of risk can be expected to rise. In addition, the discrediting, disappearance, or reduced scope for many of the financial instruments that contributed to the credit boom (see chapter 2), as well as the large losses sustained by investors throughout the world, are likely to reduce demand for speculative financial instruments going forward. As a result, banks, firms, and individuals can be expected to carry less leverage, reduce their exposure to currency and maturity mismatches, and take greater care in evaluating counterparty risk.

A sharp increase in risk aversion on the part of investors was apparent in the immediate wake of the crisis, and the spread on riskier assets such as corporate bonds and equities spiked sharply in both high-income and developing countries—as did the premium required of developing-country sovereign borrowers. Since then, borrowing costs in high-income countries have been suppressed by monetary and fiscal actions, notably the efforts by the U.S. Federal Reserve to keep securitized mortgage markets liquid and to make direct purchases of corporate bonds. Risk premiums on many assets have declined as the crisis has stabilized. The fall in risk premiums partly reflects the very loose monetary conditions in high-income countries, which have lowered yields there and prompted the kind of search for yield behavior that characterized the boom period itself. Developing-country risk premiums appear to have reached new "normal" levels that are about 150 basis points higher than during the boom period. Some further moderation may be possible, but this tendency will be countered as today's loose conditions tighten, and high-income-country yields rise. Assuming past relations continue to hold, developing-country risk premiums can be expected to rise with them.

The remainder of this section suggests that the balance of these competing forces will likely cause borrowing costs in developing countries to be higher than during the boom period, and it explores the implications that increase may have for investment and growth in these countries.

Weaker financial intermediation and increased risk aversion in high-income countries

Changes in risk management techniques, low short-term interest rates (which reduce the cost of financing a given level of risk and tend, at least temporarily, to reduce the likelihood of default), and an increasingly held but ultimately misplaced view that overall risk had declined contributed to a significant decline in the price of risk worldwide during the early 2000s. As a result, interest rates and spreads on a wide range of riskier assets in both developed and developing countries fell sharply (see discussion in chapter 2, including figures 2.5 and 2.6).

Econometric work first undertaken by the Organization for Economic Co-operation and Development (OECD 2004; Sløk and Kennedy 2005) demonstrated that as much as 82 percent of the decline in risk premiums during the first half of the 2000s for a wide range of assets (high-income investment grade and below-investment grade corporate bonds, equities, and developing-country sovereign and corporate bonds) could be explained by a single common factor, which the authors termed a synthetic price of risk (box 3.6).

This synthetic-price-of-risk measure, which continues to be updated by the OECD (2009), is used to monitor financial conditions in high-income markets. It suggests that the cost of a

Figure 3.7 The global synthetic price of risk versus the portion explained by economic fundamentals

Synthetic price of risk

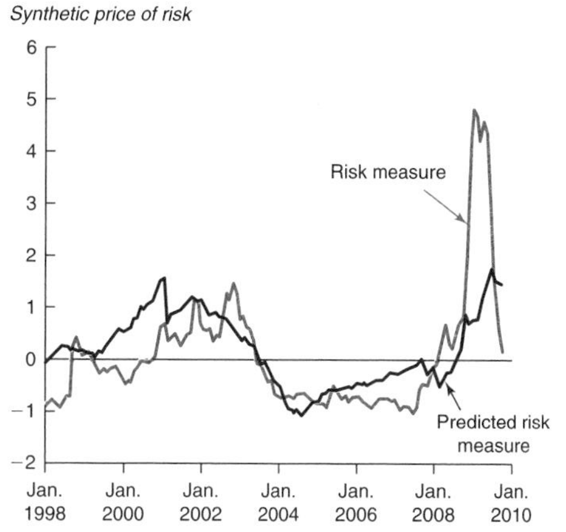

Source: Kennedy and Palerm forthcoming.

given level of risk in high-income countries declined sharply between 2002 and late 2003 and remained depressed straight through to mid-2007 before it spiked with the onset of the financial crisis (figure 3.7).

Since then, the price of risk has declined; an update of the measure commissioned for this study (Kennedy and Palerm forthcoming) put it at about 0.2 points in September 2009, or about 1 point (a full standard deviation) higher than its average rate during the boom period.

Box 3.6 The synthetic price of risk

The synthetic price of risk was calculated as the first principal component computed from a set of returns on corporate bonds (high grade and high yield) for the United States and the Euro Area versus their respective government bonds, the implied risk on equities for each economy, and the global EMBI+ (Emerging Markets Bond Index Plus) spread (versus U.S. Treasury bonds). This synthetic price of risk is a purely statistical measure of the cost of

risk.[a] which is constructed to have mean zero and standard deviation one. Thus an increase in this measure of 1 unit does not represent a 100 basis point increase in risk premiums. One goal in constructing this statistical measure is to explore how much of the change in the price of risk can be explained by economic fundamentals, and how much may result from changes in investors' appetite for risk.

a. The first principal component is a statistical technique that analyzes the covariance of a group of data series by decomposing the series into orthogonal subgroups composed of weighted averages of the original series. The first principal component is the index of the weighting scheme that explains the largest share of the overall variance of the series being examined.

Despite being a purely statistical construct, the OECD's synthetic-price-of-risk measure can be modeled as a function of fundamental economic factors, including real policy interest rates in the United States and the Euro Area, the outlook for the cyclical position of the OECD (measured as the 12-month rate of change in the OECD's leading economic indicators); and global bond default rates. In normal times changes in these economic determinants do a reasonable job of explaining changes in the synthetic-price-of-risk measure. However, they were unable to explain much of the fall in the synthetic risk premium during the early 2000s. The difference has been attributed to reduced risk aversion among investors stemming from financial innovations and "animal spirits" during this period (Sløk and Kennedy 2005). Fundamentals only explain about half of the increase in the synthetic price of risk in the immediate post-crisis period, with the remainder explained by an increase in risk aversion.[29] Similarly, the analysis of Kennedy and Palerm (forthcoming) suggests that—through September 2009—the global price of risk fell further than was warranted by fundamentals.

The influence of the global price of risk

Kennedy and Palerm (forthcoming) extend the earlier OECD work by linking changes in the global price of risk to changes in the risk premiums of specific developing countries.[30] They show that much of the increase in developing-country risk premiums during the post-crisis period can be explained by this updated synthetic-price-of-risk measure. Simple correlations indicate that for a sample of 17 developing countries, between 10 and 80 percent of the changes in these countries' risk premiums between 1998 and 2008 can be explained by fluctuations in the OECD's synthetic-price-of-risk measure, with 40 percent or more of the variation explained in half of the countries in the sample. A more comprehensive modeling of country-specific factors (including foreign indebtedness, macroeconomic stability, political risk, and economic growth) explains more

than 45 percent of the changes in country-specific risk premiums over the period January 2002 to April 2009.

Although changes in these country-specific factors contributed to the rise in country-specific interest-rate spreads, by far the largest source of the rise resulted from the more generalized repricing of risk: the increase in the synthetic price of risk explains 75 percent or more of the rise in interest-rate spreads between July 2007 and December 2008 for all but two of the developing countries in the sample (Kennedy and Palerm forthcoming).[31]

The estimated relationship between developing-country risk premiums and the global-price-of-risk measure suggests that when global conditions tighten, developing-country risk premiums tend to rise faster than risk premiums in high-income countries. Among the main determinants of the global price of risk are monetary and fiscal conditions. The OECD estimates that an increase of 100 basis points in policy interest rates in high-income countries will result in a 0.41 increase in the global-price-of-risk measure. Combining this with the results for developing countries, a 100 basis point increase in the base interest rate would increase the risk premiums of countries with good credit histories by a further 11.1 basis points and of countries with less good records by an additional 57 basis points. These results are somewhat higher than the estimates derived by Dailami, Masson, and Padou (2008) in a slightly different context.[32]

Medium-term developing-country interest rates

The rapid decline in the synthetic-cost-of-risk measure and in developing-country risk premiums since they peaked in early 2009 has reduced borrowing costs substantially. However, as monetary policy in high-income countries tightens from its currently very loose state, interest rates and interest premiums can be expected to rise. To what extent they increase in the long run is uncertain.

Several factors point to higher borrowing costs for developing countries in the future.

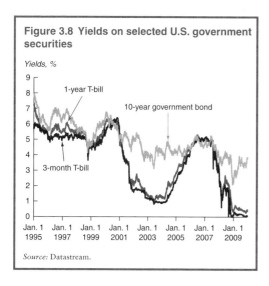

Figure 3.8 Yields on selected U.S. government securities

Yields, %

Source: Datastream.

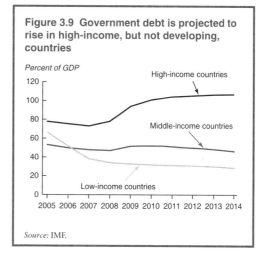

Figure 3.9 Government debt is projected to rise in high-income, but not developing, countries

Percent of GDP

Source: IMF.

- The global price of risk is currently suppressed by very loose monetary policy conditions (see figure 3.7).
- Base rates used to calculate developing-country borrowing rates are also low because of post-crisis flight to quality (figure 3.8), and this effect can be expected to dissipate over time.
- Base rates are likely to rise further because of the sharp increase in high-income countries' government debt, from under 80 percent of GDP in 2007 to perhaps as much as 109 percent of GDP by 2014 (figure 3.9). Reducing these debt levels will take some time; and as long as they and deficits remain high, so too will governments' demand for funds to cover interest payments. Moreover, high debt levels will increase investors' concern over the sustainability of fiscal policy, which also will tend to increase base interest rates.

At the same time, several factors suggest that developing-country borrowing costs may not rise as much as otherwise might have been expected.

- Improved regulation, by increasing transparency, may lower the uncertainty surrounding investment instruments by enough to lower risk premiums by more than the increased costs the regulations impose, resulting in a net reduction in borrowing costs.
- Increased indebtedness in high-income countries is likely to raise their borrowing costs and developing-country base rates, but it also may result in lower interest rate premiums for developing countries. Developing countries' government debt is not expected to increase as much as in high-income countries, largely because of a limited access to finance (see chapter 1). As a result, relative to high-income-country debt, the inherent riskiness of developing-country debt may decline, along with their risk premiums, although probably not by as much as they rise in high-income countries. Overall, developing-country borrowing costs would still be higher but the relative attractiveness of investments in developing countries would be enhanced, and they could be expected to attract a larger share of a reduced quantity of total lending (see McKibbin and Stoeckel 2009 for a modeling of this effect in a slightly different context).

In the modeling work that follows, neither the negative nor positive implications of these

Table 3.4 Historical and prospective costs of capital for developing countries

Costs	Base rate	Real base rate (deflated by core inflation)	Real Federal Funds rate (deflated by core inflation)	East Asia and Pacific	Europe and Central Asia	Latin America and Caribbean	Middle East and North Africa	South Asia	Sub-Saharan Africa
	(Percent)			(Basis points)					
Interest rates and spreads									
Average 1995–2003	5.8	2.7	2.0	274	1135	802	434	276	832
Average 2004–May 2007	4.5	2.4	0.1	224	196	384	351	215	289
Level in August 2008	3.9	1.4	−3.3	286	273	350	474	287	301
Current (Oct. 2009)	3.0	1.6	0.4	304	412	362	419	286	408
Consistent with long-term price of risk			2.0	318	523	478	496	363	470
Cost of capital				(Percent)					
Average 1995–2003	9.7	2.0		12.4	21.1	17.7	14.0	12.5	18.0
Average 2004–May 2007	9.4	0.1		11.7	11.4	13.3	13.0	11.6	12.3
Level in August 2008	8.4	−3.3		11.2	11.1	11.9	13.1	11.2	11.4
Current (Oct 2009)	8.6	0.4		11.7	12.7	12.3	12.8	11.5	12.7
Spreads constant at October 2009 level									
U.S. base rate at avg 04-07H1 level	9.4			12.5	13.6	13.1	13.6	12.3	13.5
U.S. base rate at avg 95-03 level	9.7			12.7	13.8	13.3	13.9	11.9	12.6
Spreads at level consistent with average price of risk									
U.S. base rate at avg 04-07H1 level	9.4			12.6	14.7	14.2	14.4	13.1	14.1
U.S. base rate at avg 95-03 level	9.7			12.9	14.9	14.5	14.7	13.3	15.4

Source: World Bank.

factors on borrowing costs are taken into account explicitly. Rather, a range of estimates for future borrowing costs is presented, based upon different historical "norms" for real base interest rates and recent relationships between developing-country spreads and the price of global risk.

The top panel of table 3.4 reports historical real interest rates and interest rate spreads for selected developing-country regions. During the boom period 2004–May 2007 the real yields on long-term U.S. treasury bills were 30 basis points lower than during the previous nine-year period. Spreads on developing-country debt were about 370 basis points lower, implying that during the pre-crisis period, borrowers coming to international markets were paying some 400 basis points less for U.S. dollar loans than in the preceding nine-year period. As of early October 2009, risk premiums remain on average about 110 basis points higher than they were during the

pre-crisis period, notwithstanding significant declines from their peak levels during the most acute phase of the crisis.

As discussed in chapter 2, the widespread fall in borrowing costs before the crisis was associated with an investment boom and a significant increase in capital-to-output ratios in developing countries (figure 3.10). Many factors, including the tax regime, inflation, the rate of depreciation of the asset in question, and other regulatory features that impinge on profitability (Jorgenson 1963; Lau 2000) go into determining the cost of capital in a given country (or firm for that matter); however, most of these factors are relatively constant over time, and there is very limited information on their appropriate values at the country level. As a result, the second panel of table 3.4 converts the historical interest rates and interest rate spreads of the first panel into estimates for the cost of capital based on very strong simplifying assumptions. Specifically, the cost

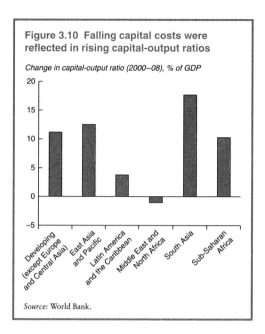

Figure 3.10 Falling capital costs were reflected in rising capital-output ratios

Change in capital-output ratio (2000–08), % of GDP

Source: World Bank.

of capital at the country level is defined as the real dollar borrowing cost (deflated by core inflation from the U.S. consumer price index) plus depreciation, which is assumed to be 7 percent throughout the developing world.[33] In addition to abstracting away from many of the determinants of the cost of capital, this definition also assumes that developing-country borrowers (both domestic and external) pay the U.S. Treasury-bill rate plus the interest rate spread. In reality, formal domestic interest rates tend to be higher, and informal borrowing rates significantly higher still.

Table 3.5 calculates the change in the cost of capital by region between the boom period and three alternative futures. The first assumes

that spreads remain at their current levels but that real base rates in the United States return to their pre-boom-period levels. In the second scenario, the same assumption about base rates is applied but spreads are assumed to rise in response to a return to the levels consistent with the long-term price of global risk. And the final scenario builds on the previous two by assuming that U.S. base rates rise by a further 100 basis points above their pre-crisis average levels, reflecting the potential impact of higher high-income-country debt and tighter regulations.

In the first scenario, the cost of capital rises a great deal in some regions (notably by as much as 240 basis points in Europe and Central Asia), while in others it changes relatively little. In the second scenario, interest rate spreads rise from current levels to levels consistent with fundamentals. This implies a further capital cost increase of 50–100 basis points in every region other than East Asia and the Pacific. In the final scenario, the cost increases are augmented by a 100-basis-point increase in the base interest rate—assumed to be caused by concerns about debt servicing, long-term inflation, and the influence of tighter regulation raising the cost of capital in high-income countries.

Implications of higher borrowing costs for growth and potential GDP in the medium term

Economic theory suggests that higher capital costs would cause the desired capital-output

Table 3.5 Possible impact of tighter financial conditions on developing-country capital costs

Alternative scenarios	Real base rate	East Asia and Pacific	Europe and Central Asia	Latin America and Caribbean	Middle East and North Africa	South Asia	Sub-Saharan Africa
			Change in cost of capital compared to the boom period (percentage points)				
Spreads contant at today's level	0.3	1.1	2.4	0.0	0.9	0.3	0.3
Spreads consistent with long-term average price of risk	0.3	1.2	3.5	1.2	1.7	1.7	2.1
Higher base rates and spreads consistent with long-term price of risk	1.3	2.2	4.5	2.2	2.7	2.7	3.1

Source: World Bank.

Box 3.7   Higher borrowing costs will constrain domestic and external finance

The expected rise in risk aversion and in the cost of capital will likely slow, possibly even reduce, the gains in domestic intermediation that the low interest rates of the boom period facilitated (see chapter 2). Already, the sudden increase in borrowing costs and increased risk aversion that followed the crisis have cut into lending (and borrowing) throughout the developing world (see also chapter 1). Since September 2008 the pace of credit expansion in the 69 developing countries for which data are available fell by almost half, from a monthly increase of around 1.1 percent between January and September 2008 to a much more modest 0.6 monthly pace between September 2008 and October 2009 (box figure 3.7.1). The decline was particularly pronounced in middle-income countries, perhaps because their more integrated financial systems were most directly affected by the change in global financial conditions. While sovereign bond flows have picked up recently, corporate bond issues and especially bank lending remain sharply lower than during the boom period.

As policy interest rates in high-income countries rise, the differential between long-term yields on developing-country debt and short-term dollar-denominated borrowing costs will decline, and the financial incentive that is currently boosting capital flows to developing countries will ease. As a result, borrowing costs are expected to be relatively high over the medium term, and therefore the growth of domestic financial intermediation is also likely to moderate on a sustained basis. While these events are likely to have negative consequences for development in many countries, they may have some benefits in those countries, including many in Europe and

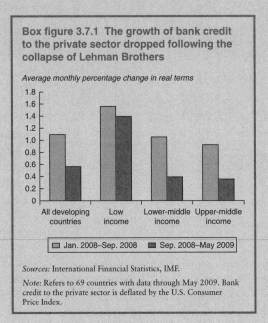

Box figure 3.7.1 The growth of bank credit to the private sector dropped following the collapse of Lehman Brothers

Average monthly percentage change in real terms

☐ Jan. 2008–Sep. 2008   ■ Sep. 2008–May 2009

Sources: International Financial Statistics, IMF.

Note: Refers to 69 countries with data through May 2009. Bank credit to the private sector is deflated by the U.S. Consumer Price Index.

Central Asia, that were unable to sustain the very strong capital inflows of the first part of this decade.

As seen in the discussion of the boom in chapter 2, higher financing costs will affect international capital flows as well. Higher interest rates will reduce the demand for external finance, while banks are likely to lower the supply of loans because marginally creditworthy developing countries will be able to reliably service a smaller quantity of debt. Thus the expected rise in borrowing costs will compound the reductions in external finance owing to tighter regulation in industrial countries (described above).

ratio in the economy to fall. As a result, if costs do rise in the longer run, entrepreneurs will have less capital to work with than if interest rates had remained low (box 3.7).[34] This implies that the level of output that the economy will be able to sustain is likely to decline and that during the transition period to the new lower capital-output ratio, the reduced rate of growth of potential output will be temporarily lower.

Table 3.6 reports on three simulations undertaken to provide some insight into the likely quantitative impact of the higher cost of capital on growth. The interest rate scenarios that drive the simulations are those outlined in table 3.4.

In these simulations, higher borrowing costs serve to lower long-term developing-country potential output (measured as the

Table 3.6 Impact on potential output of a return to normal pricing of risk and higher base rates

	Spreads remain at October 2009 level, but base rates rise to pre-crisis levels		Spreads return to "normal" levels, and base rates rise to pre-boom levels		Spreads return to "normal" levels and base rates rise 100 basis points above pre-boom period levels	
	Short-term impact on potential growth[a]	Long-term level of potential[b]	Short-term impact on potential growth[a]	Long-term level of potential[b]	Short-term impact on potential growth[a]	Long-term level of potential[b]
			(percent)			
Developing countries	−0.2	−3.4	−0.4	−5.2	−0.7	−8.0
Middle-income countries	−0.3	−3.5	−0.4	−5.2	−0.7	−8.0
Low-income countries	−0.1	−1.0	−0.5	−5.7	−0.7	−8.2
East Asia and Pacific	−0.3	−3.9	−0.4	−4.3	−0.6	−7.5
Europe and Central Asia	−0.5	−6.5	−0.8	−9.2	−1.0	−11.4
Latin America and Caribbean	0.0	0.0	−0.3	−3.6	−0.6	−6.3
Middle East and North Africa	−0.2	−3.0	−0.4	−5.4	−0.7	−8.2
South Asia	−0.1	−1.0	−0.4	−5.1	−0.6	−7.8
Sub-Saharan Africa	−0.1	−0.5	−0.4	−3.4	−0.5	−4.9

Source: World Bank.
a. Short-term impact on potential growth rate change is measured in percentage points during the transition to new lower level of potential output (about 5–7 years).
b. Percent change in long-term level of potential output.

difference between the simulated 2050 level of potential in the base case versus the scenario)[35] by between 3.4 and 8.0 percent overall, with regional declines as large as 11.4 percent. The impact on trend growth during the period in which economies transition down to these lower long-term levels of potential (about 5–7 years in these simulations) is less marked, averaging between a 0.2 and 0.7 percentage point annual decline.

The first simulation can be understood as a relatively benign outcome. It assumes that developing-country spreads remain at to-day's levels—somewhat lower than might be expected when high-income monetary policy tightens and interest rates rise—and that interest rates in high-income countries rise to their pre-crisis average level between 2002 and 2005. Even with this modest tightening of liquidity conditions, long-term potential output in developing countries falls 3.4 percent compared with a scenario where the cost of capital remained at the very low levels observed during the boom period. During the transition to new lower capital ratios, the annual rate of growth of potential output declines by about 0.2 percentage points for about seven years.

The second scenario assumes that developing-country spreads rise somewhat as monetary conditions tighten, in line with the historical relationship between developing-country spreads and high-income policy rates. Overall, potential output falls 5.2 percent in the long run, and transitional growth rates are expected to be about 0.4 percentage points lower than they would have been otherwise. In this second scenario, low-income countries are hit somewhat harder relative to the first scenario because their interest rate premiums are projected to rise by more than those of middle-income countries.

In the third scenario, weaker fundamentals are assumed to raise borrowing costs in high-income countries an additional 100 basis points. This causes borrowing costs to rise globally, with developing-country long-run potential output falling by around 8 percent and annual potential growth rates falling by 0.7 percentage points for about seven years.

The impact of higher interest rates, investment, and the capital stock is illustrated in figure 3.11, which is drawn from the second scenario. The declining capital stock causes the level of output that the economy can sustain

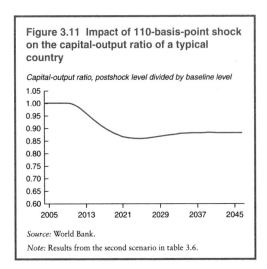

Figure 3.11 Impact of 110-basis-point shock on the capital-output ratio of a typical country

Capital-output ratio, postshock level divided by baseline level

Source: World Bank.

Note: Results from the second scenario in table 3.6.

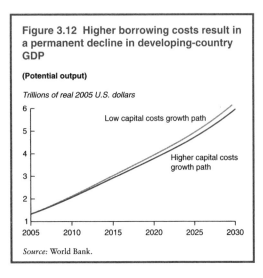

Figure 3.12 Higher borrowing costs result in a permanent decline in developing-country GDP

(Potential output)

Trillions of real 2005 U.S. dollars

Source: World Bank.

in the long run to be lower than it would have been had borrowing costs remained unchanged. Overall, the capital-output ratio falls by about 12 percent compared with the baseline—a baseline that already includes the post-crisis recession but assumes that the long-term cost of capital returns to its boom-period level. Initially the capital-output ratio rises in response to the shock because the decline in investment it provokes causes GDP to fall more quickly than the capital stock. Relatively quickly the combination of depreciation of the existing capital stock and slower investment growth causes the capital stock to fall.[36]

As the new capital-output ratio is achieved, the pre-crisis potential output growth rate is regained. Nevertheless, as presented in table 3.6, there is a permanent 5.2 percent loss in GDP (figure 3.12).

Of course, this process may occur more quickly in the real world owing to a more rapid depreciation of the existing capital stock stemming from the closing down of industries that are no longer competitive. An important implication of this logic is that a policy designed to assist existing firms that are placed in long-term difficulty by less liquid global conditions will tend only to prolong the period of slow growth through which an economy must pass in these circumstances. In contrast, a policy that combined efforts to facilitate the

movement of both people and capital from less to more productive uses, especially if it succeeded at the same time in boosting aggregate productivity, would help to speed the transition toward a new equilibrium.

The long-run declines in potential output vis-à-vis the baseline reported in the first and second scenarios of table 3.6 are broadly consistent with results produced by McKibbin and Stoeckel (2009) in their analysis of the global financial crisis—even though their focus is not on the impact on potential output in developing countries and the shock is not framed in precisely the same manner. In part, this similarity reflects the fact that their model includes many of the same mechanisms as the one presented here. These results are also very similar in size to the average post-financial-crisis decline in potential output identified by the International Monetary Fund in its September 2009 *World Economic Outlook* (IMF 2009), although that work, which was based on a decomposition analysis of the economic outturns following past crises, attributed a smaller share of the total decline to the decline in the capital output ratio. The analysis presented here differs by explicitly modeling in a forward-looking manner the main mechanism through which lower potential output is reached and relating it to the primary driver of both the boom and the bust—the decline and subsequent sharp rise in the global price of risk.[37]

Table 3.7 Higher borrowing costs and slower population growth imply slower growth in potential output over the longer term

	Developing countries	Middle income	Low income	East Asia and Pacific	Europe and Central Asia	Latin America and Caribbean	Middle East and North Africa	South Asia	Sub-Saharan Africa
(Average rate of growth of potential output, percent)									
Baseline scenario: spreads and base interest rates constant at boom period levels									
1980–95	2.6	2.6	2.6	8.3	−0.6	2.4	2.6	5.1	1.8
1996–2002	4.6	4.6	3.9	7.8	3.1	3.0	4.2	5.8	3.4
2003–08	6.2	6.2	5.4	8.7	5.9	3.5	5.0	7.4	5.6
2009–15	6.3	6.3	5.8	8.1	5.7	3.8	5.4	7.4	6.5
2016–50	4.5	4.5	5.2	5.5	4.5	1.6	2.9	4.9	5.1
Pre-crisis base rates and return to normal spreads[a]									
1980–95	2.6	2.6	2.6	8.3	−0.6	2.4	2.6	5.1	1.8
1996–2002	4.6	4.6	3.9	7.8	3.1	3.0	4.2	5.8	3.4
2003–08	6.2	6.2	5.4	8.7	5.9	3.5	5.0	7.4	5.6
2009–15	5.9	5.9	5.4	7.8	5.2	3.3	4.9	7.0	6.3
2016–50	4.5	4.4	5.2	5.4	4.4	1.5	2.8	4.8	5.1
(Percentage point difference in average potential output growth rates)									
Difference compared with baseline									
2003–08	0.0	0.0	0.0	0.0	0.0	0.0	0.0	0.0	0.0
2009–15	−0.4	−0.4	−0.4	−0.3	−0.5	−0.5	−0.4	−0.4	−0.3
2016–50	−0.1	−0.1	−0.1	−0.1	−0.1	−0.1	−0.1	−0.1	0.0

Source: World Bank.
a. Results from the second scenario in table 3.6.

The top panel of table 3.7 illustrates the influence of slower population growth and an aging population on potential output in the baseline scenario, where borrowing costs are assumed to remain unchanged at their 2008 level and where total factor productivity trends remains unchanged. In this scenario, developing-country growth is set to slow by 1.7 percentage points between the boom period and the 2016–50 period, mainly because of slower growth of the working-age population reflecting both aging and slower population growth. Total factor productivity is assumed to be constant.[38] The second panel shows average potential output growth rates assuming the same increase in capital costs as in the second scenario of table 3.6. Although the long-term growth rate of potential output after adjustment of the capital stock to its new levels is broadly the same as in the baseline case, potential output growth is 0.4 percentage points slower during the transition period and potential output in the end period is some 5.2 percent lower than in the baseline.

Slower future growth and lower income levels imply potentially large long-term impacts on poverty and disease in developing countries. Recent estimates suggest the recession will likely result in some 30,000–50,000 additional childhood deaths in 2009 and 2010 in Africa (Friedman and Schady 2009). And, assuming the 4.2 percent of GDP decline in potential output reported in the second scenario of table 3.7, by 2015 the crisis and its aftermath can be expected to have prevented some 46 million poor people from emerging from poverty (table 3.8).

The higher borrowing rates under the scenarios outlined above are unlikely to have a major impact on debt sustainability, even for the most highly indebted developing countries.

Assuming that borrowing costs rise by 2.7 percentage points (roughly equivalent to the most pessimistic of the scenarios in table 3.6), private-source-debt-to-GNI ratios among developing countries would rise by at most 6 percentage points. In most of the 20 developing countries with the highest ratio of private-source debt to GNI, the rise is about

Table 3.8 The crisis could increase poverty by 46 million in the long term

Region	Impact on poverty of a 5.2 percent decline in potential output as of 2015	
	Change in head count (millions)	Percent change in head count
East Asia and Pacific	6.3	19.3
Europe and Central Asia	0.9	27.7
Latin America and Caribbean	3.4	14.3
Middle East and North Africa	0.8	46.8
South Asia	16.3	31.2
Sub-Saharan Africa	18.2	11.7
Developing countries	46.0	17.0

Source: World Bank.
Note: Estimates based on the GIDD model.

1 percentage point (figure 3.13). However, the impact of higher interest rates for countries with external borrowing constraints could be more disruptive if it occurs quickly. If borrowing costs rise 270 basis points, a country with a private-source-debt-to-GNI ratio of about 40 percent (the median of the 20 most indebted countries) would have to reduce its foreign exchange expenditures by 1.1 percent of GNI. Assuming a 4 percent import elasticity, this would imply a 4.4 percent cut in domestic demand.[39]

Strategies for dealing with a weaker international finance system

While individual developing countries can do little to influence developments in the global financial system, they can do a great deal at the local level to influence intermediation costs and offset, possibly even reverse, the expected increase in capital costs—perhaps not immediately but over the longer term.

As discussed in chapter 2, the most important influence on changes in borrowing costs in developing countries during the past 10 years has been changes in the international cost of risk. However, inefficiencies in domestic financial systems are more important than international financial conditions in explaining the *levels* of borrowing costs in many developing countries. Fundamentals still matter—in determining both the risk premium attached to financial transactions with individual countries and the relative cost effectiveness of a given investment project. Even the financial systems of the most advanced developing countries underperform the financial systems in high-income countries. For example 11 of the 14 developing countries included in an aggregate index of financial system efficiency scored in the bottom half of the rankings (Dorrucci, Meyer-Cirkel, and Santabarbara 2009).

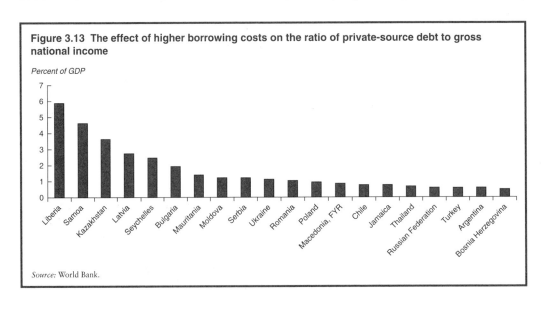

Figure 3.13 The effect of higher borrowing costs on the ratio of private-source debt to gross national income

Percent of GDP

Source: World Bank.

Table 3.9 Selected indicators of banking sector efficiency
(Operational ratios of commercial banks, average 2006–08)

Region	Net interest margin (%)	Net interest revenue/ average assets (%)	Other operating income/average assets (%)	Noninterest expenses/ average assets (%)	Profit margin (before tax and non-operational items
East Asia and Pacific	3.85	3.34	1.52	3.09	1.77
Europe and Central Asia	6.94	5.86	11.05	14.18	2.73
Latin America and Caribbean	8.38	6.69	3.51	8.44	1.77
Middle East and North Africa	3.21	2.58	1.66	2.66	1.58
South Asia	3.47	3.05	1.88	3.26	1.68
Sub-Saharan Africa	7.17	5.80	4.23	6.58	3.45
Developing countries	6.62	5.50	7.12	10.22	2.40
High income	3.57	3.25	1.94	4.06	1.13
Low income	6.16	5.02	3.46	5.47	3.01
Lower-middle income	5.57	4.37	2.42	5.21	1.58
Upper-middle income	7.00	5.91	9.05	12.39	2.57

Source: World Bank calculations using data from Bankscope.

Table 3.9 reports information on net interest revenues (the difference between interest income paid on deposits and earned on loans), other income, and noninterest expenditures (principally overhead), all expressed as a percent of the total value of banks' assets. On average, the difference between interest paid on deposits and charged on loans by developing-country banks is 225 basis points higher than in high-income countries. Overhead expenditures are more than twice as large as in high-income countries, and profit rates are twice as high. In addition, in some developing countries banks rely much more heavily on nonbanking activities for revenues and profits. Indeed, if developing-country banks did not have these other revenues, they would be making losses in all but one of the developing regions.

High overhead costs (as a share of total asset ratios) reflect a variety of factors, and their relative weight varies across banks and countries. In countries and regions that also show high profit rates (Sub-Saharan Africa and to a lesser extent Europe and Central Asia), these high overheads may reflect a lack of competitive pressure as well as a thin market. High levels of noninterest income such as in Europe and Central Asia, Latin America, and Africa suggest that shortcomings in the regulatory environment, including in the protection of property rights, may make nonbanking activities more profitable than traditional deposit and loan making,

reducing the overall level of intermediation that banks might otherwise accomplish.

Although interest rate margins and overhead costs provide only rough indicators of the economic costs imposed by inefficient financial systems, they do suggest considerable potential for reducing borrowing costs by improving efficiency. For example, if the spread between deposit and lending rates in Sub-Saharan Africa, Latin America, and Europe and Central Asia were reduced to the levels observed in East Asia or South Asia, borrowing costs in these regions would be lowered by between 300 and 450 basis points, much more than the estimated increase from tighter global financial conditions in even the most pessimistic scenario discussed earlier. Based on the econometric work reported in chapter 2, such a reduction in borrowing costs could prompt an increase in the level of domestic intermediation equivalent to 2.5 percent of GDP.

Moreover, the differences in banks' net interest margins between developing and high-income countries are considerable understatements of differences in the costs of borrowing. Particularly in low-income countries, small formal banking systems tend to drive borrowers to informal lenders. Because the interest rates charged by informal lenders are often several multiples of interest rates in high-income countries, improvements in efficiency that expanded developing countries' banking systems could result in very large reductions in interest rates facing less-creditworthy borrowers. In addition, many potential borrowers are denied finance altogether, so efficiency improvements that expanded the volume of credit would have large welfare effects.

The impact of improvements in the regulatory environment would likely be even more positive, because weak protection of property rights and excessive levels of corruption reduce the profitability of investment projects in ways other than through higher borrowing costs. Thus, according to the regression analysis in chapter 2, in addition to a lower cost of capital, a one-standard-deviation improvement in the business environment would increase the profitability of investments by enough to increase investment-to-GDP ratios by another 4 percentage points.

Table 3.10 gives a sense of the potential growth implications if developing countries were successful in reducing borrowing costs

Table 3.10   Potential impact of improved fundamentals on long-term growth prospects

	Developing countries	Middle income	Low income	East Asia and Pacific	Europe and Central Asia	Latin America and Caribbean	Middle East and North Africa	South Asia	Sub-Saharan Africa
(Average rate of growth of potential output, percent)									
Baseline scenario: spreads and base interest rates constant at their 2008 level									
1980–95	2.6	2.6	2.6	8.3	−0.6	2.4	2.6	5.1	1.8
1996–2002	4.6	4.6	3.9	7.8	3.1	3.0	4.2	5.8	3.4
2003–08	6.2	6.2	5.4	8.7	5.9	3.5	5.0	7.4	5.6
2009–15	6.3	6.3	5.8	8.1	5.7	3.8	5.4	7.4	6.5
2016–50	4.5	4.5	5.2	5.5	4.5	1.6	2.9	4.9	5.1
Higher base rates and return to "normal" spreads									
1980–95	2.6	2.6	2.6	8.3	−0.6	2.4	2.6	5.1	1.8
1996–2002	4.6	4.6	3.9	7.8	3.1	3.0	4.2	5.8	3.4
2003–08	6.2	6.2	5.4	8.7	5.9	3.5	5.0	7.4	5.6
2009–15	5.9	5.9	5.4	7.8	5.2	3.3	4.9	7.0	6.3
2016–50	4.5	4.4	5.2	5.4	4.4	1.5	2.8	4.8	5.1
Higher base rates, initially "normal" spreads that fall subsequently due to improved policies									
1980–95	2.6	2.6	2.6	8.3	−0.6	2.4	2.6	5.1	1.8
1996–2002	4.6	4.6	3.9	7.8	3.1	3.0	4.2	5.8	3.4
2003–08	6.2	6.2	5.4	8.7	5.9	3.5	5.0	7.4	5.6
2009–15	6.0	6.0	5.5	8.1	5.3	3.4	5.1	7.1	6.3
2016–50	4.9	4.8	6.0	5.6	5.1	1.9	3.3	5.5	5.5
(Percentage point difference in average potential output growth rates)									
Difference compared with baseline									
Higher base rates and return to normal spreads									
2003–08	0.0	0.0	0.0	0.0	0.0	0.0	0.0	0.0	0.0
2009–15	−0.4	−0.4	−0.4	−0.3	−0.5	−0.5	−0.4	−0.4	−0.3
2016–50	−0.1	−0.1	−0.1	−0.1	−0.1	−0.1	−0.1	−0.1	0.0
Higher base rates, initially "normal" spreads that fall subsequently due to improved policies									
2003–08	0.0	0.0	0.0	0.0	0.0	0.0	0.0	0.0	0.0
2009–15	−0.3	−0.3	−0.3	0.0	−0.4	−0.4	−0.3	−0.3	−0.2
2016–50	0.3	0.3	0.7	0.1	0.5	0.3	0.4	0.6	0.3
(Cumulative change in potential output)									
Change in final potential output compared with baseline									
Higher rates scenario									
	−4.8	−4.8	−4.9	−4.3	−6.0	−6.3	−5.7	−5.4	−2.8
Higher rates plus improved policy scenario									
	7.4	7.0	20.4	1.5	14.8	7.9	8.8	17.2	8.1

Source: World Bank.

through a mixture of regulatory reform and improved macroeconomic management. It compares the outcomes from the third scenario in table 3.6 (the scenario with higher base rates and a return to "normal" interest rate spreads) and a scenario that builds upon the same increase in base rates and interest rate spreads but assumes that developing countries continue to make strides in reducing borrowing costs (by 25 basis points a year until spreads reach 150 basis points). In this simulation, developing countries still experience a period of significantly slower growth in the five to seven years following the crisis, but the assumed cumulative improvements in fundamentals result in a gradual increase in growth rates relative to both the higher base rates and baseline scenarios. Overall, these improvements mean that potential output is actually some 7.4 percent higher than in the original baseline scenario and 12.2 percent higher than in the higher rates scenario, with the largest gains accruing to those countries and regions currently facing the highest spreads.

Implications for the global balance between savings and investment

The preceding analysis focused on the impact of increasing costs of capital on potential output. However, GDP growth may fall short of historical levels for reasons other than a decline in the capital-output ratio during the transition period. The adjustment process, during which investment rates are suppressed, may also have an impact on effective demand, and thus on utilization rates, although that impact is more speculative than the analysis of potential growth.

Especially in middle-income countries, investment rates are likely to remain substantially lower during the next five years than during the boom period as the capital stock adjusts to higher borrowing costs and slowing population growth. The impact of lower investment rates on the global balance between savings and investments could be substantial because middle-income countries have become the source of more than half of global investment growth. Moreover, lower investment rates will likely have an impact on regional imbalances. In Europe and Central Asia lower rates will contribute to a reduction in current account deficits, in a way similar to what happened in East Asia after the 1998 financial crisis. In East Asia, where annual growth rates during the next five years are expected to be almost 1 percentage point lower than during the boom, lower investment rates will increase current account surpluses—unless savings rates decline.

In low-income countries, capital needs remain substantial. The impact of higher borrowing costs could be counteracted by total factor productivity gains that are already in the pipeline and by sustained population growth.

The increase in borrowing costs described in the preceding pages reflects both an increase in the cost of intermediation (stemming from stricter regulation of financial markets and consolidation in the banking sector) and an increase in the price of a given quantity of risk (caused by the disappearance of some risk-management instruments and a generalized increase in risk aversion). The risk-free interest rate that is relevant for savers is not affected directly by these factors. It is affected indirectly, however, because higher intermediation costs and risk premiums will increase the wedge between borrowers' costs and the risk-free interest rate that motivates savers. If savings are interest-rate elastic, this will provoke a rightward movement along both the demand and supply of savings curves, reducing the risk-free rate of interest (from r^s_1 to r^s_2 in figure 3.14). This decline will reduce savings and increase domestic demand—at least partially compensating for the decline in investment and working to eliminate current account surpluses. The overall impact on global imbalances will depend on the balance of these affects across current account surplus and deficit countries.

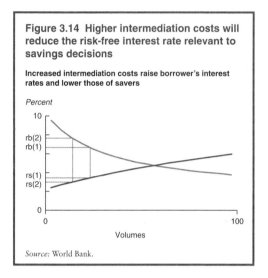

Figure 3.14 Higher intermediation costs will reduce the risk-free interest rate relevant to savings decisions

Increased intermediation costs raise borrower's interest rates and lower those of savers

Source: World Bank.

Apart from increasing consumption shares in some of the emerging economies, measures to counteract the potential decline in investments may be needed too. The possibility of ineffective demand provides another reason to accelerate productivity growth, either by eliminating bottlenecks or by opening up new areas of growth. Only with such growth impulses can investment rates in developing countries return to the levels seen during the boom. In that sense the most successful strategy to create sufficient effective demand in the medium run is consistent with policies that aim to maximize potential growth.

Conclusion

Developing countries are likely to face a much more constrained financial environment over the next decade or so than they did during the pre-crisis boom. The discrediting of many of the financial innovations that led investors to believe that the ultimate cost of holding a risky asset had declined sharply, a tighter regulatory environment, more risk aversion on the part of investors, and the necessity of both the high-income banking and household sectors to consolidate and rebuild their balance sheets is expected to result in a more stable and ultimately more robust global financial environment, but also one characterized by less liquid and more expensive financing conditions.

The combination of a more constrained and more expensive financing environment is likely to have important real-side implications for developing countries. For low-income countries with relatively weak domestic financial sectors and binding capital constraints, weaker bank finance and FDI flows will be particularly problematic. In some of these countries FDI inflows represent more than 40 percent of total investment, so the projected 30 percent cut in flows from pre-crisis levels could have particularly strong repercussions. For middle-income countries with access to international financial markets and better developed domestic markets, the main impact is likely to be through the increased cost of borrowing. Here, estimates suggest that the adjustment to higher capital costs could reduce potential growth rates in developing countries by between 0.2 and 0.7 percentage points over the next five to seven years, and that, longer term, potential output in these countries could be lower by between 3.4 and 8.0 percent.

The extent to which domestic finance will be able to step in to supplement a weaker international financial system is very uncertain. Countries with strong policies and institutions have the most to lose from a weakening of the international financial system because they benefit most from it. However, in general they also have the strongest domestic intermediation systems and are well placed to compensate for a weaker international system by expanding this sector. Increased domestic intermediation could ultimately generate larger benefits than the cost that reduced access to international capital might impose. For many low-income countries the domestic financial sector may be too weak to respond effectively. Moreover, while the immediate costs from reduced international flows may be smaller—because these countries have little access and therefore little to lose—the longer-terms costs could be significant. In particular, if international finance and the expertise and spillover effects that can accompany it are not available or are available to a lesser degree, in the future this could hamper the ability of low-income, weakly intermediated countries to make the transition to middle-income countries with more robust financial systems.

Developing countries themselves can be expected to react to the crisis in ways that are not necessarily beneficial. The crisis has made clear once again the lesson that financial flows can be very volatile and that this volatility can generate extremely costly real-side adjustments. With GDP growth off by as much as 4 percent, it is a small consolation to a country that has pursued prudent macroeconomic and structural policies that the growth recession that it has experienced was much smaller than that of countries that went into the crisis with large current account and budget deficits.

Throughout the world public pressure and prudent policy making will force a rethinking of the costs and benefits of both financial and trade openness. The evidence supports a cautious approach to capital account liberalization, while supporting the view that relatively flexible exchange rate regimes are less susceptible to the kind of crises that have been observed in the past. Countries with weak domestic institutions and limited intermediation can find a too rapid capital account liberalization to be destabilizing, while those with more mature domestic systems can benefit from the additional competition and in some cases funding that a more liberalized external account can provide. Similarly, while a buildup of reserves gives a country additional room for maneuver, in the event of a crisis these reserves can be very expensive to maintain and, of course, cannot prevent exchange rate revaluations in the presence of overwhelming fundamental forces.

Although individual developing countries may be powerless to influence global developments, much can done at the domestic level to mitigate these costs. The sensitivity of developing-country GDP and growth prospects to borrowing costs and the high cost of intermediation suggests that policies that succeed in increasing the efficiency of the domestic banking sector—through improved enforcement of property rights, enhanced competition, or better regulation—could have significant impacts on domestic intermediation, investment levels, and growth potential. Borrowing costs in many regions could be reduced by more than 300 basis points, a reduction that could be associated with a long-term increase in potential output of 8 percent or more. Of course, implementing the reforms to take advantage of this potential will be a slow and difficult process—especially if they run afoul of domestic interests.

Notes

1. It was possible to retain the risk of off-balance-sheet assets but avoid capital requirements by abusing exceptions to the "true sale" rule governing securitization; that rule states that to avoid capital requirements the seller of loans must not retain any responsibility for subsequent loan performance or collateral. U.S. regulators were aware of this practice but found it difficult to control (Calomiris and Mason 2004).

2. Calomiris and Mason (2004) argued that the use of securitization with implicit recourse to evade capital requirements was socially beneficial, essentially because regulatory capital requirements were too high.

3. Efforts by regulators to close insolvent banks and impose capital requirements that are commonly based on the risk of an individual bank can fail to mitigate systemic risk (Acharya 2009).

4. For a broad view of potential changes in financial sector regulation, see the G-20 statement on "Strengthening the Financial System," issued at the London Summit on April 2, 2009; "A New Foundation: Rebuilding Financial Supervision and Regulation" (issued by the Obama administration in June 2009); and "The Turner Review: A Regulatory Response to the Global Banking Crisis" (issued by the United Kingdom's Financial Services Authority in March 2009). One example of legislative progress is passage by the US House of Representatives of a bill to strengthen consumer protection, extend regulation to some over the counter derivatives, and create a process for addressing troubled firms that may pose systemic risks. The bill may yet undergo significant modification before a compatible version is passed by the U.S. senate and it becomes law.

5. See cross-country studies in Claessens, Demirgüç-Kunt, and Huizinga (1998); Barth, Caprio, and Levine

(2001); and Claessens and Laeven (2003). Bayraktar and Wang (2004) find that domestic banks' efficiency gains from foreign entry are greatest in countries that liberalized their stock markets before domestic financial markets.

6. The data on local claims on foreign-owned banks include only banks reporting to the BIS and thus exclude claims by some foreign-owned banks (particularly from many developing countries). Also, these data on the stock of claims are not adjusted for changes in exchange rates. Thus the appreciation of the dollar during the second half of 2008 contributed to reducing the level of claims. It is unclear, however, whether the currency denomination of claims differed greatly between foreign and locally owned banks.

7. Up to 20 percent of the $15.8 trillion of world merchandise trade in 2008 involved secured documentary transactions (such as letters of credit), and other forms of trade finance play an important role (either in financing inventories or accounts receivables) in helping bridge the gap between the time when costs are incurred in producing a product and the time when final payment is made upon receipt.

8. World Bank calculations using data from Dealogic.

9. Mutual funds based in developed countries began investing in the 1980s in the form of closed-end funds (whose shares cannot be redeemed), to limit turnover in the relatively illiquid markets in many developing countries (Kaminsky, Lyons, and Schmuckler 2001). As liquidity increased, open-end funds became more common. Other major foreign investors in emerging stock markets (many of whom invest through mutual funds) include pension funds, insurance companies, hedge funds, and individual investors.

10. This includes evidence that stock market liberalizations reduce the cost of capital (Henry 2000, Bekaert and Harvey 2000). Kose, Prasad, and Terrones (2008) find a positive relationship between portfolio equity liabilities and total factor productivity growth in a sample of industrial and developing countries.

11. For example, Gupta and Yuan (2005) find that following equity market liberalizations, industries that depend on external finance grow faster than industries dependent on finance internal to the firm. Similarly, Vanassche (2004) finds that financial openness has a positive effect on growth of industrial sectors generally, and that this impact is greatest in industries that rely more on external finance. Eichengreen, Gullapalli, and Panizza (2009) find that capital account openness has a positive impact on the growth of financially dependent industries only in high-income countries and that this effect disappears during periods of crisis.

12. There remains some theoretical argument over this effect, however, because the opportunity to exit at low cost may also reduce incentives for monitoring managers, leading to weaker corporate governance and less productive investments (Levine and Zervos 1998).

13. Levine and Zervos (1998) find that stock market liquidity (along with banking sector development) is positively associated with growth, capital accumulation, and productivity improvements in a cross-country regression. Demirgüç-Kunt and Maksimovic (1996) find that active stock markets are associated with higher-than-predicted rates of firm growth. Kassimkatis and Spyrous (2001) find that equity markets boost growth only in relatively liberalized economies. In addition, some authors have found that the lifting of restrictions on stock market development is positively associated with growth, either temporarily or over the long term (Fuchs-Schundeln and Funke 2003).

14. Foreign investors may spur investment in infrastructure services such as clearing and settlement systems, as countries compete for the limited pool of foreign investors willing to devote resources to developing-country markets, and provide information on practices in more developed markets. In a cross-country regression, Chinn and Ito (2006) find that openness to external financial flows contributes to the development of equity markets.

15. While the database does not distinguish whether the acquisition is cross-border or domestic, we assume that multinational firms borrow internationally mostly for cross-border acquisitions.

16. Outward FDI from developing countries actually increased in 2008 to $164 billion (from $138 billion in 2007), in contrast to the 25 percent fall in outflows from developed countries, and is expected to slow only slightly in 2009. Chinese companies have spent more than $20 billion on oil assets overseas since December 2008, including in Kazakhstan, Nigeria, and the Syrian Arab Republic.

17. The superior technology (and marketing and management practices) often used by foreign firms is transmitted to domestic firms either through observation or because domestic firms hire workers trained by foreign firms (Fosfuri, Motta, and Ronde 2001). Foreign firm entry also can increase the intensity of competition in an industry, potentially forcing domestic firms to improve their efficiency (Blomström, Kokko, and Zejan 2000; Javorcik, Keller, and Tybout 2006). The extent of efficiency gains from FDI depends on the quality of domestic policies and institutions, including policies toward FDI (Beamish 1998); policies promoting the diffusion of technology (Lall 2003); the level of human capital (Borensztein, DeGregorio, and Lee 1998); the level of technology in the recipient country and how close it is to technology used by foreign firms (Saggi 2002); trade policy (Moran 2002); and financial development (Alfaro and others 2002).

18. See World Bank (2004) for a discussion of infrastructure financing in developing countries, and Dailami and Hauswald (2007) for an example of how complex financing arrangements helped ensure the success and lower the costs of a major project finance transaction in Qatar.

19. For example, the share in dollar terms of developing-country institutions in project finance transactions increased from about 0.5 percent in 1997 to 9 percent in 2008 (Project Finance International, http://www.pfie.com). Moreover, participation by firms in high-income countries that recently were viewed as developing—for example the Republic of Korea; Taiwan, China; and Singapore—also increased markedly.

20. The high levels of volatility in consumption in developing countries imply large welfare benefits to consumption smoothing (Pallage and Robe 2003). Consumption smoothing may also facilitate specialization and hence development by reducing the impact on welfare of higher volatility that may be associated with specialization.

21. The correlation between ratios of short-term debt to reserves and the change in GDP growth is -0.2. And using our forecasts of GDP growth in 2009, the correlation between reserves-to-import ratios in 2007 and the fall in GDP growth in 2008–09 is zero.

22. This last term reflects the difference between the interest on domestic-currency securities issued in the course of past efforts to sterilize capital inflows and the domestic-currency return on the international reserves.

23. Hauner's country groups do not correspond to the World Bank's distinction between developing and high-income countries.

24. This figure, which refers to reserves holdings where the currency composition is known, is taken from the International Monetary Fund's COFER database.

25. World Bank calculations based on table 7A of the Locational Banking Statistics from the Bank for International Settlements.

26. The Chinn-Ito index aggregates information on restrictions on financial transactions reported in the IMF's Annual Report on Exchange Arrangements to produce a single indicator of financial openness for most of the world's countries. The data can be found at www. http://web.pdx.edu/~ito/.

27. Information asymmetries may be smaller at regional levels than at the global level (Ocampo 2006).

28. As reported in the *People's Daily Online*, May 4, 2008 (http://english.people.com.cn/90001/90780/91421/6650574.html). ASEAN + 3 refers to the ASEAN countries plus China, Japan, and the Republic of Korea.

29. The observed increase in the synthetic price of risk in the fourth quarter of 2008 was equivalent to what might have been expected if high-income policy rates increased by some 600 basis points. In fact during the period, the effective Federal Reserve rate actually fell by close to 180 basis points, although corporate bond defaults (another important fundamental) did rise significantly.

30. Prediction errors are largest for Brazil, Hungary, and to a lesser extent Bulgaria and Malaysia; for more see Kennedy and Palerm 2009.

31. The interest rate spread rose by more than 30 percent more than expected by the model in Argentina and Brazil and by 30 percent less than expected in the case of Poland.

32. The basic OECD model has the form SynRiskIndex = $-1.24 + 0.41*$BaseRate + Other variables. In Kennedy and Palerm (2009), developing-country spreads (EMBI spreads) are a function of the SynRiskIndex (and indirectly, the BaseRate). Two specifications were retained: one for countries with good credit histories, and one for those with less good histories: EMBI(poor risk) = $140*$ SynRiskIndex + Other variables; and EMBI(better risk) = $27*$ SynRiskIndex + Other variables. Combining the two equations results in a reduced form equation for EMBI spreads as a function of the BaseRate: ΔEMBI(poor risk) = $140* 0.41*\Delta$BaseRate = $57.4*\Delta$BaseRate and ΔEMBI(better risk) = $27* 0.41*\Delta$BaseRate = $11.1*\Delta$BaseRate. Dailami, Masson, and Padou (2008) modeled the relationship between fluctuations in high-income policy interest rates and developing-country risk premiums directly, in contrast with the less direct approach here, which first estimates the impact of policy rates on the global price of risk and then the impact of the price of risk on specific developing-country risk premiums.

33. Empirically, depreciation rates range from 3 to 13 percent in the manufacturing sector (Nadiri and Prucha 1993) for manufacturing in the United States to as high as 18 to 36 percent in the high-tech research and development sector. Economy-wide depreciation rates represent a weighted average of very long depreciation rates on physical capital such as roads and building and other much shorter ones on high technology. The aggregate depreciation rate varies from country to country with these values and the weight of different activities in overall output. While the 7 percent assumption used here is a rough approximation, it corresponds to the assumption used in IMF (2005) in a slightly different modeling exercise and is broadly consistent with implicit values used in the OECD interlink model.

34. In the model of potential output described in chapter 2, a 100 basis point fall in the cost of capital for a country with a cost of capital of 1,000 basis points should result in a 4 percent increase in its capital-output ratio over the long term (assuming capital's share in

value added of 40 percent, a real interest rate of 3 percent, and an average depreciation rate of 7 percent).

35. The simulations are run out to 2050 to allow medium-term dynamics to resolve themselves.

36. The dynamic interaction between investment rates and the desired capital stock actually causes the ratio to overshoot its final level about by 3 percent of the baseline capital output ratio.

37. The IMF analysis is based on an ex post analysis of the factors that explain past post-crisis declines in potential output, among which is the same fall in capital-output ratios described here.

38. See World Bank (2007) for a more in-depth discussion of likely long-term scenarios and their long-term implications for poverty.

39. Based on an assumed import elasticity of 4.

References

Acharya, Viral V. 2009. "A Theory of Systemic Risk and Design of Prudential Bank Regulation." *Journal of Financial Stability* 5 (3): 224–55.

Alfaro, Laura, Areendam Chanda, Sebnem Kalemli-Ozcan, and Selin Sayek. 2004. "FDI and Economic Growth: The Role of Local Financial Markets." *Journal of International Economics* 64 (October): 89–112.

Al-Yousif, Khalifa Yousif. 2002. "Financial Development and Economic Growth: Another Look at the Evidence from Developing Countries." *Review of Financial Economics* 11 (2): 131–50.

Arena, Marco, Carmen Reinhart, and Francisco Vazquez. 2007. "The Lending Channel in Emerging Economies: Are Foreign Banks Different?" IMF Staff Working Paper 07/48. International Monetary Fund, Washington, DC.

Barth, James R., Gerard Caprio, and Ross Levine. 2001. "Bank Regulation and Supervision: What Works Best?" Policy Research Working Paper 2775. World Bank, Washington, DC (August).

Bayraktar, Nihal, and Yan Wang. 2004. "Foreign Bank Entry, Performance of Domestic Banks and the Sequence of Financial Liberalization." Policy Research Working Paper 3416. World Bank, Washington, DC.

Beamish, P. W. 1988. *Multinational Joint Ventures in Developing Countries*. London: Routledge.

Bekaert, Geert, and Campbell R. Harvey. 2000. "Foreign Speculators and Emerging Equity Markets." *Journal of Finance* 55 (2): 565–613.

Blanchard, Olivier, Hamid Faruqee, and Vladimir Klyuev. 2009. "Did Foreign Reserves Help Weather the Crisis?" *IMF Survey Magazine* (October 8).

Blomström, M., A. Kokko, and M. Zejan. 2000. *Foreign Direct Investment: Firm and Host Country Strategies*. London: Macmillan.

Borensztein, E., J. De Gregorio, and J. W. Lee. 1998. "How Does Foreign Direct Investment Affect Economic Growth?" *Journal of International Economics* 45: 115–35.

Brunnermeier, Markus K, Andrew Crockett, Charles A Goodhart, Avinash Persaud, and Hyun Song Shin. 2009. "The Fundamental Principles of Financial Regulation." *Geneva Reports on the World Economy*. Geneva: International Center for Monetary and Banking Studies.

Calomiris, Charles W., and Joseph R. Mason. 2004. "Credit Card Securitization and Regulatory Arbitrage." *Journal of Financial Services Research* 26 (1): 5–27.

Calvo, Guillermo. 1996. "Varieties of Capital Market Crises." In *The Debt Burden and its Consequences for Monetary Policy,* ed. Calvo Guillermo and Mervyn King. London: Macmillan in association with the International Economic Association.

Cetorelli, Nicola, and Linda Goldberg. 2009. "Globalized Banks: Lending to Emerging Markets in the Crisis." Staff Report 377. Federal Reserve Bank of New York, New York.

Chinn, Menzie D., and Hiro Ito. 2006. "What Matters for Financial Development? Capital Controls, Institutions, and Interactions." *Journal of Development Economics* 81: 163–92.

Claessens, Stijn, and Luc Laeven. 2003. "What Drives Bank Competition? Some International Evidence." *Journal of Money, Credit and Banking* 36 (3): 563–83.

Corm, George. 2006. "The Arab Experience." In Ocampo, *Regional Financial Cooperation*.

Cortavarria, Luis, Simon Gray, Barry Johnston, Laura Kodres, Aditya Narain, Mahmood Pradhan, and Ian Tower. 2009. *Lessons of the Financial Crisis for Future Regulation of Financial Institutions and Markets and for Liquidity Management*. Washington, DC: International Monetary Fund.

Crystal, Jennifer S., B. Gerard Dages, and Linda S. Goldberg. 2002. "Has Foreign Bank Entry Led to Sounder Banks in Latin America?" *Current Issues in Economics and Finance* 8 (1):1–6.

Cull, Robert, and Maria Soledad Martinez Peria. 2007. "Foreign Bank Participation and Crises in Developing Countries." World Bank, Washington, DC.

Dailami, Mansoor, and Robert Hauswald. 2007. "Credit-spread Determinants and Interlocking Contracts: A Study of the Ras Gas Project." *Journal of Financial Economics* 86: 248–78.

Dailami, Mansoor, Paul R. Masson, and Jean Jose Padou. 2008. "Global Monetary Conditions versus

Country-Specific Factors in the Determination of Emerging Market Debt Spreads." *Journal of International Money and Finance* 27: 1325–36.

De Haas, Ralph, and Iman van Lelyveld. 2006. "Foreign Banks and Credit Stability in Central and Eastren Europe: A Panel Data Analysis." *Journal of Banking and Finance* 30: 1927–52.

Demirgüç-Kunt, Asli, and Vojislav Maksimovic. 1996. "Financial Constraints, Uses of Funds and Firm Growth: An International Comparison." Policy Research Working Paper 1671. World Bank, Washington, DC.

Demirgüç-Kunt, Asli, Harry Huizinga, and Stijn Claessens. 1998. "How Does Foreign Entry Affect the Domestic Banking Sector?" Policy Research Working Paper 1918. World Bank, Washington, DC.

Detragiache, Enrica, and Poonam Gupta. 2004. "Foreign Banks in Emerging Market Crises: Evidence from Malaysia." IMF Working Paper 04/129. International Monetary Fund, Washington, DC.

Di Giovanni, Julian. 2005. "What Drives Capital Flows? The Case Of Cross-Border M&A Activity and Financial Deepening." *Journal of International Economics* 65 (1): 127–49.

Dorrucci, Ettore, Alexis Meyer-Cirkel, and Daniel Santabarbara. 2009. "Domestic Financial Development in Emerging Economies: Evidence and Implications." Occasional Paper Series 102, European Central Bank, Frankfurt (April).

Edwards, Sebastian. 2005. "Capital Controls, Sudden Stops, and Current Account Reversals." NBER Working Paper 11170. National Bureau of Economic Research, Cambridge, MA.

Eichengreen, Barry, Rachita Gullapalli, and Ugo Panizza. 2009. "Capital Account Liberalization, Financial Development and Industry Growth: A Synthetic View." University of California at Berkeley, Berkeley, CA.

Eichengreen, Barry, and David Leblang. 2002. "Capital Account Liberalization and Growth: Was Mr. Mahathir Right?" NBER Working Paper 9427. National Bureau of Economic Research, Cambridge, MA.

Ellis, Nan S., Lisa M. Fairchild, and Harold D. Flether. 2008. "The NYSE Response to Specialist Misconduct: An Example of the Failure of Self-Regulation." www.works.bepres.com\cgi.

Fimetrix. 2009. www.fimetrix.com.

Fosfuri, Andrea, Massimo Motta, and Thomas Ronde. 2001. "Foreign Direct Investment and Spillovers through Workers' Mobility." *Journal of International Economics* 53 (1): 205–22.

Friedman, Jed, and Norbert Schady. 2009. "How Many More Infants Are Likely to Die in Africa as a Result of the Global Financial Crisis?" Research Paper 60. World Bank, Development Research Group, Washington, DC.

Fuchs-Schundeln, Nicola, and Norbert Funke. 2003. "Stock Market Liberalizations: Financial and Macroeconomic Implications." *Review of World Economics* 139 (4): 730–61.

Fung, Laurence Kang-por, Chi-sang Tam, and Ip-wing Yu. 2008. "Assessing the Integration of Asia's Equity and Bond Markets." In *Regional Financial Integration in Asia: Present and Future.* BIS Papers 42. Bank for International Settlements, Basel.

Furman, Jason, and Joseph Stiglitz. 1998. "Economic Crises: Evidence and Insights from East Asia." In *Brookings Papers on Economic Activity,* ed. William C. Brainard and George Perry. Washington, DC: Brookings Institution.

Glick, Reuven, and Michael Hutchison. 2001. "Banking and Currency Crises: How Common Are Twins?" In *Financial Crises in Emerging Markets,* ed. Reuven Glick, Ramon Moreno, and Mark M. Spiegel. New York: Cambridge University Press.

Goldberg, Linda, B. Gerard Dages, and Daniel Kinney. 2000. "Foreign and Domestic Bank Participation in Emerging Markets: Lessons from Mexico and Argentina." NBER Working Paper 7714. National Bureau of Economic Research, Cambridge, MA.

Gupta, Nandini, and Kathy Yuan. 2005. "On the Growth Effects of Liberalizations." Available at SSRN: http://ssrn.com/abstract=774605.

Hauner, David. 2005. "A Fiscal Price Tag for International Reserves." IMF Working Paper 05/81. International Monetary Fund, Washington, DC.

Hellman, T., K. Murdock, and J. Stiglitz. 2000. "Liberalization, Moral Hazard in Banking and Prudential Regulation: Are Capital Requirements Enough?" *American Economic Review* 90(1): 147–65.

Henry, Peter B. 2000. "Stock Market Liberalization, Economic Reform, and Emerging Market Equity Prices." *Journal of Finance* 55 (2): 529–64.

———. 2007. "Capital Account Liberalization: Theory, Evidence and Speculation." *Journal of Economic Literature* 45 (4): 887–935.

IMF (International Monetary Fund). 2005. *World Economic Outlook.* Washington, DC.

———. 2009. *World Economic Outlook: Sustaining the Recovery.* Washington, DC (October).

IMF/BAFT (International Monetary Fund–Bankers' Association for Finance and Trade). 2009. "IMF-BAFT Trade Finance Survey: A Survey among Banks Assessing the Current Trade Finance Environment" (http://baft.org/content_folders/Issues/IMFBAFTSurveyResults20090331.ppt).

Javorcik, Beata Smarzynska, Wolfgang Keller, and James R. Tybout. 2006. "Openness and

Industrial Responses in a Wal-Mart World: A Case Study of Mexican Soaps, Detergents and Surfactant Producers." NBER Working Paper 12457. National Bureau of Economic Research, Cambridge, MA.

Jeanne, Olivier. 2007. "International Reserves in Emerging Market Economies: Too Much of a Good Thing?" *Brookings Papers on Economic: 1*, ed. William C. Brainard and George Perry. Washington, DC: Brookings Institution.

Jeon, Bang Nam. 2002. "Progress and Prospects of Regional Financial Arrangements and Cooperation: A Critical Suvey." Paper prepared for the 2002 International Finance Seminar ADBI/ADB in Penang, Malaysia. http://ssrn.com/abstract=1305688.

Jickling, Mark. 2009. "Causes of the Financial Crisis." Congressional Research Service, Washington, DC. http://digitalcommons.ilr.cornell.edu/key workplace/600.

Jorgenson, Dale W. 1963. "Capital Theory and Investment Behavior." *American Economic Review* 53: 247–57.

Kaminsky, Graciela A., Richard K. Lyons, and Sergio L. Schmukler. 2001. "Mutual Fund Investment in Emerging Markets: An Overview." *World Bank Economic Review* 15 (2): 315–40.

Kaminsky, Graciela L. and Sergio L. Schmukler. 2002. "Short-Run Pain, Long-Run Gain: The Effects of Financial Liberalization." NBER Working Paper 9787. National Bureau of Economic Research, Cambridge, MA.

Kassimatis, Konstantinos, and Spyros I. Spyrou. 2001. "Stock and Credit Market Expansion and Economic Development in Emerging Markets: Further Evidence Utilizing Cointegration Analysis." *Applied Economics* 33: 1057–64.

Kennedy, Michael, and Angel Palerm. Forthcoming. "Emerging Market Bond Spreads: The Role of World Financial Market Conditions and Country-Specific Factors." World Bank Prospects Working Paper, Washington, DC.

Klein, Michael W., and Giovanni P. Olivei. 2008. "Capital Account Liberalization, Financial Depth and Economic Growth." *Journal of International Money and Finance* 27: 861–75.

Klein, M. W., J. Peek, and E. S. Rosengren. 2002. "Troubled Banks, Impaired Foreign Direct Investment: The Role of Relative Access to Credit." *American Economic Review* 92: 8.

Kose, M. Ayhan, Eswar Prasad, Kenneth Rogoff, and Shang-Jin Wei. 2006. "Financial Globalization: A Reappraisal." IMF Working Paper 06/189. International Monetary Fund, Washington, DC.

Kose, M. Ayhan, Eswar Prasad, and Ashley D. Taylor. 2009. "Thresholds in the Process of International Financial Integration." Working Paper 14916. National Bureau of Economic Research, Cambridge, MA.

Kose, M. Ayhan, Eswar Prasad, and Marco E. Terrones. 2005. "Growth Volatility in an Era of Globalization." IMF Staff Papers 52. International Monetary Fund, Washington, DC (September).

———. 2008. "Does Openness to International Financial Flows Raise Productivity Growth?" NBER Working Paper 14558. National Bureau of Economic Research, Cambridge, MA.

Lall, Sanjaya. 2003. "The Technological Structure and Performance of Developing Country Manufacturing Exports, 1985–98." QEH Working Paper 44. Queen Elizabeth House, Oxford University, Oxford, U.K.

Lau, Lawrence J. 2000. "Research on the Cost of Capital: Past, Present and Future." Chapter in *Econometrics and the Cost of Capital: Essays in Honor of Dale Jorgenson.* Cambridge, MA: Massachusetts Institute of Technology Press.

Levine, Ross. 1996. "Foreign Banks, Financial Development and Economic Growth." In *International Financial Markets,* ed. Claude E. Barfied. Washington, DC.: AEI Press.

Levine, Ross, and Sara Zervos. 1998. "Stock Markets, Banks, and Economic Growth." *American Economic Review* 88 (3): 537–58.

Machinea, Jose Luis, and Guillermo Rozenwurcel. 2006. "Macroeconomic Coordination in Latin America: Does It Have a Future?" In Ocampo, *Regional Financial Cooperation.*

Magud, Nicolas, and Carmen M. Reinhart. 2006. "Capital Controls: An Evaluation." NBER Working Paper 11973. National Bureau of Economic Research, Cambridge, MA.

Malouche, Mariem. 2009. Trade and Trade Finance Developments in 14 Developing Countries post September 2008: A World Bank Survey." Policy Research Working Paper 5138. World Bank, Washington, DC.

Martinez Peria, Maria Soledad, Andrew Powell, and Ivanna Vladkova-Hollar. 2002. "Banking on Foreigners: The Behavior of International Bank Lending to Latin America, 1985–2000." IMF Staff Papers 52. International Monetary Fund, Washington, DC.

McKibbin, Warwick J., and Andrew Stoeckel. 2009. "The Potential Impact of the Global Financial Crisis on World Trade." Mimeo.

Miyachi, Masato. 2007. "Regional Cooperation in Developing Asian Bond Market." Presentation for the Asian Development Bank, given in Shanghai September 25.

Moran Theodore. 2002. *How to Investigate the Impact of Foreign Direct Investment on Development and Use the Results to Guide Policy.* Washington, D.C.: Brookings Trade Forum.

Mukerji, Purba. 2008. "Ready for Capital Account Convertibility?" *Journal of International Money and Finance.*

Nadiri, Ishaq, and Ingmar Prucha. 2007. "Sources of Growth of Output and Convergence of Productivity in Major OECD Countries." *International Journal of Production Economics* 52 (1997): 133–46.

Ocampo, Jose Antonio. 2006. "Regional Financial Cooperation: Experiences and Challenges." In *Regional Financial Cooperation*, ed. Jose Antonio Ocampo. Washington, DC: The Brookings Institution.

OECD. 2004. *OECD Economic Outlook* No. 75. Paris.

———. 2009. *OECD Economic Outlook* No. 85. Paris.

Pallage, Stephane, and Michael A. Robe. 2003. "On the Welfare Cost of Economic Fluctuations in Developing Countries." *International Economic Review* 44 (2): 677–98.

Peek, Joe, and Eric S. Rosengreen. 2000. "Implications of the Globalization of the Banking Sector: The Latin American Experience." *Proceedings.* Federal Reserve Bank of Boston Conference Series (June): 145–70.

Rodrik, Dani. 2006. "The Social Cost of Foreign Exchange Reserves." CEPR Discussion Paper 5483. Centre for Economic Policy Research, London.

Saggi, Kamal. 2002. "Trade, Foreign Direct Investment and International Technology Transfer: A Survey." *World Bank Research Observer* 17 (2): 191–235.

SEC (Security and Exchange Commission). 2008. "Summary Report of Issues Identified in the Commission's Staff Examinations of Select Credit Rating Agencies." Washington, DC (July).

Shakya, Malika. 2009. "Integration of Developing Countries into Global Supply Chains: A Global Buyers' and Producers' Perspective." International Trade Department, World Bank, unpublished working paper.

Sløk, Torsten, and Michael Kennedy. 2005. "Factors Driving Risk Premia." OECD Economics Department Working Papers, No. 385. Paris, OECD.

UNCTAD (United Nations Conference on Trade and Development). 2009. *World Investment Report.* New York: Unied Nations.

Vanassche, Ellen. 2004. "The Impact of International Financial Integration on Industry Growth." Center for Economic Studies Discussion Paper 04.12. Catholic University of Leuven, Leuven, Belgium.

World Bank. 2004. *Global Development Finance: Harnessing Cyclical Gains for Development.* Washington, DC: World Bank.

———. 2006. *Global Development Finance: The Development Potential of Surging Capital Flows.* Washington, DC: World Bank.

———. 2007. *Global Development Finance: The Globalization of Corporate Development Finance in Developing Countries.* Washington, DC: World Bank.

———. 2008. *Global Economic Prospects: Techology Diffusion in the Developing World.* Washington, DC: World Bank.

Appendix
Regional Economic Prospects

East Asia and the Pacific

Recent developments

As chapter 1 outlined, economies in the East Asia and Pacific region were particularly hard hit by the collapse of global business investment in the fall of 2008. The crisis curtailed financing flows to private firms worldwide, and together with depressed growth expectations, investment plans were marked down sharply. Household wealth, incomes, and demand for consumer durables were affected just as adversely. Outside of China, investment in the East Asia region was hit exceptionally hard. Local equity markets fell by almost 60 percent from January to October 2008; currencies tumbled between 5 and 25 percent against the dollar through the first quarter of 2009. And bond spreads increased by 515 basis points from January 2007 to reach 645 points by November 2008.[1]

As one of the key producing regions for durable and capital goods—highly integrated into global production networks—East Asian economies experienced dramatic declines in trade and production between September 2008 and March 2009. Dollar-based exports dropped 25 percent, while production (excluding China) plummeted 15–30 percent over the period. High-income economies within the region—including Japan; Republic of Korea; Singapore; Taiwan, China; and Hong Kong, China—were equally or more severely hit by these developments (figure A1).[2]

East Asia's rebound from the global downturn over the course of 2009 was quicker and more robust than in other parts of the world. China led the global recovery in industrial production, with contributions to growth from the high-income OECD countries emerging only later in the year. The recovery in East Asia was underpinned by domestic stimulus programs put in place by a number of economies, most notably by China; a shift from large inventory reduction to restocking by firms; and a return to positive growth in exports and production by the second quarter of 2009.[3] Against this background, GDP losses for East Asia were limited in 2009, with current growth estimates placed at 6.8 percent, down from 8 percent in 2008. China grew by an estimated 8.4 percent during the year, while performance in Indonesia (4.5 percent) and Vietnam (5.5 percent) was strong. Output contractions were limited to Cambodia (−2.2 percent), Malaysia (−2.3 percent), Thailand (−2.7 percent), and several Pacific islands. However, when China is excluded from the 2009 growth estimates, GDP numbers for the remainder of the region offer a better reflection of the crisis, with an advance of just 1.3 percent following 4.8 percent growth in 2008 (table A1).

As the global downturn took hold across East Asia in late 2008, many developing countries, together with major developed economies, began to implement large-scale fiscal and monetary stimulus measures to support domestic demand and to counter the drag from the

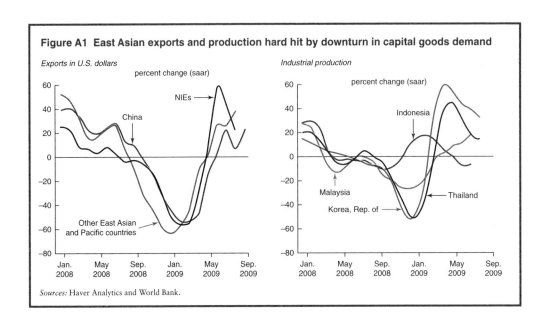

Figure A1 East Asian exports and production hard hit by downturn in capital goods demand

Sources: Haver Analytics and World Bank.

Table A1 East Asia and Pacific forecast summary
(annual percent change unless indicated otherwise)

	1995–2005[a]	2006	2007	2008	2009[e]	2010[f]	2011[f]
GDP at market prices (2005 US$)[b]	7.4	10.1	11.4	8.0	6.8	8.1	8.2
GDP per capita (units in US$)	6.3	9.2	10.5	7.2	6.0	7.2	7.3
PPP GDP[c]	7.3	10.1	11.3	8.0	6.8	8.0	8.2
Private consumption	5.7	8.1	8.7	6.7	5.9	7.3	7.5
Public consumption	8.1	8.2	9.8	7.8	11.1	8.4	7.3
Fixed investment	8.1	12.4	8.7	5.3	14.3	9.3	9.3
Exports, GNFS[d]	12.5	18.8	15.4	7.4	−13.5	6.6	8.8
Imports, GNFS[d]	9.7	12.7	11.0	4.9	−12.1	6.2	8.5
Net exports, contribution to growth	0.7	3.4	3.0	1.7	−2.0	0.7	0.8
Current account balance/GDP (%)	2.2	8.4	9.9	8.8	7.1	6.5	6.4
GDP deflator (median, LCU)	5.9	4.4	3.5	4.3	3.2	3.3	3.4
Fiscal balance/GDP (%)	−1.8	−0.7	0.0	−0.6	−3.3	−3.7	−3.1
Memo items: GDP							
East Asia excluding China	3.5	5.7	6.2	4.8	1.3	4.7	5.1
China	9.1	11.6	13.0	9.0	8.4	9.0	9.0
Indonesia	2.7	5.5	6.3	6.1	4.5	5.6	5.8
Thailand	2.7	5.3	4.9	2.6	−2.7	3.5	4.0

Source: World Bank.

a. Growth rates over intervals are compound average; growth contributions, ratios, and the GDP deflator are averages.
b. GDP measured in constant 2005 U.S. dollars.
c. GDP measured at PPP exchange rates.
d. Exports and imports of goods and non-factor services (GNFS).
e. Estimate.
f. Forecast.

collapse of export markets. The Chinese stimulus package is of special note; it entails some $575 billion to be spread proportionally over time from late 2008 through 2010, financed in part by a surge in credit expansion, with total new lending equivalent to 30 percent of GDP in 2009. Elsewhere in the region, government deficits (as a share of GDP) increased

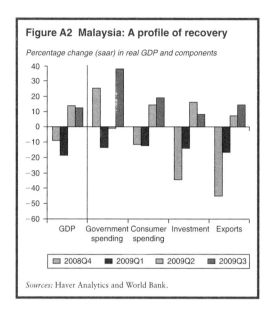

Figure A2 Malaysia: A profile of recovery

Percentage change (saar) in real GDP and components

Sources: Haver Analytics and World Bank.

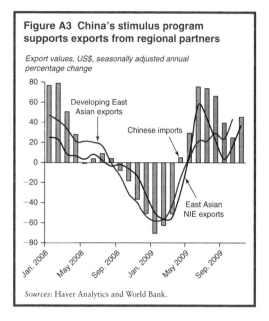

Figure A3 China's stimulus program supports exports from regional partners

Export values, US$, seasonally adjusted annual percentage change

Sources: Haver Analytics and World Bank.

significantly, reflecting both automatic stabilizers and countercyclical measures.

Over the course of 2009, East Asia's stimulus measures began to bear fruit, supporting incomes and helping to boost household spending, underpinning infrastructure development though public investment outlays, and providing support for the financial sector (figure A2 shows the recovery for Malaysia). China's stimulus had regionwide impacts, by boosting demand for East Asian exports. China's infrastructure outlays also underpinned demand for regional commodities and raw materials used in construction, from countries such as Indonesia, Papua New Guinea, and Lao People's Democratic Republic (as well as Australia). As replenishment of inventories got under way, firms in China began to restock parts and components from regional suppliers, notably electronic goods from countries such as Malaysia and Thailand (as well as NIEs). Also, rising Chinese consumer expenditure stimulated demand for a variety of consumer durable goods across the region (figure A3).

In Malaysia, fixed investment declined by 35 percent during the fourth quarter of 2008 (saar) as an indirect result of the surge in international capital costs, combined (more

importantly) with existing excess capacity, and expectations among Malaysian business that conditions in the main developed markets for electronics and other equipment would be in decline for an extended period (see figure A2). Exports fell abruptly, by 45 percent (saar), as the synchronous global shutdown of demand for capital and related goods took hold. GDP declined by a sharp 9.1 percent during the quarter. However, fiscal stimulus measures were implemented that helped to shore up confidence and provide direct support to the construction sector. The overall impact on the economy during the first two quarters of 2009 was limited, as decision and implementation lags affected the speed and rate of disbursement. While the steep decline in exports deeply affected the manufacturing sector, the impact on the economy as a whole was mitigated by the compression in processing imports.

Still, GDP declined by 18.3 percent (saar) in the first quarter of 2009, as exports continued in sharp decline, even though the falloff in investment was mitigated by a second fiscal measure (RM15 billion, or 2.3 percent of GDP). By the second and third quarters, Malaysia had emerged to recovery, after additional government spending and effects of earlier stimulus helped to turn around investment and consumer spending, while exports rebounded sharply (in part because of Chinese demand). The annualized pace of GDP growth rebounded strongly to 14.0 and 12.2 percent, respectively, in the second and third quarters.

Capital flows are returning to East Asia, with a notable pickup during the fall of 2009. East Asian bond and initial public offerings (IPO) increased as conditions in international markets became more hospitable, with spreads much reduced from crisis levels and underlying demand conditions firming. Some $12.8 billion in bonds were issued in the year to October, representing a doubling of issuance from the like period of 2008. IPO issuance increased to $38 billion, largely from China, but also from Malaysia and Indonesia, up 65 percent from the same period in 2008. But cross-border bank lending disappointed, largely reflecting risk aversion on the part of international commercial banks, where deleveraging continues to be the order of the day. Syndicated loans to East Asian entities amounted to $12.8 billion during the year through October, down substantially from the $37 billion raised in the same period of 2008. Total gross flows to developing East Asia amounted to $63 billion over the year through October—a 4.5 percent decline from the $66 billion accrued in the same period of 2008.

Local financial market developments have provided further impetus to the recovery. A return of capital from the United States, where funds had earlier fled to safe-haven securities has underpinned a rapid rebound in regional equity markets following steep declines in 2008 and early 2009 (figure A4). Bourses in Indonesia and Thailand are close to regaining levels that prevailed in January 2008, while Indonesia's market has more than doubled from October 2008 troughs, as have equity markets in Thailand and Singapore. The rebound in equity markets and falling interest rate spreads have helped reduce the cost of

Figure A4 Equity markets have nearly recovered from earlier declines

Local currency–based equity prices

Index, Jan. 1, 2008 = 100

Sources: Morgan-Stanley through Thomson/Datastream.

capital for firms, restore a significant portion of earlier wealth losses, and lift overall confidence. The return of foreign capital also helped to reverse some of the earlier sharp declines in local currencies (figure A5). Under

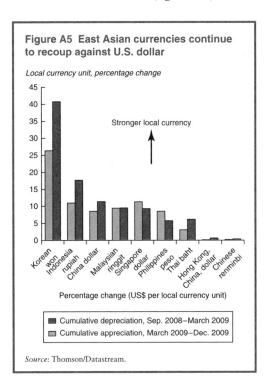

Figure A5 East Asian currencies continue to recoup against U.S. dollar

Local currency unit, percentage change

Stronger local currency

Percentage change (US$ per local currency unit)

■ Cumulative depreciation, Sep. 2008–March 2009
□ Cumulative appreciation, March 2009–Dec. 2009

Source: Thomson/Datastream.

these circumstances the potential formation of a "new" financial market bubble in the region is an increasing cause for concern.

Inflation has eased broadly in East Asia, given the slowing in activity and lower food and fuel prices, although conditions vary widely across countries. Increases in the consumer price index for 2009 range between highs of 20 and 12 percent in Cambodia and Vietnam, to 3 and zero percent (or slightly negative) in China, the Philippines, and Thailand.

In step with the cyclical downturn (a sharp drop in government revenues) and with large discretionary stimulus packages, fiscal deficits have widened across both middle- and low-income countries in the region—this even as fiscal space for the latter countries such as Cambodia and Lao PDR appears limited. The World Bank's East Asia and Pacific Department in a recent "East Asia Update" (November 2009) estimates that fiscal stimulus in the regions' middle-income countries amounted to 2.1 percent of GDP in 2009, up from an earlier estimate of 1.7 percent. China's fiscal shortfall is projected to have reached a record 3.3 percent of GDP during 2009, but a number of countries exceeded this deficit when the deficit is expressed as a proportion of GDP (figure A6). Examples

include Vietnam at 9.4 percent of GDP, Malaysia at 7.8 percent, Thailand (4.2 percent) and the Philippines (3.8 percent). The unwinding of these fiscal support measures will play an important role in shaping the economic recovery over the forecast period.

Although trade conditions have improved over the course of 2009 as Chinese imports recovered, regional export volumes (goods and services) dropped 13.5 percent during the year, while imports fell 12.1 percent, leading to a narrowing of the aggregate current account position from a surplus of 8.8 percent of GDP in 2008 to 7.1 percent for 2009. This was aided in particular by a sharp decline in China's current account surplus, which fell from 9.8 percent of GDP in 2008 to 6.4 percent of GDP during the first six months of 2009.

Medium-term outlook

Momentum underlying economic activity in the region should be sustained, as a gradual decline in the effects of domestic stimulus measures is countered over the course of 2010 by the return to growth (albeit moderate) in East Asia's main OECD export markets. But contrasted with earlier episodes of global downturns (for example the 2001–03 "dot-com" bust), the rebound and recovery path of GDP in East Asia is expected to be more muted, reflecting weaker global demand and less buoyant financial conditions. Continued strong advances in China's domestic demand, and associated imports, should play an important role in underpinning a second export-led revival phase for the remainder of the region. At the same time, world trade growth is anticipated to revive from the estimated 14.4 percent decline in 2009 to a gain of 6.2 percent by 2011.

Against this background, East Asian export volumes are forecast to advance by 6.6 percent in 2010 and 8.8 percent in 2011, picking up additional market share. The regional current account surplus position is anticipated to moderate from 7.1 percent of GDP in 2009 to

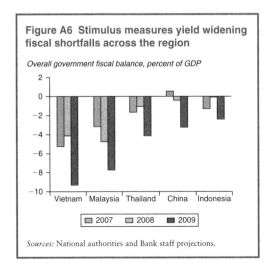

Figure A6 Stimulus measures yield widening fiscal shortfalls across the region

Overall government fiscal balance, percent of GDP

Vietnam · Malaysia · Thailand · China · Indonesia

☐ 2007 ☐ 2008 ■ 2009

Sources: National authorities and Bank staff projections.

6.4 percent by 2011 (see table A1), reflecting an increased contribution to overall growth from domestic demand.

The recovery in business investment is expected to be gradual (by historic standards), as excess capacity will first have to be worked down. Growth of public sector outlays should ease from 2009 peaks of 11.1 percent to 7.3 percent by 2011. Recognizing that prospects for an export-led recovery are less favorable than in the past, policy is likely to shift further toward fostering growth in household demand, helping, in turn, to offset the profile of weaker government spending.

On balance, regional GDP growth is expected to increase to 8.2 percent by 2011 from the 6.8 percent registered in 2009. This is a modest recovery by historic standards, but, at the end of the first year of financial crisis, the regional downturn has been equally moderate, compared, for example, with the East Asian crisis of the late 1990s. Domestic demand will be the key growth driver, with more modest net trade contributions. China will lead the regional advance with GDP growth of 9 percent by 2010 (figure A7; table A2). Growth excluding China is anticipated to pick up to 5.1 percent by 2011, from an estimated 1.3 percent in 2009. In particular, shifts from negative to positive growth in Malaysia and Thailand and a solid acceleration in activity in Indonesia and Vietnam should underpin the turnaround.

Risks

Downside risks facing the region have diminished owing to improvements in the global financial environment and positive growth developments within East Asia and the Pacific. The possibility of a "double-dip" global recession remains, particularly as mature economies will be unwinding both monetary and fiscal stimulus. Also within the region, the Chinese stimulus program,

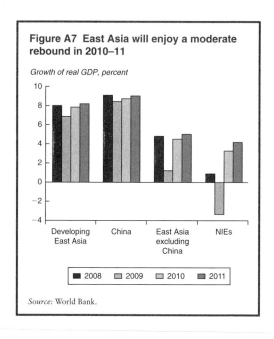

Figure A7 East Asia will enjoy a moderate rebound in 2010–11

Growth of real GDP, percent

Source: World Bank.

and in particular the surge in liquidity over the course of 2009, raises uncertainties regarding the future growth path. Prospects for low-income countries (Cambodia, Lao PDR, and Vietnam) will depend heavily on improvements in the international environment for bank lending. Recent developments in Dubai and credit rating downgrades for Greece are indicative of continued uncertainties, which, should they become widespread, may have serious implications for bank lending and growth around the globe, particularly in developing countries. Consequently, banking flows may remain sluggish for an extended period of time as commercial banks remain cautious and rebuild balance sheets. Furthermore, for middle-income countries currently benefiting from the return of large-scale inflows, driven by international investors' search for yields above those available in mature markets, there is a risk of yet another round of "asset bubbles," this time in emerging markets, the bursting of which could carry adverse effects over the short to medium term.

Table A2   East Asia and Pacific country forecasts
(annual percent change unless indicated otherwise)

	1995–2005[a]	2006	2007	2008	2009[c]	2010[d]	2011[d]
Cambodia							
GDP at market prices (2005 US$)[b]	8.3	10.8	10.2	6.7	−2.2	4.2	6.0
Current account balance/GDP (%)	−4.4	−3.6	−6.3	−10.2	−3.5	−4.0	−4.0
China							
GDP at market prices (2005 US$)[b]	9.1	11.6	13.0	9.0	8.4	9.0	9.0
Current account balance/GDP (%)	2.6	9.7	11.0	9.8	5.6	4.1	4.0
Fiji							
GDP at market prices (2005 US$)[b]	2.3	3.6	−6.6	0.2	−0.3	1.8	2.2
Current account balance/GDP (%)	−4.8	−22.5	−14.4	−19.6	−25.4	−24.8	−27.7
Indonesia							
GDP at market prices (2005 US$)[b]	2.7	5.5	6.3	6.1	4.5	5.6	5.8
Current account balance/GDP (%)	1.5	3.0	2.4	0.1	1.4	0.5	0.3
Lao PDR							
GDP at market prices (2005 US$)[b]	6.2	8.4	7.6	7.3	6.4	7.5	7.3
Current account balance/GDP (%)	−9.8	1.4	2.5	−12.5	−8.1	−6.0	−7.0
Malaysia							
GDP at market prices (2005 US$)[b]	4.8	5.8	6.2	4.6	−2.3	4.1	4.8
Current account balance/GDP (%)	6.5	16.3	15.5	17.5	15.3	15.5	15.0
Papua New Guinea							
GDP at market prices (2005 US$)[b]	0.7	2.6	6.5	6.6	3.9	3.7	3.3
Current account balance/GDP (%)	3.0	2.2	1.8	2.8	−6.7	−4.7	−4.3
Philippines							
GDP at market prices (2005 US$)[b]	4.2	5.3	7.1	3.8	1.0	3.5	3.8
Current account balance/GDP (%)	−1.4	4.5	4.9	2.5	3.4	2.8	2.3
Thailand							
GDP at market prices (2005 US$)[b]	2.7	5.3	4.9	2.6	−2.7	3.5	4.0
Current account balance/GDP (%)	1.9	1.1	5.7	−0.1	5.5	3.5	3.0
Vanuatu							
GDP at market prices (2005 US$)[b]	1.5	7.4	6.8	6.6	4.2	4.5	5.5
Current account balance/GDP (%)	−9.8	−4.1	−5.3	−5.9	−4.7	−4.4	−3.4
Vietnam							
GDP at market prices (2005 US$)[b]	7.2	8.2	8.5	6.2	5.5	6.5	7.0
Current account balance/GDP (%)	−2.5	−0.3	−9.8	−11.9	−5.1	−4.5	−4.4

Source: World Bank.

Note: World Bank forecasts are frequently updated based on new information and changing (global) circumstances. Consequently, projections presented here may differ from those contained in other Bank documents, even if basic assessments of countries' prospects do not significantly differ at any given moment in time.

American Samoa; Micronesia, Fed. Sts.; Kiribati; Marshall Islands; Myanmar; Mongolia; N. Mariana Islands; Palau; Korea, Dem. Rep.; Solomon Islands; Timor-Leste; and Tonga are not forecast owing to data limitations.

a. Growth rates over intervals are compound average; growth contributions, ratios, and the GDP deflator are averages.
b. GDP measured in constant 2005 U.S. dollars.
c. Estimate.
d. Forecast.

Europe and Central Asia

Recent developments

Among developing regions, the Europe and Central Asia region[4] has been the most negatively affected by the global financial crisis, albeit with large variations across the region in the degree of impact. Aggregate GDP is estimated to have contracted 6.2 percent in 2009, nearly twice as much as the 3.3 percent estimated decline in high-income countries, and sharply more negative than the (2.2 percent) contraction for the remaining developing countries excluding China and India (table A3).

Table A3 Europe and Central Asia forecast summary
(annual percent change unless indicated otherwise)

	1995–2005[a]	2006	2007	2008	2009[e]	2010[f]	2011[f]
GDP at market prices (2005 US$)[b]	4.1	7.6	7.1	4.2	−6.2	2.7	3.6
GDP per capita (units in US$)	4.0	7.5	7.1	4.2	−6.2	2.6	3.5
PPP GDP[c]	4.0	7.7	7.4	4.5	−6.5	2.7	3.6
Private consumption	4.8	7.5	9.2	6.4	−4.6	2.2	3.3
Public consumption	2.0	6.0	5.2	4.1	2.3	2.1	2.6
Fixed investment	4.7	16.5	14.2	8.7	−16.5	4.1	4.7
Exports, GNFS[d]	7.9	8.1	7.1	3.9	−13.2	4.3	6.6
Imports, GNFS[d]	8.7	13.9	17.9	9.0	−12.9	3.7	6.0
Net exports, contribution to growth	0.1	−1.5	−3.4	−1.9	0.3	0.1	0.0
Current account balance/GDP (%)	0.9	1.1	−0.6	−0.3	0.5	0.4	−0.2
GDP deflator (median, LCU)	18.8	9.3	7.7	9.5	3.5	6.7	4.0
Fiscal balance/GDP (%)	−5.5	3.0	2.4	0.7	−6.2	−4.5	−3.4
Memo items: GDP							
Transition countries	4.0	6.9	5.7	3.0	−4.1	2.2	3.8
Central and Eastern Europe	3.8	6.8	6.8	5.0	−2.5	1.3	3.5
Commonwealth of Independent States	4.1	8.3	8.4	5.4	−8.1	3.1	3.3
Russian Federation	3.9	7.7	8.1	5.6	−8.7	3.2	3.0
Turkey	4.3	6.9	4.7	0.9	−5.8	3.3	4.2
Poland	4.3	6.2	6.7	4.9	1.6	2.2	3.4

Source: World Bank.

a. Growth rates over intervals are compound average; growth contributions, ratios, and the GDP deflator are averages.
b. GDP measured in constant 2005 U.S. dollars.
c. GDP measured at PPP exchange rates.
d. Exports and imports of goods and nonfactor services.
e. Estimate.
f. Forecast.

The severity of the impact of the crisis in the region reflects significant preexisting vulnerabilities in many countries. Many economies were heavily reliant on foreign finance (a result of excessive credit expansion that had been enabled by foreign banks, large current account deficits, elevated external debt levels, and considerable currency mismatches in both corporate and household debt). As a result, this region was particularly vulnerable to the reversal in capital flows that accompanied the initial phases of the financial crisis.

Sharply reduced external demand for exports, a halving of foreign direct investment inflows, and falling remittances exacerbated the collapse in investor confidence and credit tightening, forcing a sharp contraction of 4.6 percent in regional private consumption, and a decline in gross fixed investment of 16.5 percent in 2009—down from expansions of 6.4 percent and 8.7 percent, respectively, in 2008. The impact of the crisis was most negative in countries where households

and corporations held large foreign currency obligations (Armenia, Bulgaria, Croatia, Latvia, Lithuania, Romania, Turkey, and Ukraine), and where pre-crisis growth relied heavily on foreign capital inflows (Bulgaria, Georgia, Latvia, Lithuania, the former Yugoslav Republic of Macedonia, Moldova, Montenegro, and Romania are among the largest, with current account deficits equivalent to 10 percent or more of GDP in 2008). At the same time, petroleum exporters (Kazakhstan, the Russian Federation) were also hit hard by the plunge in international commodity prices.

Sharp declines in international financing have forced large adjustments in domestic demand. Gross capital inflows to the region fell 54 percent during 2009, versus the 19 percent increase posted by other developing countries (figure A8). This decline in inflows primarily reflects the drying up of syndicated bank lending, which represented 60 percent of total flows to the region in 2007, before the crisis. Partly

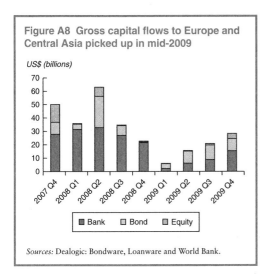

Figure A8 Gross capital flows to Europe and Central Asia picked up in mid-2009

US$ (billions)

Sources: Dealogic: Bondware, Loanware and World Bank.

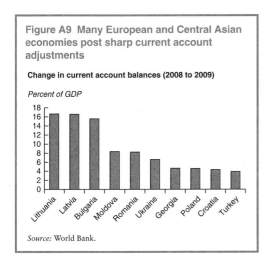

Figure A9 Many European and Central Asian economies post sharp current account adjustments

Change in current account balances (2008 to 2009)

Percent of GDP

Source: World Bank.

reflecting substantial support from international financial institutions, bond and equity flows to countries in the region began recovering in the third quarter of 2009, although bank lending remains very weak.

Reflecting the cut in capital inflows (and the associated cuts in domestic demand), regional current account deficits have narrowed, with Bulgaria, Latvia, and Lithuania posting double-digit improvements in current account positions measured as a share of GDP (figure A9). As a result of the cuts in spending,

the region's ex post financing needs declined, while at the same time external assistance and moral suasion helped prevent access to external finance from declining as sharply as had been initially expected.

Reflecting these developments, financing conditions have improved. Spreads on sovereign debt, which rose sharply in the third quarter of 2008 and into the first quarter of 2009, have since narrowed. In the case of Ukraine, for example, spreads over U.S. Treasuries jumped by as much as 3,100–3,660 basis points in March 2009 but have since reversed to a spread of 768 points, as of early January. These improved market conditions have also been supported by an easing of inflationary pressures, which has enabled monetary policies to focus on cushioning the downturn. Many governments also implemented countercyclical fiscal policies to support domestic demand. Reflecting these measures, as well as the depth of the recession and much weaker commodity prices, government deficits have increased by about 7 percent of GDP, moving from a surplus of 0.7 percent in 2008 to a 6.2 percent of GDP deficit in 2009.

Although economic activity in Europe and Central Asia remains depressed, the pace of contraction is moderating. Thus, although industrial production in the region began expanding at a 4.8 percent annualized pace in the second quarter of 2009, output in October 2009 remained 6.0 percent below its pre-crisis level in October 2008 (figure A10).

In Russia, the 2009 recession is estimated to have been much sharper than was the one following the 1998 crisis. During the 2009 recession, GDP is estimated to have fallen 8.7 percent, compared with 5.3 percent in the 1998 crisis, and represents the largest decline in growth since the breakup of the Soviet Union.[5] The contraction reflects both external factors (import demand among Russia's main trading partners decreased by an estimated 15 percent in 2009) and domestic factors (an 18 percent decline in investment and a 4.7 percent contraction in private consumption). Reflecting widespread economic slack, inflation

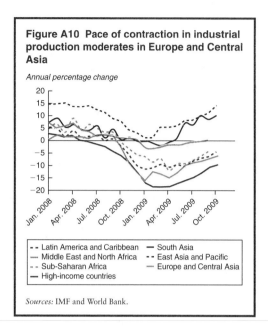

Figure A10 Pace of contraction in industrial production moderates in Europe and Central Asia

Annual percentage change

- - Latin America and Caribbean
--- Middle East and North Africa
- - Sub-Saharan Africa
— High-income countries
— South Asia
- - East Asia and Pacific
— Europe and Central Asia

Sources: IMF and World Bank.

has fallen below the 10 percent level, and the Russian central bank has repeatedly lowered its refinancing rate, so that it is nearly zero in real terms. The government has also put in place a large fiscal stimulus program, and as a result the fiscal budget is projected to move from a surplus of 4.3 percent of GDP in 2008 to a deficit equivalent to 7 percent of GDP in 2009.

Turkey's economy is projected to have contracted by 5.8 percent in 2009, nearly on par with the 5.7 percent decline posted during the 2001 economic crisis and its largest contraction on record since 1969. The economy has been hit by an investor pullback and sharp decline in demand from export markets, notably from western and eastern Europe, where economies have posted some of the sharpest slowdowns globally. The pace of contraction in growth hit the trough in the first quarter of 2009, at 14.7 percent compared with the previous year, but has eased significantly to a 3.3 percent rate of contraction in the third quarter—a relatively rapid turnaround. Unemployment has surged, contributing to the marked decline in private consumption and fixed investment. With import volumes contracting even faster than export volumes, the current account deficit improved to

1.9 percent of GDP in 2009 from an estimated 5.8 percent of GDP in 2008. To support domestic demand, the Central Bank of Turkey has more than halved its key policy interest rate, cutting it by a cumulative 1,025 basis points from 16.75 percent in October 2008 to 6.5 percent as of January 2010.

Economic conditions remained difficult over the first three quarters of 2009 for the five new members of the European Union that are developing countries, although the pace of contraction in real output moderated from 12.6 percent year-over-year in the first quarter to 4.4 in the third quarter. Partly in response to strengthening demand in high-income Europe, industrial production grew at a 6.5 percent annualized rate in the three months ending in October.

Among the five European Union accession members that are developing countries,[6] Poland has best weathered the economic storm and is one of a handful of the 24 developing countries in Europe and Central Asia not to witness a contraction in output. Poland's good performance reflects comparatively resilient service and agricultural sectors, compared with industrial output, which fell by 9 percent in the first half of 2009 over the first half of 2008. Exports were also relatively resilient, and as a result, net exports contributed positively to growth.

Outside of Poland, the other four developing European Union accession economies posted marked contractions in output during 2009, given the bursting of the credit boom and contraction in demand from Western Europe. The economies of Latvia and Lithuania were under significant stress before the onset of the acute phase of the crisis—a situation that was exacerbated by heightened international risk aversion (and concerns about the sustainability of their pegs to the euro given huge accumulated imbalances). GDP in both countries is estimated to have declined by well over 10 percent in 2009. All four countries entered the crisis with very large current account deficits. While the collapse in domestic demand has improved their external positions, substantial external debt obligations remain, further undermining the business and investment environment.

Among the Commonwealth of Independent States, Ukraine is projected to post the deepest contraction in GDP of 15 percent in 2009—indeed one of the sharpest contractions in the world. The plunge in metal prices in 2008 took a toll on the economy, where nonprecious metals represent over 40 percent of goods exports. Further, political strains in the lead-up to the January 2010 presidential elections have delayed the government from meeting the full set of IMF policy measures (such as raising household gas prices) under its $11 billion November 2008 stand-by facility. Thus, while the government has made some progress in meeting its commitments to the IMF, it appears that the release of the latest $3.7 billion tranche will be postponed until after the elections. This uncertainty—along with ongoing political instability—has undermined confidence and contributed to the depreciation and heightened volatility in the hryvnya, which depreciated by 50 percent against the U.S. dollar in 2009.

Economic growth in the five Central Asian countries has been relatively more robust than in the rest of the region.[7] However, this aggregate picture masks wide differences in economic performances at the country level. Turkmenistan and Uzbekistan—among the least open economies in the Commonwealth of Independent States and exporters of natural gas—were only modestly affected by the global crisis. In addition, these economies benefited from the implementation of fiscal stimulus measures and are estimated to have posted the strongest GDP growth outcomes in the Europe and Central Asia region, with 8 percent and 5.5 percent, respectively, in 2009. Growth in Tajikistan and Kyrgyz Republic was buoyed by an upswing in agricultural output stemming from good harvests. In contrast, GDP in Kazakhstan is estimated to have contracted, led by the negative fiscal effects from the collapse in oil prices.

Among the three Caucasus countries,[8] the global crisis has had a particularly pronounced impact on Armenia and to a lesser extent Georgia—with economic conditions in the latter also negatively affected by the conflict with Russia in 2008. In most of the other Central Asian and Caucasus countries, weaker economic conditions—notably a sharp reduction in trade demand from Russia, lower oil and commodity prices, and significant reductions in investment and remittance flows—have been partially offset by sustained economic assistance from Russia.

Overall, the number of poor or vulnerable people in the Europe and Central Asia region is estimated to have increased by some 10 million in 2009—compared with what might have been had the crisis not arisen (based on a $5-a-day poverty line). The contraction in economic activity has led to a 2.5 percentage point jump in the median unemployment rate of the 10 countries reporting data (compared with August 2008). Unemployment is expected to remain high for some time, curtailing household expenditures and contributing to higher poverty rates. Partly as a result of higher unemployment in destination countries (notably the European Union and Russia) for migrants, remittances are projected to decline by 15 percent in 2009—placing additional pressure on poor households. The macroeconomic impact from the decline in remittances will be largest in countries such as Albania, Armenia, Moldova, and Tajikistan, where remittances represent between 9 percent of GDP (Armenia) and as much as 50 percent of GDP (Tajikistan). In Tajikistan an estimated 30 percent contraction in remittances may cause an additional 5 percent of the population to move into poverty.[9]

Medium-term outlook

The recovery in economic growth in the region is expected to be slow and marked by a rise in poverty. GDP is projected to rise a modest 2.7 percent and 3.6 percent in 2010 and 2011, respectively. This growth path contrasts sharply with the average growth rate for the region of 7 percent from 2003 through 2007, and with the aggregate growth of 5.6 percent and 6.1 percent projected for other developing countries in 2010 and 2011, respectively. While resurgent demand in parts of Europe and Asia—combined with stable and/or modestly rising commodity prices—should support a turn-around in the region's exports, the projected weak recovery for developed Europe will result in relatively muted overall export growth. Similarly, foreign direct investment—which correlates strongly with trade activity—and credit inflows are expected to remain significantly lower than the levels observed before the crisis.

Given the region's overleveraged private sector, weakness in the banking sector, and household indebtedness, the recovery in domestic demand is expected to be muted. Higher tax rates, cuts in public spending, higher unemployment, and lower wages will curb private consumption, which is projected to firm to 2.2 percent in 2010 and 3.3 percent in 2011—half the unsustainable 8.4 percent pace recorded in 2006–07. Excess capacity and crowding-out from increased government borrowing will constrain investment, which is projected to grow by 4.1 percent in 2010 and by 4.7 percent in 2011—well below the double-digit growth rates recorded in the pre-crisis years.

Because of weak domestic demand and relatively tight financial conditions, the regional current account balance is forecast to remain close to zero over the forecast horizon. Across the region, however, there is greater variety (table A4). For instance, hydrocarbon exporting economies are expected to record rising surpluses or reductions in deficits resulting from somewhat higher petroleum prices and increased production (Azerbaijan, Kazakhstan, Russia, Turkmenistan, and Uzbekistan). This improvement is projected to be offset by an expansion in the current account deficits—given a more rapid recovery in domestic demand leading to import volumes that exceed exports—in Moldova, Poland, Romania, Ukraine, and Turkey. For developing European countries with important automotive industries, sales are expected to decelerate as cash-for-clunkers programs in high-income European countries unwind.

Most countries have little room for further fiscal expansion. Indeed, government spending is projected to moderate as a result of planned structural fiscal consolidation. Combined with a projected firming of growth, which should support stronger revenues, fiscal consolidation is projected to progressively reduce the regional fiscal deficit from 6.2 percent of GDP in 2009 to 4.5 percent in 2010 and to 3.4 percent in 2011. However, the adjustment in an environment characterized by large negative output gaps and low growth will be difficult, particularly as the recovery in tax revenues may initially underperform, and that recovery will be exacerbated by additional pressure in the medium term emanating from extensive social assistance and pension regimes to support the aging population.

Monetary policy is expected to remain accommodative in most regional economies over much of the forecast horizon. Inflationary pressures should remain subdued, given large excess capacity, weak domestic demand, and a relatively open economy. In countries facing continued adjustment in demand to reduce external and internal imbalances, monetary policy is expected to remain relatively restrictive to help dampen activity. Monetary policy in countries with IMF programs will be guided by the framework defined by the ongoing Stand-by Arrangements. For those economies that are moving toward adoption of the euro, or whose currencies are pegged to the euro (Bosnia and Herzegovina, Bulgaria, Latvia, and Lithuania), monetary policy will be influenced by the European Central Bank's policy stance—which is expected to remain supportive of growth over the forecast horizon, but incrementally withdraw stimulus measures (including reversal of policy interest rate cuts) as demand conditions permit. A moderate uptick in median regional headline inflation is projected for 2010, as the downward pressure from the fall in oil prices in the second half of 2008 ceases and the recent uptick in commodity prices starts to work through the system. These pressures should be partly neutralized by the strong appreciation in currencies since March 2009 (particularly the Russian ruble and the Turkish lira), which will help to reduce import costs. However, core inflation will continue to be subject to disinflationary

Table A4   Europe and Central Asia country forecasts
(annual percent change unless indicated otherwise)

	1995–2005[a]	2006	2007	2008	2009[c]	2010[d]	2011[d]
Albania							
GDP at market prices (2005 US$)[b]	5.4	5.0	6.0	6.5	2.2	3.0	4.5
Current account balance/GDP (%)	−5.5	−5.9	−8.6	−13.4	−12.8	−7.6	−6.7
Armenia							
GDP at market prices (2005 US$)[b]	8.6	13.2	13.8	6.8	−13.0	1.5	3.5
Current account balance/GDP (%)	−11.7	−1.8	−2.6	−4.9	−2.8	−0.6	3.7
Azerbaijan							
GDP at market prices (2005 US$)[b]	10.2	34.5	25.0	10.8	3.1	5.2	8.5
Current account balance/GDP (%)	−16.6	17.7	28.5	37.6	19.5	27.2	26.2
Belarus							
GDP at market prices (2005 US$)[b]	6.9	10.0	8.6	10.0	−1.0	2.0	4.0
Current account balance/GDP (%)	−3.2	−4.0	−6.8	−8.4	−9.2	−6.3	−5.1
Bulgaria							
GDP at market prices (2005 US$)[b]	2.2	6.7	6.2	6.0	−6.5	−2.0	3.6
Current account balance/GDP (%)	−3.6	−18.4	−25.2	−25.4	−9.8	−5.2	−4.9
Georgia							
GDP at market prices (2005 US$)[b]	6.6	9.4	12.3	2.2	−4.0	2.0	3.5
Current account balance/GDP (%)	−10.0	−16.2	−16.9	−22.8	−18.2	−15.8	−16.7
Kazakhstan							
GDP at market prices (2005 US$)[b]	6.4	10.7	8.2	3.0	−1.9	1.8	3.5
Current account balance/GDP (%)	−2.3	−2.5	−7.0	9.5	−1.3	2.2	1.4
Kyrgyz Republic							
GDP at market prices (2005 US$)[b]	4.7	3.1	8.5	7.6	0.6	2.4	2.8
Current account balance/GDP (%)	−10.2	−10.6	0.6	4.6	5.2	2.4	4.9
Latvia							
GDP at market prices (2005 US$)[b]	6.9	12.2	10.3	−4.6	−17.5	−3.9	2.4
Current account balance/GDP (%)	−7.5	−22.7	−21.5	−11.3	5.3	6.0	7.0
Lithuania							
GDP at market prices (2005 US$)[b]	6.0	7.8	8.9	3.0	−17.5	−3.5	2.2
Current account balance/GDP (%)	−7.9	−10.7	−14.6	−16.1	0.5	0.3	−0.5
Macedonia, FYR							
GDP at market prices (2005 US$)[b]	2.2	4.0	5.9	5.0	−1.3	1.9	3.8
Current account balance/GDP (%)	−5.9	−0.5	−4.4	−12.5	−9.4	−8.3	−7.3
Moldova							
GDP at market prices (2005 US$)[b]	2.3	4.8	3.0	7.2	−9.0	1.4	2.8
Current account balance/GDP (%)	−7.9	−11.3	−16.5	−17.4	−9.0	−10.2	−11.1
Poland							
GDP at market prices (2005 US$)[b]	4.3	6.2	6.7	4.9	1.6	2.2	3.4
Current account balance/GDP (%)	−3.3	−2.7	−4.7	−5.5	−0.9	−2.6	−2.5
Romania							
GDP at market prices (2005 US$)[b]	2.2	7.9	6.2	7.1	−7.8	0.5	4.2
Current account balance/GDP (%)	−5.8	−10.4	−13.5	−12.4	−4.2	−4.9	−5.5
Russian Federation							
GDP at market prices (2005 US$)[b]	3.9	7.7	8.1	5.6	−8.7	3.2	3.0
Current account balance/GDP (%)	7.6	9.6	5.9	6.2	3.1	2.5	1.7
Tajikistan							
GDP at market prices (2005 US$)[b]	4.6	7.0	7.8	7.9	2.0	5.0	5.0
Current account balance/GDP (%)	−4.5	−2.8	−8.6	−7.9	−10.9	−11.1	−10.2
Turkey							
GDP at market prices (2005 US$)[b]	4.3	6.9	4.7	0.9	−5.8	3.3	4.2
Current account balance/GDP (%)	−1.5	−6.0	−6.1	−5.8	−1.9	−2.5	−2.8
Ukraine							
GDP at market prices (2005 US$)[b]	2.7	7.3	7.9	2.1	−15.0	2.2	3.0
Current account balance/GDP (%)	2.7	−1.5	−3.7	−7.2	−0.6	0.1	−2.1
Uzbekistan							
GDP at market prices (2005 US$)[b]	4.6	7.3	9.5	9.0	5.5	6.5	6.5
Current account balance/GDP (%)	3.3	14.4	19.5	26.3	16.9	20.4	19.2

Source: World Bank.

Note: World Bank forecasts are frequently updated based on new information and changing (global) circumstances. Consequently, projections presented here may differ from those contained in other Bank documents, even if basic assessments of countries' prospects do not significantly differ at any given moment in time.

Bosnia and Herzegovina, Turkmenistan, and Yugoslavia, FR (Serbia/Montenegro) are not forecast owing to data limitations.

a. Growth rates over intervals are compound average; growth contributions, ratios, and the GDP deflator are averages.

b. GDP measured in constant 2005 U.S. dollars.

c. Estimate.

d. Forecast.

tendencies and headline inflation is expected to ease into 2011.

Risks

Despite the weak baseline forecasts for the region, risks remain tilted toward the downside, a result of financing constraints, the limited scope for supportive fiscal policy, large and rising banking sector vulnerabilities, and a lack of economic diversification. If the domestic recovery is slow and subdued with continued high interest rates stifling investment growth, potential output could suffer—leading to a rise in structural unemployment. A more protracted and deeper-than-projected recession could place further pressure on banking systems and on currencies in those countries with relatively inflexible exchange rate regimes. Balance-sheet consolidation by parent banks of foreign subsidiaries may manifest as further cuts in financial flows to the region in the months ahead. Rising domestic nonperforming loans and inadequate provisioning thereof pose significant risks to regional growth by restricting capital availability or, in a worst case scenario, leading to a freezing of banking systems (figure A11). This already somber scenario may be further darkened if it coincides with a global double-dip scenario, particularly if the region's major export markets (such as Germany) are severely affected.

A related and enduring risk for the region derives from the high level of household and corporate foreign-currency-denominated debt. Exposure to foreign exchange loans exceeds 50 percent of total lending in Hungary, Kazakhstan, Latvia, Lithuania, Romania, and Ukraine for both corporate and household borrowers. For households in particular, high levels of foreign exchange debt post significant risks, because unlike corporations, households are unlikely to have hedged against exchange rate movement.[10] For countries with relatively inflexible exchange rate regimes, outturns could find these regimes under assault, which in turn would limit the ability of regional central banks to conduct accommodative monetary policy.

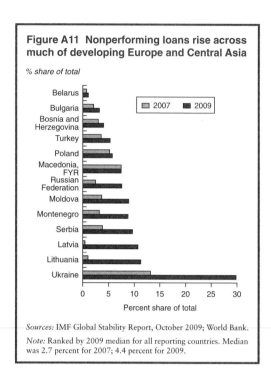

Figure A11 Nonperforming loans rise across much of developing Europe and Central Asia

% share of total

Legend: 2007, 2009

Countries (top to bottom): Belarus, Bulgaria, Bosnia and Herzegovina, Turkey, Poland, Macedonia, FYR, Russian Federation, Moldova, Montenegro, Serbia, Latvia, Lithuania, Ukraine

x-axis: 0, 5, 10, 15, 20, 25, 30

Percent share of total

Sources: IMF Global Stability Report, October 2009; World Bank.

Note: Ranked by 2009 median for all reporting countries. Median was 2.7 percent for 2007; 4.4 percent for 2009.

Reinvigorating the reform programs that have stalled with the global crisis could help deliver stronger growth outturns than projected.[11] Regional governments have space to introduce institutional reforms to improve the regulatory framework and reduce red tape, tighten legal standards and further adopt international contract and property rights norms, and clamp down on corruption to improve competition and efficiency, among other reforms. Failure to reform the pension systems poses a long-term threat to growth, given high social security financing burdens. Successful implementation of these reforms may lower precautionary savings, with positive spin-offs for private consumption and growth. Higher private consumption in the region is indeed identified as a possible upside risk and incorporated in the global "more buoyant private-sector reaction" scenario (see chapter 1).

Finally, given the degree of dislocation engendered by the crisis, black market activity is expected to rise, posing challenges for policy makers and undermining greater fiscal consolidation. In the Commonwealth of Independent States, a lack of economic diversification outside of mineral-export-led activities is a common structural weakness and remains a key vulnerability.

Latin America and the Caribbean

Recent developments

Thanks to sound macroeconomic fundamentals in place before the onset of the crisis, the Latin America and Caribbean region has been able to weather the global financial crisis much better than previous external shocks. Nevertheless, economic activity in the region decelerated sharply in the aftermath of the crisis. For the 2009 calendar year, GDP is estimated to have fallen 2.6 percent, following an expansion of 3.9 percent in 2008 (table A5). This aggregate result masks a high degree of heterogeneity among countries in the region with respect to the timing and magnitude of

the contraction in domestic output. Central American economies (including Mexico) were the worst affected, with output contracting a sharp 6.4 percent, while growth in the Caribbean economies stagnated.

In the immediate aftermath of the crisis, the region was hit by a sharp slowdown in private capital inflows, while increased uncertainty and credit tightening led to a marked contraction in private consumption and private investment. The capital outflows induced a sharp depreciation of currencies in the region, a decline in equity markets, and much higher borrowing costs. Nevertheless, the region managed to avoid falling into a balance of payments and/or financial crisis.

Private consumption contracted by nearly 2 percent, while fixed investment declined sharply by 13.6 percent, after growing at double-digit rates in the previous years. The region was also affected by the collapse in external demand for commodity exports, falling

Table A5   Latin America and the Caribbean forecast summary
(annual percent change unless indicated otherwise)

	1995–2005[a]	2006	2007	2008	2009[e]	2010[f]	2011[f]
GDP at market prices (2005 US$)[b]	2.9	5.4	5.5	3.9	−2.6	3.1	3.6
GDP per capita (units in US$)	1.4	4.0	4.1	2.6	−3.8	1.8	2.3
PPP GDP[c]	2.9	5.5	5.7	4.2	−2.3	3.0	3.5
Private consumption	3.4	6.1	3.5	4.2	−1.9	3.2	3.4
Public consumption	2.2	2.8	2.9	4.1	2.9	2.8	2.6
Fixed investment	3.3	13.4	20.7	11.7	−13.6	6.1	5.8
Exports, GNFS[d]	6.0	6.7	4.9	1.6	−11.2	7.8	5.0
Imports, GNFS[d]	6.2	14.0	11.9	9.2	−15.8	10.3	5.6
Net exports, contribution to growth	0.2	−1.5	−1.7	−2.0	1.6	−0.7	−0.3
Current account balance/GDP (%)	−1.6	1.4	0.4	−0.6	−0.9	−1.0	−1.0
GDP deflator (median, LCU)	7.1	7.2	5.4	8.4	7.2	3.0	4.0
Fiscal balance/GDP (%)	−3.5	−1.1	−1.1	−0.9	−3.3	−2.8	−2.5
Memo items: GDP							
Latin America excluding Argentina	3.0	5.2	5.2	3.7	−2.6	3.2	3.7
Central America	3.6	5.0	3.7	1.7	−6.4	3.3	3.6
Caribbean	4.2	9.0	6.1	3.6	−0.1	2.3	3.3
Brazil	2.4	4.0	5.7	5.1	0.1	3.6	3.9
Mexico	3.6	4.8	3.3	1.4	−7.1	3.5	3.6
Argentina	2.3	8.5	8.7	6.8	−2.2	2.3	2.4

Source: World Bank.

a. Growth rates over intervals are compound average; growth contributions, ratios, and the GDP deflator are averages.
b. GDP measured in constant 2005 U.S. dollars.
c. GDP measured at PPP exchange rates.
d. Exports and imports of goods and nonfactor services.
e. Estimate.
f. Forecast.

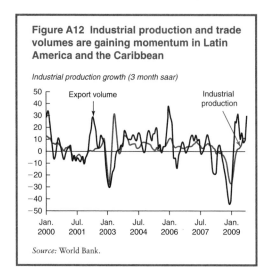

Figure A12 Industrial production and trade volumes are gaining momentum in Latin America and the Caribbean

Industrial production growth (3 month saar)

Source: World Bank.

Exports collapsed in the first half of the year, dragging output down 7 percentage points, while the collapse in import volumes boosted growth by close to 9 percentage points. In 2009 private consumption is estimated to have contracted by 6.9 percent, as the labor market was severely affected by the economic slowdown, with formal unemployment almost doubling to 6.4 percent by September, and as remittances fell 13.4 percent in the first nine months of the year.

In Argentina, the global recession in conjunction with policy-related uncertainty took a toll on investment and trade. Collapsing imports and declining fiscal revenues point to weak domestic demand and relatively poor output performance in the first half of 2009, while a severe drought added to the economy's weak performance.

In República Bolivariana de Venezuela, GDP is estimated to have declined 2.4 percent as a result of the collapse in external demand, weak private consumption, and lower investment spending. Manufacturing and retail sales plunged owing to weak domestic demand, and output fell at a 4.5 percent annualized pace in the third quarter of 2009. The oil sector is becoming increasingly dominant in the economy. Supply bottlenecks, a difficult business environment, and a lack of private investor confidence are undermining new investment, impairing much-needed economic diversification.

Strong retrenchment in private investment spending and a steep drawdown in stocks (close to 1 percent of GDP) caused Chile's output to decline 4.7 percent year-on-year in the second quarter of 2009. Marked weakness in domestic demand resulted in a sharp contraction in imports that exceeded the plunge in exports.

Peru's economic growth decelerated from a double-digit pace in the first half of 2008 to a standstill in the first half of 2009, with the sharp contraction in investment spending leading to a 5.4 percent contraction in domestic demand. Weak external demand resulted

commodity prices, lower remittance inflows, and declining tourism activity. The decline in domestic demand translated into a sharp 15.8 percent contraction in import volumes. As a result, and despite an 11.2 percent contraction in export volumes, net trade contributed 1.6 percent to growth. Reflecting these developments industrial activity fell rapidly, plunging at a 20 percent saar rate in the last quarter of 2008 and at 16 percent in the first quarter of 2009 (figure A12).

Countries that rely heavily on trade with the United States were especially hard hit by the crisis. Mexico's economy suffered the steepest contraction in the region (7.1 percent) and its worst economic performance in seven and a half decades, both because of its close economic ties with the United States in the sectors most affected by the crisis (construction, automotive, and electrical appliances) and because of the AH1N1 flu outbreak in the second quarter of 2009. The flu outbreak hit the tourism sector especially hard and is estimated to have reduced overall GDP by 0.5 percent. Furthermore Mexican firms suffered foreign derivatives losses in December 2008 after the global crisis drove the peso to record lows.

in a 6.3 percent decline in exports, although imports contracted more sharply on account of weak domestic demand.

Countries in Central America and the Caribbean were afflicted by the recession in the United States and major economic partners in the European Union, particularly Spain, which has resulted in a contraction in trade, tourism, FDI, and remittances. The Caribbean economies contracted only 0.1 percent in 2009, down from the 3.6 percent growth recorded in 2008. Jamaica recorded one of the sharpest declines in GDP in the subregion, attributable to its heavy dependence on the U.S. economy (remittances declined 17 percent in the first half of 2009), and to sharp cuts in mining production. In the Dominican Republic, economic performance deteriorated sharply, with output down by 0.1 percent after 5 percent growth in 2008, reflecting developments in the U.S. economy that affected remittances, FDI, and tourism. The improvement in the terms of trade, as the oil price declined, has had a positive impact on economic performance, however. Caribbean economies benefited somewhat from the AH1N1 outbreak in Mexico as visitors shifted holiday destinations from Mexico to the Caribbean islands, and consequently in the early stages of the crisis, tourism and offshore financial services proved somewhat resilient.

The Central American economies, excluding Mexico, contracted by 1.0 percent in 2009. External demand for their exports was hit by the global economic crisis, while remittances and tourism revenues also declined. Costa Rica's economy was afflicted by a 10.3 percent decline in U.S. tourist arrivals in the first nine months of 2009, but investment in the services sector continued and back-office services were resilient. The decline in tourist arrivals has prompted large price cuts for tourism packages as countries competed for a declining number of tourists. Remittances have also suffered because of weak labor markets in high-income countries. Compared with a year earlier, remittances to Guatemala and El Salvador were down by 9.5 and 10.3 percent,

respectively, during the first half of 2009. In the first quarter of 2009, FDI inflows to Costa Rica fell by 19 percent (year-on-year), and by 41 percent to the Dominican Republic.

In response to the crisis, many governments in the region implemented countercyclical macro-economic policies in an effort to support domestic demand, with government spending being the only demand component that registered growth during 2009. The aggressiveness of the fiscal policies implemented depended on the fiscal space available in each country and the extent to which they had access to financial markets. That said, the region entered the crisis much better prepared with respect to both the fiscal and external accounts. In Mexico, the declining oil revenues constrained the countercyclical response. In Chile, fiscal stimulus has helped limit the output contraction, and the government also provided credit support to SMEs through the development bank Banco Estado. The implementation of the fiscal stimulus in Peru was to some extent hindered as budget appropriation and distribution rules limited the increase in government spending, even as procurement rules have become more lax. Furthermore the government provided credit support to SMEs through the development bank Banco de la Nacion to help ease the impact of the credit crunch.

To support domestic demand at the time that external demand was collapsing, countries more integrated in the global economy lowered interest rates aggressively and allowed real exchange rates to depreciate (figure A13, figure A14). During the monetary-easing cycle, the central bank of Colombia cut rates by a cumulative 6.5 percentage points. Chile cut rates by 7.75 percentage points since the beginning of 2009, while Peru also eased monetary policy substantially. Brazil cut the SELIC[12] rate by an unprecedented 500 basis points to 8.75 percent.

As elsewhere, many economies in the region showed signs that the recession bottomed out in the second half of 2009, with external demand rebounding faster and more strongly than initially anticipated (figure A15).

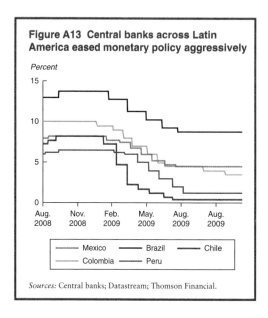

Figure A13 Central banks across Latin America eased monetary policy aggressively

Percent

Sources: Central banks; Datastream; Thomson Financial.

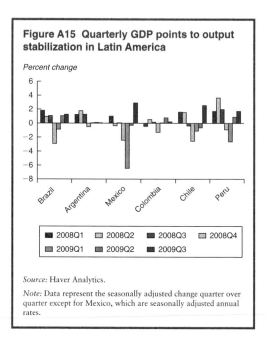

Figure A15 Quarterly GDP points to output stabilization in Latin America

Percent change

Source: Haver Analytics.

Note: Data represent the seasonally adjusted change quarter over quarter except for Mexico, which are seasonally adjusted annual rates.

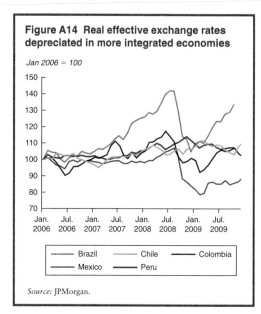

Figure A14 Real effective exchange rates depreciated in more integrated economies

Jan 2006 = 100

Source: JPMorgan.

In Brazil, a swift rebound in domestic demand was boosted by expansionary monetary policy and countercyclical fiscal policy. These steps pulled the economy out of recession in the second quarter of 2009. Brazil's economy is also benefiting from the shift in the inventory cycle. This in conjunction with the stimulus for the automotive sector has set the stage for a sharp recovery in industrial production, which increased by an annualized 17.6 percent in the second quarter and by 20.5 percent in the third quarter. However, because of base effects and a rather moderate recovery in external demand, as Chinese restocking tailed off, output is estimated to have remained relatively flat in 2009, implying the worst economic performance since the early 1990s.

In Mexico, the rate of contraction moderated in the second and third quarters, supported by less dramatic output declines in the manufacturing and service industries. In Argentina, an improved external environment has ignited a modest recovery and led to improvements in external balances, as commodity prices firmed and demand for exports increased, in particular from its main trading partner Brazil. In Chile significant fiscal and monetary stimulus contributed to the moderation in output contraction to 1.7 percent year-on-year in the third quarter, bringing the decline in GDP over the first three quarters of the year to 2.7 percent. In Colombia the improved external environment and the lagged effect of aggressive monetary easing helped the economy recover in early 2009. Output growth in the first two quarters of 2009 was also boosted by strong growth in public investment spending, even though private consumption and investment remained weak. In Peru a significant rebuilding of inadequate stocks is projected to contribute to growth in the second half of 2009. Uruguay's economy expanded by 0.5 percent in the second quarter of 2009 relative to the previous quarter, bolstered by growth in construction and transportation, reflecting the impact of several megaprojects, which offset output declines elsewhere, particularly in energy, agriculture, and manufacturing.

Corporate and sovereign spreads have retreated to pre-crisis levels in countries more integrated into the global financial system—demonstrative of a return of investors' confidence, while access to the international debt market has also improved. Lower-rated countries in the region continue to be perceived as risky by investors and this is reflected in spreads remaining above pre-crisis levels.

Overall, capital inflows to the region have returned, especially in economies that proved resilient to the crisis, such as Brazil, with total capital inflows rising to $57.4 billion in the fourth quarter of 2009, up from $15.7 billion in the second quarter. Bond issuance increased almost sixfold, nearing $30 billion, while equity inflows more than tripled to $14.8 billion. Bank lending recovered modestly, totaling $13.2 billion, down 33 percent compared with the second quarter of 2008 (figure A16).

Medium-term outlook

Fiscal stimulus, lagged impacts of accommodative monetary policy, the shift in the inventory cycle, improvements in the terms of trade, rising consumer and business confidence, stronger demand from high-income countries, and an easing of external financing conditions are all expected to support growth in the region over the next few quarters. GDP growth in the region is projected to accelerate to 3.1 percent in 2010, following an estimated 2.6 percent contraction in 2009, but growth will not regain the growth rates recorded during the boom years, in part because of

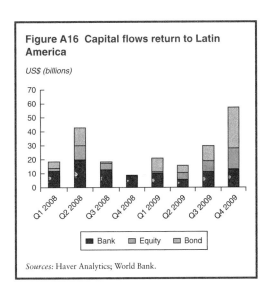

Figure A16 Capital flows return to Latin America

US$ (billions)

Sources: Haver Analytics; World Bank.

weaker investment growth. The shape of the recovery will, to a large extent, be determined by the growth path of the United States and other major economic partners of the region. Growth is expected to remain strong for the next couple of quarters but to weaken in the second half of 2010, as the impact of stimulus measures and the rebuilding of depleted inventories cease to bolster growth. A double dip or a more buoyant growth scenario is also possible as a result of close linkages with high-income countries.

Economies more integrated through trade and financial linkages with the global economy, which have been the worst affected by the global downturn are expected to benefit most from the global economic recovery. The region's exports are projected to rebound strongly, expanding by 7.8 percent in 2010 as demand from major trading partners recovers. Higher commodity prices will also benefit commodity exporters in the region, easing pressures on external balances and in some cases fiscal balances. A weakening of growth momentum or even a double dip in high-income countries (see chapter 1) could lead to a deceleration in export growth in the second half of 2010 and into 2011.

Private consumption in the region is projected to bounce back strongly, rising 3.2 percent in 2010, partly because of a low base effect (it contracted by an estimated 1.9 percent in 2009) but also owing to improvements in labor markets throughout the region and in migrant-destination countries. Domestic demand growth may be supported by a pronounced bounce back in fixed investment as confidence returns and financing constraints ease (see chapter 1 regarding a more buoyant private sector reaction scenario). Less restrictive financing conditions compared with the crisis period and a return of investor confidence together with resumptions in delayed investment, are projected to boost fixed investment by 6.1 percent in 2010. However, investment growth will remain below the double-digit pace recorded in the boom years, as excess capacity lingers. Large output gaps, weak international financing conditions, and weak public sector investment will all weigh on prospects. The lagged impact of the substantial monetary easing in some countries, along with stronger fiscal stimulus, and a one-off benefit from inventories accumulation will bolster growth into 2010. In other countries, such as Chile, there will be fiscal consolidation in 2010, which will moderate the contribution of government spending to growth.

The tourism sectors in many countries in the region are expected to stage a recovery after a sharp decline in tourist arrivals in 2009, although a recovery in Mexico's tourism sector may weaken the recovery in some of the Caribbean countries that had seen a lower-than-expected decline in tourist arrivals in 2009, as they managed to attract tourists by offering discounted packages.

Remittances are expected to recover only modestly in the 2010–11 period, undermined by weak labor market conditions in the United States and other high-income countries, although the bottoming out of the housing sector in the United States bodes well for countries receiving remittances from the construction sector. The weak recovery in remittances will limit the strength of the recovery in

private consumption in many countries in the Caribbean and Central America.

The recovery in the United States will help Mexico exit the deep recession it entered following the collapse in U.S. demand. Mexico's economy is forecast to expand by 3.5 percent in 2010 and growth will accelerate marginally to 3.6 percent in 2011 (table A6). Government spending is not expected to grow as it implements fiscal adjustments to compensate for lower oil revenues associated with declining oil production. Both exports and imports are projected to rebound strongly in 2010, as external and domestic demand strengthen, but net trade will be a drag to growth, as the acceleration in imports due to stronger domestic demand will outpace export growth. A strong rebound in the service sector is projected, after a subdued performance in 2009 on account of the negative impact of the AH1N1 flu. Mexico's growth outlook is clouded, however, by concerns about the long-term sustainability of fiscal accounts. The fiscal shortfall over the 2009–10 period is estimated at a cumulative 6.6 percent of GDP, with almost half of the deterioration related to lower oil prices and production. The expected fiscal reform should reduce government discretionary spending, which may have a negative impact on growth over the short(er) term.

Domestic demand in Brazil should benefit from strong fiscal and monetary stimuli, while exports are projected to rise in response to strong external demand from China. Overall, the economy is projected to stage a comeback in 2010, with growth accelerating to 3.6 percent. Economic growth will be largely driven by the recovery in private consumption and investment, as well as stronger external demand.

Recovery in external demand will help Argentina's economic recovery strengthen into 2010 as job creation in export-oriented industries will underpin a mild recovery in private consumption. The expected recovery in the agriculture sector will boost economic activity, as will less restrictive external financing conditions. The recovery will be fragile, however, with investment remaining a drag on growth

Table A6　Latin America and the Caribbean country forecasts
(annual percent change unless indicated otherwise)

	1995–2005[a]	2006	2007	2008	2009[c]	2010[d]	2011[d]
Argentina							
GDP at market prices (2005 US$)[b]	2.3	8.5	8.7	6.8	−2.2	2.3	2.4
Current account balance/GDP (%)	−0.2	3.6	2.8	2.2	2.3	2.2	2.2
Belize							
GDP at market prices (2005 US$)[b]	5.6	4.7	1.2	3.8	−0.1	1.7	2.3
Current account balance/GDP (%)	−12.1	−2.1	−4.0	−10.8	−7.7	−7.7	−7.6
Bolivia							
GDP at market prices (2005 US$)[b]	3.8	4.6	4.6	6.1	2.6	3.2	3.8
Current account balance/GDP (%)	−3.0	11.5	12.5	12.0	2.6	1.8	2.9
Brazil							
GDP at market prices (2005 US$)[b]	2.4	4.0	5.7	5.1	0.1	3.6	3.9
Current account balance/GDP (%)	−2.0	1.3	0.1	−1.7	−1.1	−1.6	−1.8
Chile							
GDP at market prices (2005 US$)[b]	4.2	4.6	4.7	3.2	−1.8	4.7	4.5
Current account balance/GDP (%)	−1.5	4.9	4.4	−2.0	1.5	1.1	1.4
Colombia							
GDP at market prices (2005 US$)[b]	2.4	6.9	7.5	2.5	−0.1	2.6	3.9
Current account balance/GDP (%)	−2.2	−1.8	−2.9	−2.7	−2.9	−2.6	−2.3
Costa Rica							
GDP at market prices (2005 US$)[b]	4.5	8.8	7.8	2.6	−1.8	2.1	2.9
Current account balance/GDP (%)	−4.0	−4.5	−6.3	−9.2	−4.2	−5.1	−6.3
Dominica							
GDP at market prices (2005 US$)[b]	1.4	3.2	0.9	3.1	−1.7	1.4	3.0
Current account balance/GDP (%)	−19.8	−17.3	−28.5	−36.5	−24.2	−24.1	−23.8
Dominican Republic							
GDP at market prices (2005 US$)[b]	5.2	10.7	8.5	5.0	−0.1	2.4	2.6
Current account balance/GDP (%)	−0.8	−3.6	−5.1	−10.1	−6.8	−7.2	−6.7
Ecuador							
GDP at market prices (2005 US$)[b]	3.2	3.9	2.5	6.5	−2.2	1.7	3.0
Current account balance/GDP (%)	−1.4	3.9	3.6	2.2	−3.0	−3.3	−3.4
El Salvador							
GDP at market prices (2005 US$)[b]	2.7	4.2	4.7	2.5	−2.1	0.8	2.3
Current account balance/GDP (%)	−2.5	−3.6	−5.4	−7.2	−2.6	−3.5	−4.7
Guatemala							
GDP at market prices (2005 US$)[b]	3.5	5.4	6.3	3.8	−0.4	1.6	3.0
Current account balance/GDP (%)	−4.9	−5.2	−5.4	−4.8	−2.8	−4.1	−4.4
Guyana							
GDP at market prices (2005 US$)[b]	1.7	−2.4	5.4	3.2	1.1	2.5	3.0
Current account balance/GDP (%)	−9.4	−19.8	−17.8	−20.2	−12.6	−18.1	−18.2
Haiti							
GDP at market prices (2005 US$)[b]	0.9	2.3	3.2	1.4	−0.3	1.9	2.1
Current account balance/GDP (%)	−4.0	−9.0	−5.7	−8.2	−7.9	−9.1	−10.6
Honduras							
GDP at market prices (2005 US$)[b]	3.8	6.3	6.3	4.0	−2.5	1.8	2.8
Current account balance/GDP (%)	−6.7	−4.7	−9.8	−14.3	−8.7	−10.9	−9.3
Jamaica							
GDP at market prices (2005 US$)[b]	0.8	2.7	1.5	−1.0	−3.7	0.3	2.2
Current account balance/GDP (%)	−5.5	−9.9	−15.3	−19.8	−14.3	−12.6	−9.9
Mexico							
GDP at market prices (2005 US$)[b]	3.6	4.8	3.3	1.4	−7.1	3.5	3.6
Current account balance/GDP (%)	−1.9	−0.5	−0.8	−1.5	−1.4	−1.7	−1.9

(continued)

137

Table A6 (*continued*)
(annual percent change unless indicated otherwise)

	1995–2005[a]	2006	2007	2008	2009[c]	2010[d]	2011[d]
Nicaragua							
GDP at market prices (2005 US$)[b]	4.1	3.7	3.2	3.2	−2.5	1.7	1.7
Current account balance/GDP (%)	−20.2	−13.4	−17.6	−23.8	−15.2	−19.8	−21.7
Panama							
GDP at market prices (2005 US$)[b]	4.5	8.5	11.5	9.2	1.2	2.7	3.8
Current account balance/GDP (%)	−5.3	−3.1	−7.3	−12.3	−7.4	−10.1	−10.0
Paraguay							
GDP at market prices (2005 US$)[b]	1.2	4.3	6.8	5.8	−3.8	2.6	3.7
Current account balance/GDP (%)	−1.5	1.4	0.8	−2.1	−0.3	−1.5	−1.9
Peru							
GDP at market prices (2005 US$)[b]	3.3	7.7	9.0	9.8	1.2	3.9	5.2
Current account balance/GDP (%)	−3.3	3.0	1.6	−3.4	−2.4	−2.5	−2.3
St. Lucia							
GDP at market prices (2005 US$)[b]	2.9	2.2	1.7	0.7	−1.4	1.5	2.7
Current account balance/GDP (%)	−13.8	−33.1	−32.6	−33.6	−26.5	−27.9	−29.0
St. Vincent and the Grenadines							
GDP at market prices (2005 US$)[b]	4.2	10.8	6.7	2.3	−1.0	1.2	1.8
Current account balance/GDP (%)	−18.3	−24.1	−26.3	−27.8	−20.1	−21.4	−21.8
Uruguay							
GDP at market prices (2005 US$)[b]	1.5	4.6	7.6	8.9	1.3	3.2	3.4
Current account balance/GDP (%)	−0.9	−2.0	−0.9	−3.8	−1.4	−2.4	−2.5
Venezuela, R. B. de							
GDP at market prices (2005 US$)[b]	1.6	10.3	8.4	4.8	−2.4	−0.2	1.4
Current account balance/GDP (%)	7.5	14.3	8.7	12.4	2.2	3.5	2.5

Source: World Bank.

Note: World Bank forecasts are frequently updated based on new information and changing (global) circumstances. Consequently, projections presented here may differ from those contained in other Bank documents, even if basic assessments of countries' prospects do not significantly differ at any given moment in time.

Barbados, Cuba, Grenada, and Suriname are not forecast owing to data limitations.

a. Growth rates over intervals are compound average; growth contributions, ratios, and the GDP deflator are averages.
b. GDP measured in constant 2000 U.S. dollars.
c. Estimate.
d. Forecast.

owing to policy uncertainty. Furthermore, the unsustainable fiscal stimulus implemented ahead of the presidential elections will likely fade in the second half of the year, weakening one of the growth engines.

República Bolivariana de Venezuela is expected to buck the regional trend of economic recovery and is likely to continue to contract for a second consecutive year in 2010, as private consumption, investment, and exports continue to shrink. Macroeconomic imbalances—the result of inadequate macroeconomic policies and high inflation (notwithstanding economic contraction)—will undermine investment. Also, the strong growth of government spending,

funded by an increasing public debt issuance as well as price and exchange controls, is undermining growth. Inflationary pressures are likely to continue to be fueled by currency mismanagement as well as rising import costs, partly stemming from the government's decision to import through Argentina instead of Colombia. Furthermore, inadequate investments will exacerbate domestic shortages, thereby exerting further upward pressure on prices.

Small open economies like Chile are likely to benefit most from the global economic recovery as their business cycles are highly correlated with the global economy. Chile's recovery will also be supported by domestic factors because aggressive and front-loaded countercyclical policies are boosting domestic demand. Improved terms of trade as well as rising consumer and business confidence should also bolster the recovery, bringing growth closer to potential.

Peru's recovery will benefit from stronger demand for commodity exports, particularly from Asia. Furthermore, the Free Trade Agreement with China, which comes into operation in January 2010, will further boost exports, in particular those of fishmeal and minerals. Government consumption and investment should be firm in 2010 as the government maintains efforts to support economic growth through new spending on public works and social programs, and it should remain a high priority ahead of the April 2011 presidential and congressional elections.

Growth in Central America is expected to bounce back in 2010 in line with developments in the United States and other major economic partners. Recovery in the region is highly dependent on workers' remittances from the United States and Europe (El Salvador, Guatemala, Honduras, and Nicaragua), and is projected to be more gradual, as the expected jobless recovery in high-income countries will put pressure on remittances, thereby delaying the recovery in private consumption in these countries. Similarly, tourism in the region (of particular importance for the Caribbean) is expected to recover only moderately as labor markets in client countries recover only gradually. FDI, which was a major source of growth over the 2003–08 period, is unlikely to return to pre-crisis levels while excess capacity lingers. The recovery in most countries in Central America will thus be anemic at best. In Jamaica, low alumina and bauxite production and export prices will constrain the recovery. Growth in these regions will continue to be undermined further by crime, corruption, weak democratic institutions, and a lack of competitiveness.

Risks

In countries where domestic demand is strengthening rapidly, delays in withdrawing policy stimulus represent an upside risk to growth and inflation. In such cases, output gaps could close

faster than anticipated, leading to an inflationary environment. In particular, the risks for Brazil have shifted to the upside as domestic demand is rebounding strongly, while the effects of already enacted monetary loosening and countercyclical fiscal policy easing have not yet run their course. Another upside risk emanates from commodity prices, should the world economy (particularly in resource-intensive economies such as China) stage a stronger-than-expected rebound.

The recent run-up in equity markets and stronger capital inflows in general, stemming in part from still large interest rate differentials, have put upward pressure on real effective exchange rates in some countries. The surge in capital inflows to the region, which reached $87.2 billion in the second half of 2009 (of which $34.3 billion came in December), compared with $36.8 billion in the first half of the year, has prompted the Brazilian government to impose a 2 percent financial transaction tax on foreign portfolio inflows. However, this measure has been ineffective in preventing capital inflows and real currency appreciation. Should such flows persist, this may lead to renewed asset price bubbles. Also, some economies may lose external competitiveness because of real currency appreciation at a time when external demand recovery remains fragile.

Middle East and North Africa

Recent developments

The impact of the global financial crisis for the developing economies of the Middle East and North Africa region varied across oil exporters and importers of the region.[13] Initially, the decline in regional equity markets was sharper than the average for emerging markets (figure A17). Since then, recovery in these markets has been hesitant owing to the unfolding of the Dubai World debt problems in the United Arab Emirates as well as concerns regarding growth prospects for the broader region.

Conditions at the outset of the financial crisis were less than propitious for the Middle East and North Africa. The "food-fuel" crisis

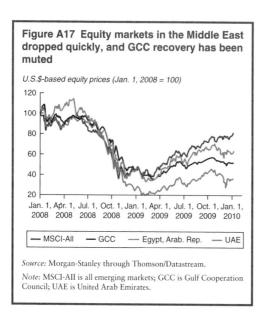

Figure A17 Equity markets in the Middle East dropped quickly, and GCC recovery has been muted

U.S.$-based equity prices (Jan. 1, 2008 = 100)

Source: Morgan-Stanley through Thomson/Datastream.

Note: MSCI-All is all emerging markets; GCC is Gulf Cooperation Council; UAE is United Arab Emirates.

of 2007–08 was a challenge for the region, the largest net exporter of oil and the largest net importer of food. Oil exporters were less adversely affected, but food import bills rose sharply. Hardest hit were countries in the Maghreb, as well as Jordan and Lebanon, which are large importers of both food and fuel; and the Arab Republic of Egypt (high food-import dependence). The policy environment had to shift quickly from mitigating the effects of higher commodity prices to shoring up banking systems and applying fiscal stimulus to bolster domestic demand.

Over the course of 2009, net terms-of-trade movements for the developing oil exporters (Algeria, Islamic Republic of Iran, Syrian Arab Republic, and Republic of Yemen) and the Gulf Cooperation Council (GCC) were favorable, as oil prices increased and food prices declined. But high oil prices have been maintained at the expense of much reduced output. Because of falling oil production, key GCC oil exporters suffered modest GDP declines during the year, only partially offset by fiscal stimulus programs and more buoyant non-oil sectors. Developing oil exporters in contrast saw a marked downturn in oil sectors of their

economies, but stimulus measures and stronger non-oil developments helped to maintain positive overall growth. For the more diversified economies (Egypt, Jordan, Lebanon, Morocco, and Tunisia) steep declines in external demand (notably from the dominant Euro Area) had a negative effect on merchandise exports, compounded by falling tourism volumes, lower worker remittances, and declining FDI inflows, notably those from the GCC economies. The decline in FDI was at first linked to falling oil revenues among the GCC and softer conditions in host markets. This came to be further clouded by the question of sovereign debt sustainability on the part of Dubai, owing to past overinvestment in real estate and tourism ventures within the United Arab Emirates.

Against this background, GDP growth in 2009 for the *developing countries* of the region is estimated to have eased to 2.9 percent, from 4.3 percent in 2008. For developing oil exporters, growth almost halved, to 1.6 percent from 2.9 percent in 2008. GDP gains for the oil importers (diversified economies) faltered by almost 2 percentage points in the year, from a strong 6.6 percent outturn in 2008 (powered by growth of more than 7 percent in Egypt) to 4.7 percent in 2009. And for the *high-income* GCC economies covered in this report, GDP is estimated to have contracted by 0.6 percent in 2009 following a firm 4.6 percent growth in the preceding year, as the sharp slide in oil production and revenues dampened output (table A7).

Developments among regional oil exporters. The global economic crisis ended the oil boom that saw oil prices peak at more than $150 a barrel on an intra-day basis in mid-2008 (figure A18), and prices have settled into a range of $65–$80 a barrel, supported by OPEC (Organization of Petroleum-Exporting Countries) production cuts. As part of this effort, regional oil exporters scaled back production by nearly 10 percent (11 percent among high-income producers and 7.3 percent among the developing exporters of the region). The combination of much lower prices and reduced output caused oil and gas

Table A7 Middle East and North Africa forecast summary
(annual percent change unless indicated otherwise)

	1995–2005[a]	2006	2007	2008	2009[g]	2010[h]	2011[h]
GDP at market prices (2005 US$)[b]	4.4	5.2	5.9	4.3	2.9	3.7	4.4
GDP per capita (units in US$)	2.7	3.5	4.1	2.6	1.2	2.0	2.8
PPP GDP[c]	4.5	5.4	6.2	4.3	2.7	3.6	4.4
Private consumption	4.2	4.8	6.3	1.2	4.6	4.5	5.1
Public consumption	3.3	5.7	2.2	11.3	10.6	7.5	6.4
Fixed investment	6.5	5.9	18.7	19.4	8.0	4.0	4.6
Exports, GNFS[d]	4.9	5.9	6.5	0.2	−8.8	2.3	5.2
Imports, GNFS[d]	5.7	7.0	12.4	9.0	1.1	5.2	6.7
Net exports, contribution to growth	−0.2	−0.1	−1.6	−3.0	−3.5	−1.1	−0.8
Current account balance/GDP (%)	2.9	11.6	10.1	10.5	−0.1	1.5	1.0
GDP deflator (median, LCU)	5.2	8.3	6.1	16.0	6.7	6.2	3.9
Fiscal balance/GDP (%)	−2.2	−0.9	0.4	1.9	−6.1	−4.1	−3.7
Memo items: GDP							
Middle East and North Africa geographic region[e]	4.0	4.6	4.9	4.4	1.4	3.5	4.3
Selected GCC Countries[f]	3.6	3.8	3.6	4.6	−0.6	3.2	4.1
Egypt, Arab Rep.	4.4	6.8	7.1	7.2	4.7	5.2	6.0
Iran, Islamic Rep. of	4.8	5.9	7.8	2.5	1.0	2.2	3.2
Algeria	4.0	2.0	3.0	3.0	2.1	3.9	4.0

Source: World Bank.

a. Growth rates over intervals are compound average; growth contributions, ratios, and the GDP deflator are averages.

b. GDP measured in constant 2005 U.S. dollars.

c. GDP measured at PPP exchange rates.

d. Exports and imports of goods and non-factor services.

e. Geographic region includes high-income countries: Bahrain, Kuwait, Oman, and Saudi Arabia.

f. Selected GCC countries: Bahrain, Kuwait, Oman and Saudi Arabia.

g. Estimate.

h. Forecast.

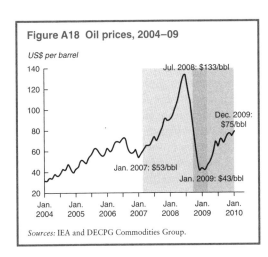

Figure A18 Oil prices, 2004–09

US$ per barrel

Jul. 2008: $133/bbl

Dec. 2009: $75/bbl

Jan. 2007: $53/bbl

Jan. 2009: $43/bbl

Sources: IEA and DECPG Commodities Group.

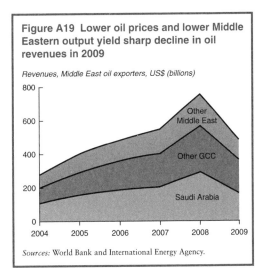

Figure A19 Lower oil prices and lower Middle Eastern output yield sharp decline in oil revenues in 2009

Revenues, Middle East oil exporters, US$ (billions)

Other Middle East

Other GCC

Saudi Arabia

Sources: World Bank and International Energy Agency.

revenues for all exporters to drop from $755 billion in 2008 to $485 billion in 2009—a decline equivalent to 30 percent of the group's GDP (figure A19). For the developing exporters, the decline in revenues was less severe, but nonetheless a substantial 12.5 percent of GDP. Current account surplus positions fell sharply across the region for all oil exporters, from

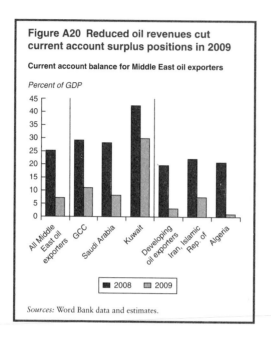

Figure A20 Reduced oil revenues cut current account surplus positions in 2009

Current account balance for Middle East oil exporters

Percent of GDP

Sources: Word Bank data and estimates.

revenues plummeted 40 percent. This placed substantial pressures on budget revenues, which normally support domestic demand. Inflation continues at rates near 20 percent, and the current account surplus fell from 22 percent of GDP in 2008 to 7.5 percent in 2009.

Iraq is facing a major short-term financing gap in the year ahead owing to the global slowdown, with a fiscal deficit of 26 percent of GDP accrued in 2009 and a current account that moved from substantial surplus in 2008 (13.3 percent of GDP) to major deficit in 2009 (31 percent).

The diversified economies. The Euro Area is the destination for more than 70 percent of export goods from the diversified economies of the Middle East and North Africa region. Moreover, the Euro Area is also the host for overseas workers from the Maghreb and Mashreq and an important source of remittance flows and tourism arrivals to the developing region. As investment and trade plummeted in key Euro Area economies, GDP for the zone declined to 0.5 percent growth in 2008, and it is anticipated to contract by a sharp 3.9 percent in 2009, the deepest recession since WWII.

The effects of the European downturn on exports from the region have been dramatic, with Egypt's merchandise exports declining from growth of 33 percent in 2008 to minus 15 percent by July 2009 (year-on-year). Similar patterns of export decline were registered in Jordan, Morocco, and Tunisia (figure A21). Together with only modest declines in imports (supported by stimulus measures), the current account position for the group deteriorated from a deficit of 2.1 percent of GDP in 2007 to 5.2 percent by 2009. Deficits during 2009 varied between 2.5 percent of GDP in Egypt and Tunisia, 5.8 percent in Morocco, and 7.0 percent in Jordan.

Slackening economic activity and worsening labor conditions in Europe, as well as across the GCC economies over the course of 2009 caused worker remittances flows into the developing region to decline by 6.3 percent for the year—in contrast to the strong gains of 23.0 and 11.3 percent in 2007 and 2008,

25 percent to 7.3 percent of GDP between 2008 and 2009, and from 19.7 percent to 3.3 percent for developing oil exporters (figure A20). With public expenditure growing at a rapid pace, fiscal deficits for developing exporters increased sharply during 2009, to 11 percent of GDP in Algeria (though well covered by reserves of some $150 billion), 5.5 percent in Syria, 3.8 percent in the Islamic Republic of Iran, and 2 percent in the Republic of Yemen.

GDP growth in Algeria slowed to 2.1 percent in 2009 from 3 percent in 2008. A 2 percent decline in the oil sector was partly offset by non-oil activity, which increased by 5.7 percent, supported by construction and services tied to a long-running infrastructure development plan (PIP). The program has continued to be implemented in part as a stimulus measure, and in early 2009 the government announced it would put about $60 billion from its oil-linked fiscal surplus toward the investment program. Even though partial national accounts data for 2009 are not available for the Islamic Republic of Iran, growth is estimated to have slowed to 1 percent in 2009, from 2.5 percent during 2008, as crude oil production contracted 7.3 percent and oil and gas export

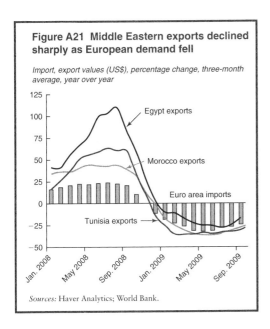

Figure A21 Middle Eastern exports declined sharply as European demand fell

Import, export values (US$), percentage change, three-month average, year over year

Sources: Haver Analytics; World Bank.

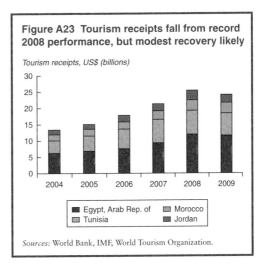

Figure A23 Tourism receipts fall from record 2008 performance, but modest recovery likely

Tourism receipts, US$ (billions)

Sources: World Bank, IMF, World Tourism Organization.

respectively (figure A22). Among the larger recipient countries, Egypt appears to have been most adversely affected, with flows declining 9 percent, while Morocco experienced an 8 percent drop in receipts. Jordan, Lebanon, and Tunisia experienced lesser declines, varying between 1 and 3 percent.

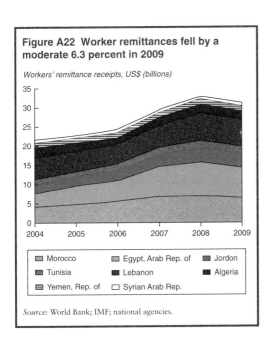

Figure A22 Worker remittances fell by a moderate 6.3 percent in 2009

Workers' remittance receipts, US$ (billions)

Source: World Bank; IMF; national agencies.

Tourism receipts are a key source of foreign currency (equivalent to 14 percent of GDP for the diversified economies of the region). With Europe suffering increasing unemployment rates, faltering wage growth, and efforts by households to repair balance sheets badly damaged by the financial market meltdown of 2008, tourism receipts are estimated to have declined by 5 percent during 2009, following strong gains in the 20 percent range since 2006 (figure A23). Tunisia appears to have bucked the downtrend with a gain of 4 percent. But declines elsewhere range from 8 percent in Morocco to 3 percent in Egypt.

Foreign direct investment (FDI) inflows to the diversified group, which is increasingly sourced from the GCC economies, fell to 4.3 percent of GDP in FY09 from 8.1 percent a year earlier. Morocco and Tunisia registered a 35 percent decline in inflows during calendar year 2009, while FDI in Jordan dropped by 80 percent during the first quarter of 2009. These declines reflect the substantial deterioration of financial conditions in the wake of the Dubai World debt-payment standstill, inducing GCC economies to scale back on current investment projects and putting earlier planned FDI endeavors on hold.

In addition to pressures on FDI, the Dubai financial crisis may have adverse consequences for the countries of the Mashreq (Jordan, Lebanon, and Syria), which hold particularly close ties to the GCC. Lower investment within the GCC portends fewer job opportunities for workers from these countries, lower remittances, and consumption in home markets.

Growth in *Egypt* slowed to 4.7 percent in FY09, from 7 percent during the three previous years. The slowdown was driven by lower external demand with exports of goods and services declining by 25 percent; growth was negative in economic sectors with a strong exposure to external markets such as the Suez Canal (down by 7.2 percent, compared with 18 percent growth in FY08) and hotels, restaurants, and related activities linked to tourism (down by 1.3 percent in real terms compared with 30 percent growth). Declining fixed investment (down 10 percent compared with 14.8 percent growth a year ago) has moved in tandem with increases in unemployment, which rose to 9.4 percent from 8.4 percent a year earlier. In response, the government implemented a crisis stimulus plan featuring fiscal, monetary, and direct support measures in the form of LE 15 billion in additional spending, including higher subsidies and social benefits. On the monetary side, the Central Bank of Egypt cut policy rates six times between February and September 2009, reducing overnight deposit and lending policy rates by 325 and 275 basis points, respectively.

Medium-term outlook

Following the tortuous conditions of 2009, prospects for both the developing and high-income economies of the Middle East and North Africa should improve through 2011. Growth is projected to increase to 4.4 percent by that year, the same pace registered on average between 1995 and 2005. Though domestic absorption will be a continuing source of strength, the forecast for regional recovery is premised on a revival in global oil demand and a rebound in key export markets. Despite the gradual withdrawal of fiscal stimulus measures, moderate advances in consumer and capital spending are expected to underpin the strengthening of growth (see table A7). But

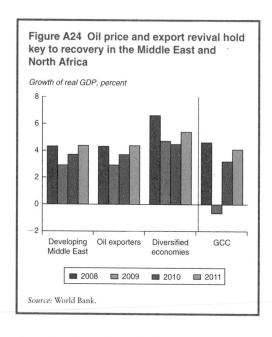

Figure A24 Oil price and export revival hold key to recovery in the Middle East and North Africa

Growth of real GDP, percent

Legend: 2008, 2009, 2010, 2011

Categories: Developing Middle East, Oil exporters, Diversified economies, GCC

Source: World Bank.

the regional profile masks both the diversity of performance across countries and the driving forces for growth.

Oil prices are expected to remain broadly stable over the forecast period, at around $75 a barrel. Stronger global activity should allow for crude oil and gas production to return to positive growth, implying moderate revenue gains. As a result, current account positions for developing oil exporters are projected to stabilize near 5 percent of GDP by 2011. GDP growth for developing oil exporters should reach 3.1 and 3.7 percent, respectively, in 2010 and 2011 (figure A24). By 2011 growth will vary from 3 percent in the Islamic Republic of Iran to 5.5 percent in Syria, grounded in developments in non-oil sectors and in investment in hydrocarbons capacity (table A8).

GDP for the high-income GCC economies is anticipated to increase by 3.2 percent in 2010 and 4.1 percent in 2011, as oil production firms and a higher average oil price help to restore revenues, albeit in more moderate increments. Current account surplus positions for the group are expected to rebound from 11 percent of GDP in 2009 to 14.5 percent by 2011, providing a means to support

Table A8   Middle East and North Africa country forecasts
(annual percent change unless indicated otherwise)

	1995–2005[a]	2006	2007	2008	2009[c]	2010[d]	2011[d]
Algeria							
GDP at market prices (2005 US$)[b]	4.0	2.0	3.0	3.0	2.1	3.9	4.0
Current account balance/GDP (%)	8.2	25.0	22.4	20.8	−3.4	2.7	5.6
Egypt, Arab Rep. of							
GDP at market prices (2005 US$)[b]	4.4	6.8	7.1	7.2	4.7	5.2	6.0
Current account balance/GDP (%)	0.4	2.4	0.3	−0.9	−3.2	−3.5	−3.2
Iran, Islamic Rep. of							
GDP at market prices (2005 US$)[b]	4.8	5.9	7.8	2.5	1.0	2.2	3.2
Current account balance/GDP (%)	7.3	9.2	12.0	22.2	7.5	3.6	3.2
Jordan							
GDP at market prices (2005 US$)[b]	4.7	8.0	8.9	7.9	3.2	3.9	4.5
Current account balance/GDP (%)	0.0	−10.8	−16.7	−11.4	−10.1	−9.7	−9.2
Lebanon							
GDP at market prices (2005 US$)[b]	3.2	0.6	7.5	8.5	7.0	7.0	7.0
Current account balance/GDP (%)	−20.0	−11.3	−11.1	−20.5	−14.5	−15.2	−14.2
Morocco							
GDP at market prices (2005 US$)[b]	4.4	7.8	2.7	5.6	5.0	3.0	4.4
Current account balance/GDP (%)	0.7	2.0	−0.3	−5.4	−5.9	−5.7	−5.2
Syrian Arab Republic							
GDP at market prices (2005 US$)[b]	3.2	5.1	4.2	5.2	3.0	4.0	5.5
Current account balance/GDP (%)	2.9	−2.8	−3.3	−4.0	−3.2	−4.3	−4.0
Tunisia							
GDP at market prices (2005 US$)[b]	5.0	5.7	6.3	4.5	3.3	3.8	5.0
Current account balance/GDP (%)	−3.0	−2.0	−2.6	−4.2	−3.5	−2.6	−2.0
Yemen, Rep. of							
GDP at market prices (2005 US$)[b]	4.9	3.2	3.3	3.6	4.2	7.3	4.5
Current account balance/GDP (%)	3.1	1.1	−7.0	−5.6	−5.2	−2.3	−2.5

Source: World Bank.

Note: World Bank forecasts are frequently updated based on new information and changing (global) circumstances. Consequently, projections presented here may differ from those contained in other Bank documents, even if basic assessments of countries' prospects do not significantly differ at any given moment in time.

Djibouti, Iraq, Libya, and West Bank and Gaza are not forecast owing to data limitations.

a. Growth rates over intervals are compound average; growth contributions, ratios, and the GDP deflator are averages.
b. GDP measured in constant 2005 U.S. dollars.
c. Estimate.
d. Forecast.

domestic growth while once more accumulating international reserves. A rekindling of interest in regional FDI may emerge as financial and economic conditions begin to normalize.

Economic recovery in Europe and among the GCC countries will be supportive of a revival for the diversified economies, suggesting a resumption of export growth, a rebound in remittances and various services receipts, and improvement in business expectations, leading to a revival in capital spending. GDP gains in Jordan, Morocco, and Tunisia are likely to be driven by domestic demand, with the help of fiscal and monetary stimulus measures, as external contributions fade. The anticipated normalization of agriculture in Morocco (following the post-drought boom of 2009) will be a drag on growth in 2010, and gains for the diversified group are projected to pick up to 4.5 percent in 2010 and 5.4 percent in 2011, respectively.

Risks

The broadly favorable outlook for the Middle East and North Africa over 2010–11 remains subject to substantial downside risks, which would pose additional challenges to policy makers already grappling with the current crisis. A deeper and more protracted global recession (the deeper growth recession discussed in chapter 1) cannot be ruled out. Within the region, political tensions remain a constant, tending to restrain international capital flows that might otherwise contribute to a deepening of capital markets and private investment. Further, needed reform efforts, some initiated during the crisis period, could receive less attention and commitment once economic conditions start to normalize.

The recent difficulties of Dubai World holding company—an entity of the Government of Dubai, United Arab Emirates—in asking its creditors for a six-month standstill on all scheduled debt payments, indicates that financial institutions in the region were not entirely unaffected by the global financial crisis. Given the very high investment levels of the past several years, as well as asset inflation (property prices increased particularly sharply in Egypt and Morocco), there may be additional large-scale financial losses that have yet to be realized. Though a systemic crisis in Dubai will likely be averted thanks to the diversified holdings of the Dubai government and emergency support from the emirate of Abu Dhabi (both bilaterally and through the federal authorities), it may have an adverse impact on the balance sheets of local and regional banks holding Dubai World debt. The financial problems facing Dubai, along with previous defaults by two large Saudi private companies, will continue to raise concern amidst the need for comprehensive corporate governance and debt restructuring reforms in the region.

South Asia

Recent developments

The global financial crisis contributed to a marked deceleration in real GDP growth in South Asia, from 8.7 percent in 2007 to 6.0 percent in 2009, which was largely driven by a pronounced decline in investment growth and, to a lesser extent, private consumption. While exports contracted sharply with external demand, the decline in imports was steeper, and net trade actually supported growth on the regional level. As the crisis took hold, equity markets and exchange rates plunged in most countries in the region. Sovereign bond spreads spiked with the contraction in capital flows, as both domestic and international investors sought safe-haven assets outside the region.

Although the global financial crisis had a sharp negative impact on South Asia, the slowdown in regional GDP growth was the least pronounced among all developing regions. This partly reflects the relatively closed nature of the region's economies. Private capital inflows—a key transmission channel of the crisis—are less significant as a share of South Asia's GDP (particularly foreign direct investment), compared with most other regions. Economic activity in South Asia is also less specialized in manufacturing and natural resources—sectors that have been particularly negatively affected by the crisis. Correspondingly, the region's greater reliance on services trade—roughly double the 7.7 percent average share of GDP for developing countries in 2008—also provided a buffer to the crisis, as services tend to be more resilient during downturns (although smaller countries with important tourism sectors, such as the Maldives, were hit hard). Domestic demand in the region was relatively resilient, having been cushioned by countercyclical macroeconomic policies. Interest rates were rapidly cut across most economies. Although fiscal space in most economies was limited, substantial fiscal stimulus measures were introduced in India (including pre-election spending), Bangladesh and Sri Lanka (in the form of incentives and safety net expenditures). Relatively robust, albeit moderating, regional remittance inflows have been supportive, particularly in Bangladesh, Nepal, and Sri Lanka, where they continue to represent over 5 percent of GDP. Real incomes were also boosted by the collapse in global commodity prices—particularly for food and fuel, which represent a large share of regional household outlays.

The extent of the downturn in the individual economies has been mixed and reflects initial conditions. Growth has been weakest in countries that entered the crisis with large internal and external imbalances and that were forced to severely constrain domestic demand, such as the Maldives, Pakistan, and Sri Lanka. Countries that entered the crisis with stronger fundamentals, such as Bangladesh Bhutan, and India, weathered the crisis better. A number of regional economies also faced ongoing internal conflicts that continued to disrupt economic activity, notably Afghanistan, Pakistan, Sri Lanka (which ended a decades-old civil war in mid-2009), and to a lesser extent Nepal (where warring factions reached a peace accord in late 2006, but are still vying for political control).

The stabilization and progressive thawing of global financial markets in early 2009 and the rebound of world trade and output growth beginning in the second half of 2009 have contributed to improving conditions in South Asia. Since the second quarter of 2009, local equity markets and capital inflows to the region began to recover—largely in line with

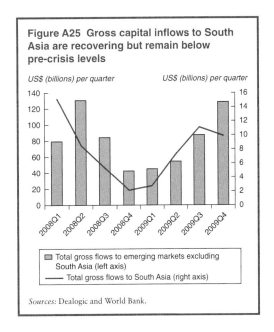

Figure A25 Gross capital inflows to South Asia are recovering but remain below pre-crisis levels

Sources: Dealogic and World Bank.

trends across developing countries (figures A25 and A26). This process has been supported by improved investor sentiment on comparatively strong growth outturns (India and Bangladesh), ongoing or new International Monetary Fund (IMF) stabilization programs (Pakistan, Sri Lanka, and most recently the Maldives), steep reductions in interest rates,

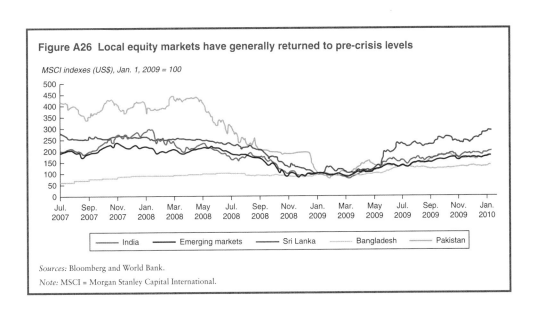

Figure A26 Local equity markets have generally returned to pre-crisis levels

Sources: Bloomberg and World Bank.

Note: MSCI = Morgan Stanley Capital International.

and improved political stability. While the region experienced a sharp decline in gross capital inflows during the first half of 2009, portfolio inflows surged in the fourth quarter and bond issuance and syndicated bank lending jumped in the fourth quarter, such that total gross inflows firmed in 2009 to an estimated $31 billion. As inflows to other regions shrank (particularly in Europe and Central Asia), South Asia's share of total capital inflows to developing countries rose to 8.9 percent in 2009 from 6.7 percent in 2008. While most local stock exchanges have recovered to pre-crisis levels, the majority remain well below peak levels posted in late 2007 and early 2008 (in both local currency and U.S. dollar terms). In Bangladesh, where capitalization of listed companies (relative to GDP) is lower than in its neighbors and where foreign participation is limited, the equity market remained stable during the crisis and posted strong growth in recent months. Sri Lanka's equity market is also an exception, with a recovery to pre-crisis highs of 2007 supported by the improvement in sentiment following the end of the civil war and the formal standby arrangement reached with the IMF in mid-2009.

Regional industrial activity, which did not contract as much as in most other developing regions, has shifted into positive growth, led by India, Bangladesh, and more recently Pakistan. Fiscal stimulus measures have supported the rebound in output by helping to revive consumer demand. Further, continued robust remittance inflows boosted construction activity, especially in Bangladesh and Nepal. The recovery in regional output is ahead of most other developing regions—with the exception of East Asia and the Pacific—and of high-income countries (figure A27). Regional agricultural output was buoyed by a good monsoon in 2008 that contributed to a good harvest in 2009 across much of the region. One exception is Afghanistan, where agricultural output contracted sharply (16.5 percent in FY2008/09). In Sri Lanka the agricultural sector benefited from the end of fighting and from acreage brought back into production.

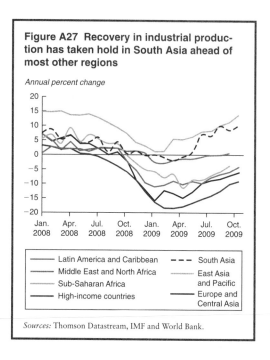

Figure A27 Recovery in industrial production has taken hold in South Asia ahead of most other regions

Annual percent change

Legend:
- Latin America and Caribbean
- Middle East and North Africa
- Sub-Saharan Africa
- High-income countries
- South Asia
- East Asia and Pacific
- Europe and Central Asia

Sources: Thomson Datastream, IMF and World Bank.

However, a poor monsoon season in India in 2009 suggests that agricultural growth will be modest in the current 2009–10 crop year (which began in late 2009). Regional services activity decelerated with the decline in global tourism, hitting the Maldives, Nepal, and Sri Lanka, in particular, where tourism is a key sector. In contrast, in India, services activity was supported by resilient outsourcing.

Merchandise trade growth remains below previous-year levels for the region, with imports down much more sharply than exports, given the sharp compression of demand in Maldives, Pakistan, and Sri Lanka in particular. Indeed, the 32 percent decline in South Asia's import volumes through July 2009 compared with the previous year is the second steepest among developing regions after that of Europe and Central Asia (39 percent). In contrast, the decline in the region's merchandise export volumes was less severe than in most other developing regions, with the exceptions of East Asia and the Pacific and Latin America and the Caribbean. This partly reflects the low manufacturing and commodity content (sectors particularly hard hit by the recession) of the region's exports. Some sectors also demonstrated marked resilience during the crisis, such as ready-made garments in Bangladesh, where competitive pricing has enabled producers to build market shares (i.e., the "Wal-Mart effect") and in Sri Lanka, where long-term strategic partnerships with mid- to high-end retailers in the United States and the European Union, (such as Victoria's Secret, Diesel, and Nike) created a buffer, and in India, where information technology software also proved relatively resilient.

Overall, the combination of a sharp fall in the value of imports, a somewhat less steep decline in exports (both reflecting favorable terms-of-trade developments), and resilient remittance inflows meant that current account balances generally improved in 2009 (figure A28). Regional external positions had come increasingly under strain from the multiyear boom in food and fuel prices before mid-2008. During 2009, the Maldives, Pakistan, and Sri Lanka posted the largest adjustments in their current account deficits. Domestic demand was sharply compressed in the three economies, where large fiscal deficits had contributed to the buildup of considerable external imbalances before the crisis. The Maldives is an extreme case, where a massive

upswing in government outlays and a surge in imports for resort-related construction materials contributed to the sharp deterioration in the current account balance.

While the adjustment was less stark, India also posted a shrinking current account deficit in 2009, as imports fell faster than exports. Bangladesh and Nepal recorded rising current account surpluses, as the moderation of export growth was less pronounced than the decline in imports, supported by continued firm remittances inflows. In contrast, Bhutan's current account deficit is estimated to have grown from 10 percent of GDP in 2008 to 12.3 percent in 2009, partly reflecting the start of interest payments for the Tala hydropower scheme (figure A28). Afghanistan's current account deficit, including official transfers (equivalent to some 50 percent of official GDP) is estimated to have shifted from a surplus of 0.9 percent of GDP in 2008 to a deficit of 1.6 percent in 2009.

Remittance inflows—a key source of foreign exchange for the region—declined in 2009, pushed down by the decline in economic activity and the rise in unemployment in migrant-host countries. However, remittance inflows remained relatively strong compared with other sources of foreign exchange, and indeed are above their 2007 levels (figure A29). Remittance inflows to South Asia contracted by a modest

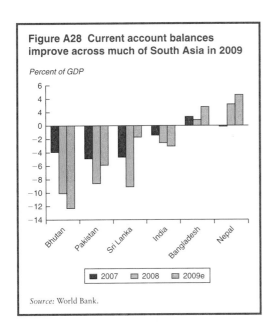

Figure A28 Current account balances improve across much of South Asia in 2009

Percent of GDP

Source: World Bank.

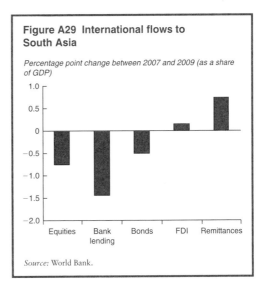

Figure A29 International flows to South Asia

Percentage point change between 2007 and 2009 (as a share of GDP)

Source: World Bank.

1.8 percent in 2009, compared with a 7.5 percent decline for developing countries excluding South Asia (World Bank 2009). Growth in the Arabian Gulf and East Asian economies, which host a significant share of South Asia's migrant workers, has not been as adversely affected as growth in other key host economies, such as the United States, the European Union, and Russia. Among South Asia's economies, India—the largest recipient of remittances in the world in dollar terms—posted a contraction in remittance inflows in 2009, while Bangladesh, Nepal, Pakistan, and Sri Lanka, experienced a slower pace of growth of remittances inflows.

With the moderation in demand and collapse in energy prices, inflationary pressures across the region subsided following the onset of the crisis, particularly in the first half of 2009. This helped reverse the buildup of inflationary pressures that became increasingly evident in 2007 and 2008, as fuel and food prices spiked—despite efforts by authorities to contain the price increases. Lower oil prices have eased pressures on fiscal deficits stemming from fuel price subsidies. The moderation in inflationary pressures and falling international commodity prices also provided scope for regional central banks to introduce expansionary measures to support domestic demand in response to the crisis. Bangladesh, India, Pakistan, and Sri Lanka cut policy interest rates. Activity in Bhutan and Nepal, where the currencies are tied to the Indian rupee, was supported by India's expansionary monetary policy stance.

Regional fiscal positions deteriorated in 2009 in response to a combination of reduced tax receipts resulting from the decline in economic activity and higher outlays. Corresponding to the introduction of more accommodative monetary policies, expansionary fiscal policy measures were introduced in Bangladesh, India, and Sri Lanka to support domestic demand through various expenditure and incentive programs. Pakistan also sought to stimulate its economy through an increase in its public sector development program. While these stimulus measures helped offset the negative effects of the global crisis, they also led to higher fiscal deficits in

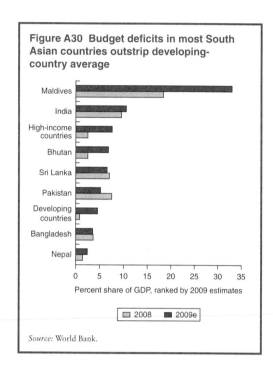

Figure A30 Budget deficits in most South Asian countries outstrip developing-country average

Percent share of GDP, ranked by 2009 estimates

☐ 2008   ■ 2009e

Source: World Bank.

nearly all of the regional economies. Even before the crisis, sizable fiscal deficits were already a problem for many South Asian economies, where weak tax administration and structure resulted in low domestic resource mobilization (figure A30).

Medium-term outlook

South Asia's GDP growth is projected to firm from an estimated 6 percent in 2009 to 7.0 percent in 2010 and 7.4 percent in 2011. External demand for goods and services is anticipated to recover, while improving consumer and business confidence, combined with the lagged effects of expansionary monetary and fiscal policy measures and a positive turn in the inventory cycle, should contribute to strengthening domestic demand. A projected firming of capital inflows will also support regional economic activity. The regional current account deficit is projected to rise modestly, from 1.2 percent in 2009 to 2.2 percent in 2010 and 2.4 percent in 2011, a result of firming domestic demand that is expected to drive import growth ahead of export growth.

Table A9 South Asia forecast summary
(annual percent change unless indicated otherwise)

	1995–2005[a]	2006	2007	2008	2009[g]	2010[h]	2011[h]
GDP at market prices (2005 US$)[b,f]	6.0	9.0	8.5	5.7	5.7	6.9	7.4
GDP in calendar year basis[c]	6.1	9.3	8.7	6.9	6.0	7.0	7.4
GDP per capita (units in US$)	4.1	7.3	6.8	4.2	4.3	5.5	6.1
PPP GDP[d]	6.0	9.0	8.5	5.7	5.7	6.9	7.4
Private consumption	4.7	6.0	7.0	2.7	4.2	6.0	6.7
Public consumption	5.0	9.9	5.6	21.1	7.1	7.3	7.2
Fixed investment	8.0	14.6	13.6	7.6	4.1	9.7	10.2
Exports, GNFS[e]	11.3	17.7	3.5	10.5	−4.6	10.3	12.1
Imports, GNFS[e]	10.6	22.7	6.8	14.9	−6.9	10.6	12.3
Net exports, contribution to growth	−0.2	−1.7	−1.0	−1.7	0.9	−0.6	−0.7
Current account balance/GDP (%)	−0.6	−1.5	−1.3	−3.3	−2.3	−3.2	−3.4
GDP deflator (median, LCU)	5.9	5.2	7.4	7.2	13.8	6.9	6.5
Fiscal balance/GDP (%)	−8.1	−5.1	−5.7	−8.9	−9.5	−8.6	−7.8
Memo items: GDP[f]							
South Asia excluding India	4.5	6.4	6.0	3.9	4.4	4.1	4.8
India	6.4	9.7	9.1	6.1	6.0	7.5	8.0
Pakistan	4.1	6.2	5.7	2.0	3.7	3.0	4.0
Bangladesh	5.3	6.6	6.4	6.2	5.9	5.5	5.8

Source: World Bank.

a. Growth rates over intervals are compound average; growth contributions, ratios, and the GDP deflator are averages.

b. GDP measured in constant 2005 U.S. dollars.

c. GDP figures are presented in calendar years (CY) based on quarterly history for India. For Bangladesh, Nepal, and Pakistan, CY data is calculated taking the average growth over the two fiscal year periods to provide an approximation of CY activity.

d. GDP measured at PPP exchange rates.

e. Exports and imports of goods and nonfactor services.

f. National income and product account data refer to fiscal years (FY) for the South Asian countries with the exception of Sri Lanka, which reports in calendar year (CY). The fiscal year runs from July 1 through June 30 in Bangladesh and Pakistan, from July 16 through July 15 in Nepal, and from April 1 through March 31 in India. Because of reporting practices, Bangladesh, Nepal, and Pakistan report FY2007/08 data in CY2008, while India reports FY2007/08 in CY2007.

g. Estimate.

h. Forecast.

Although regional GDP growth is projected to accelerate, a return to boom-period growth rates is not anticipated over the forecast horizon, as investment growth is expected to continue to be constrained by supply bottlenecks and higher capital costs in the wake of the crisis. (table A9). External demand is expected to firm, but it too will expand less quickly than during the boom years. The regional fiscal deficit is projected to narrow on planned structural fiscal consolidation and cyclical factors, as well as a reversal of stimulus measures introduced to support demand during the crisis. Nevertheless, the aggregate regional fiscal deficit is projected to continue to exceed its pre-crisis 2007 deficit of 5.7 percent.

Expected progressive tightening of monetary conditions over the forecast horizon will contribute to an easing of inflationary pressures by 2011 across the region. Further, given strong aversion to food price inflation within the region, monetary authorities are particularly responsive to signs of inflationary pressures building.

The recovery path for the individual economies will vary substantially (table A10). India, Bangladesh, and Bhutan are expected to emerge from the global crisis with stronger growth performances, backed by generally sound economic policies and greater resilience of trade, investment, and remittances. Sri Lanka is also forecast to post a relatively firm recovery, supported by the recent surge in capital inflows and improvement in investor confidence following the cessation of fighting after nearly three decades of civil war. Elsewhere in the region, conflict-affected

Table A10 South Asia country forecasts
(annual percent change unless indicated otherwise)

	1995–2005[a]	2006	2007	2008	2009[c]	2010[d]	2011[d]
Calendar year basis							
Bangladesh							
GDP at market prices (2005 USD)[b]	5.0	6.3	6.5	6.3	6.1	5.7	5.7
Current account balance/GDP (%)	−0.6	2.0	1.3	1.4	3.1	1.8	1.5
India							
GDP at market prices (2005 USD)[b]	6.7	9.9	9.3	7.3	6.4	7.6	8.0
Current account balance/GDP (%)	−0.4	−1.1	−0.7	−2.6	−2.4	−3.5	−3.6
Nepal							
GDP at market prices (2005 USD)[b]	3.9	3.4	3.5	4.3	5.0	4.3	4.3
Current account balance/GDP (%)	−3.1	−0.1	−1.5	3.7	4.4	1.0	1.4
Pakistan							
GDP at market prices (2005 USD)[b]	3.7	6.9	5.9	3.8	2.9	3.3	3.5
Current account balance/GDP (%)	−1.0	−5.7	−6.3	−10.2	−5.2	−4.1	−4.6
Sri Lanka							
GDP at market prices (2005 USD)[b]	4.5	7.7	6.8	6.0	3.6	5.0	6.0
Current account balance/GDP (%)	−3.2	−5.8	−4.7	−9.1	−1.7	−2.7	−2.9
Fiscal year basis							
Bangladesh							
Real GDP at market prices	5.3	6.6	6.4	6.2	5.9	5.5	5.8
Current account balance/GDP (%)	−0.8	1.3	1.4	0.9	2.8	2.2	1.5
India							
Real GDP at market prices	6.4	9.7	9.1	6.1	6.0	7.5	8.0
Current account balance/GDP (%)	−0.2	−1.2	−1.0	−1.4	−2.6	−3.1	−3.3
Nepal							
Real GDP at market prices	4.1	3.7	3.3	5.3	4.7	4.0	4.5
Current account balance/GDP (%)	0.2	2.3	−0.1	3.2	4.6	2.4	1.1
Pakistan							
Real GDP at market prices	4.1	6.2	5.7	2.0	3.7	3.0	4.0
Current account balance/GDP (%)	−0.8	−4.0	−4.9	−8.6	−5.9	−4.5	−4.1

Source: World Bank.

Note: World Bank forecasts are frequently updated based on new information and changing (global) circumstances. Consequently, projections presented here may differ from those contained in other Bank documents, even if basic assessments of countries' prospects do not significantly differ at any given moment in time.

Afghanistan, Bhutan, and the Maldives are not forecast owing to data limitations. National income and product account data refer to fiscal years (FY) for the South Asian countries with the exception of Sri Lanka, which reports in calendar year (CY). The fiscal year runs from July 1 through June 30 in Bangladesh and Pakistan, from July 16 through July 15 in Nepal, and April 1 through March 31 in India. Because of reporting practices, Bangladesh, Nepal, and Pakistan report FY2007/08 data in CY2008, while India reports FY2007/08 in CY2007. GDP figures are presented in calendar years (CY) based on quarterly history for India. For Bangladesh, Nepal, and Pakistan, CY data is calculated taking the average growth over the two fiscal year periods to provide an approximation of CY activity.

a. Growth rates over intervals are compound average; growth contributions, ratios, and the GDP deflators are averages.
b. GDP measured in constant 2000 U.S. dollars.
c. Estimate.
d. Forecast.

countries—Afghanistan, Pakistan, and to a lesser extent, Nepal—are expected to face more moderate growth outturns, as political uncertainty and fighting continue to disrupt economic activity.

Regional economies are projected to benefit from stronger remittance inflows over the forecast horizon, which in turn should boost private consumption and support growth—particularly in Bangladesh, Nepal, Pakistan, and Sri Lanka. However, the recovery in remittance growth is anticipated not to take hold immediately as job growth typically lags output growth in high-income markets—a lag that could be more extended than usual given the synchronicity of the global downturn. However, the slowdown in growth in the Arabian Gulf and East Asia—South Asia's key migrant destination countries—was generally less pronounced than in other labor-importing countries, which is expected to allow a relatively rapid recovery in remittances inflows to South Asia.

Risks

As the global economic recovery begins to take hold in the second half of 2009, risks to the GDP growth forecast for South Asia have lessened. Nevertheless, downside risks remain and center on the extent of the upswing and durability of the global recovery.

Downside risks to the forecast are represented by the region's large fiscal imbalances and its relatively high reliance on trade taxes. An extended period of weak external demand would likely erode these revenues and increase pressures on government coffers. The region's large fiscal imbalances also represent a potential drag on long-term growth by crowding out private investment through the public sector's large financing requirement and higher interest rates. Interest payments in South Asia represented 21.7 percent of central government expenditures in 2007, more than double the share represented in other developing regions (figure A31). By reducing the large fiscal deficits and payment obligations, regional governments could free up resources to devote to development spending. The region has a very low tax base compared with other developing regions, so improving tax collection would help alleviate fiscal pressures. Similarly, revamping the tax structure (including introduction of value-added taxes in some countries) could help boost revenue mobilization.

Remittances inflows—which provided a cushion for the region—could fail to recover in the event of a prolonged global recession or a jobless economic recovery (potentially coupled with tighter immigration controls). The debt payment problems of Dubai World in the United Arab Emirates that erupted in late-November 2009 suggest that economic activity in the Arabian Gulf economies could

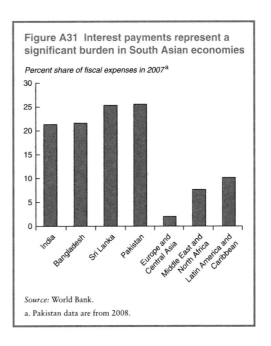

Figure A31 Interest payments represent a significant burden in South Asian economies

Percent share of fiscal expenses in 2007[a]

Source: World Bank.

a. Pakistan data are from 2008.

surprise to the downside, pointing to downside risks for South Asian migrants working in the Gulf and reduced remittances flows to their home countries. Correspondingly, should a significant portion of the stock of expatriate workers return home with accumulated savings due to the downturn in the Gulf, near-term remittances inflows might rise.

Overheating is also a risk. Should the recent surge in capital inflows to developing countries (see chapter 1) be sustained, they could lead to ballooning asset markets and appreciation of currencies (with the latter hindering export prospects), creating challenges for monetary authorities. Failure to mop up excess liquidity in banking systems or to bring down the region's large fiscal deficits could lead to higher inflationary pressures. Separately, while global rice markets appear well-supplied, and stock-to-use ratios have returned to more normal levels (along with maize and wheat stocks), a serious weather event or policy action could also cause prices to rise significantly, as only seven percent of global rice production is traded.

Table A11   Sub-Saharan Africa forecast summary
(annual percent change unless indicated otherwise)

	1995–2005[a]	2006	2007	2008	2009[e]	2010[f]	2011[f]
GDP at market prices (2005 US$)[b]	4.0	6.4	6.5	5.1	1.1	3.8	4.6
GDP per capita (units in US$)	1.4	3.9	4.0	3.1	−0.8	1.9	2.7
PPP GDP[c]	4.0	6.4	6.5	5.2	1.6	4.1	4.9
Private consumption	2.0	7.0	8.1	3.5	0.4	3.2	4.5
Public consumption	5.2	5.8	5.8	5.6	5.6	5.2	5.2
Fixed investment	6.5	16.9	19.5	12.2	0.3	6.3	5.7
Exports, GNFS[d]	4.9	4.8	3.8	4.6	−5.2	6.6	5.9
Imports, GNFS[d]	6.1	13.2	11.8	6.7	−5.2	7.5	6.6
Net exports, contribution to growth	−0.1	−2.7	−2.9	−0.9	0.2	−0.6	−0.5
Current account balance/GDP (%)	−1.7	0.7	−0.1	0.1	−3.4	−2.5	−2.4
GDP deflator (median, LCU)	7.3	7.3	7.6	9.7	6.2	6.1	4.1
Fiscal balance/GDP (%)	−2.3	4.3	0.4	0.9	−4.2	−2.1	−1.7
Memo items: GDP							
Sub-Saharan Africa excluding South Africa	4.5	6.9	7.1	5.9	2.8	4.8	5.6
Oil exporters	4.6	7.5	7.9	6.3	2.8	4.9	5.3
CFA countries	4.4	2.7	4.5	4.0	1.6	3.4	3.8
South Africa	3.3	5.6	5.5	3.7	−1.8	2.0	2.7
Nigeria	4.6	6.2	6.3	5.3	4.3	4.8	5.1
Kenya	2.9	6.4	7.1	1.7	2.8	3.7	4.8

Source: World Bank.

a. Growth rates over intervals are compound average; growth contributions, ratios, and the GDP deflator are averages.
b. GDP measured in constant 2005 U.S. dollars.
c GDP measured at PPP exchange rates.
d. Exports and imports of goods and nonfactor services.
e. Estimate.
f. Forecast.

Sub-Saharan Africa

Recent developments

The global financial crisis has had a marked, negative impact on economic performance in Sub-Saharan Africa, affecting trade, foreign direct investment, tourism, remittances, and official assistance. GDP is estimated to have grown only 1.1 percent for the region as a whole in 2009 (table A11). Notwithstanding the severity of the shock, the improved macroeconomic fundamentals in place in many countries of the region as they entered the crisis meant that the impact was less pronounced than in other regions and relative to previous external shocks. The growth slowdown has varied across countries in Sub-Saharan Africa, with oil exporters and middle-income countries affected more severely, at least initially, than low-income, fragile, and less globally integrated countries (figure A32). Per capita GDP has declined by an estimated 0.8 percent in 2009, the first decline in a decade. This is

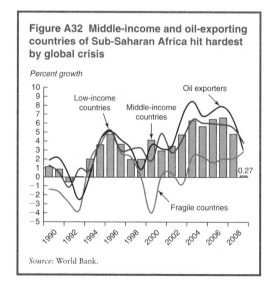

Figure A32 Middle-income and oil-exporting countries of Sub-Saharan Africa hit hardest by global crisis

Percent growth

Source: World Bank.

likely to have long-term consequences for Sub-Saharan African countries, as more people fall into poverty in the region, according to Chen and Ravallion (2009); 30,000 to 50,000 more infants are likely to die of malnutrition in 2009, with a larger impact among infant girls (Friedman and Schady 2009).

As Sub-Saharan Africa is a major commodity exporting region, lower commodity prices, declining export volumes, as well as lower tourism revenues, and declining remittances have all undermined income and private consumption, which decelerated to 0.4 percent growth in 2009, down from 3.5 percent the previous year. Weak external demand for commodities, excess capacity, scarce credit, and tight liquidity all led to delays and scaling back of investment spending. Although FDI declined by 19 percent in 2009 the decline was more muted than in other regions except South Asia, mainly because of sustained investment in the extractive sectors. Weak private consumption and investment resulted in lower imports, partially offsetting the negative growth impact emanating from the sharp contraction in export volumes (figure A33).

As expected, the contraction in both export and import volumes was more severe in middle-income countries, which are more

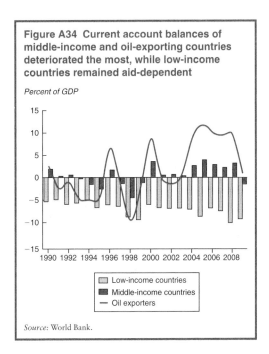

Figure A34 Current account balances of middle-income and oil-exporting countries deteriorated the most, while low-income countries remained aid-dependent

Percent of GDP

Source: World Bank.

integrated into the global economy. Because of the marked declines in oil prices, the deterioration in current account balances was most pronounced in oil-exporting countries, where it fell from 9.7 to 1.4 percent of GDP (figure A34). Meanwhile lower tourism revenues, remittances, and private current net transfers brought the current account balances in middle-income countries to a deficit of 1.2 percent of GDP—down from a surplus of 3.3 percent of GDP in 2008. Low-income countries remain dependent on foreign assistance to finance deficits of nearly 10 percent of GDP. For most of these countries the terms-of-trade boost from lower oil prices was offset by lower export prices or volumes (primarily metals and minerals, agricultural products), or both. Indeed, the marked decline in oil imports merely offset the decline in current account inflows, with current account balances improving by less than 1 percent of GDP.

Sovereign spreads rose sharply in the wake of the financial crisis but have declined significantly since the first quarter of 2009. In many cases, however, these spreads remain above the pre-crisis level (figure A35).

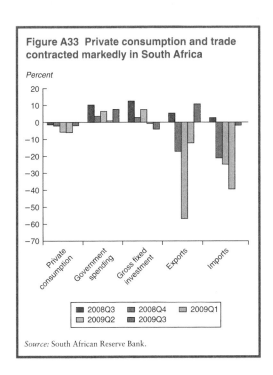

Figure A33 Private consumption and trade contracted markedly in South Africa

Percent

Private consumption | Government spending | Gross fixed investment | Exports | Imports

2008Q3   2008Q4   2009Q1   2009Q2   2009Q3

Source: South African Reserve Bank.

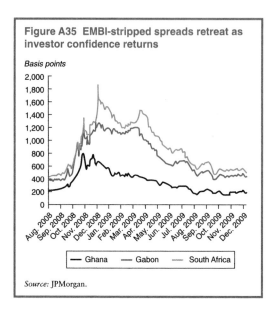

Figure A35 EMBI-stripped spreads retreat as investor confidence returns

Basis points

Legend: Ghana — Gabon — South Africa

Source: JPMorgan.

Most countries in the region have been spared from the most abrupt financial turbulences experienced by other regions, but in countries that enjoyed rapid credit expansion in the boom years (like Cape Verde, the Democratic Republic of Congo, Ethiopia, Nigeria, Rwanda, Tanzania, Uganda, and Zambia), nonperforming loans will mount in the quarters ahead, putting strains on the shallow financial systems.

Expectations about an imminent recovery in the global economy triggered a return of investors to stock markets across the world, boosting share prices. In South Africa share prices rose by 56 percent in dollar terms since January 2009. The capital inflows have also supported the rand, which gained 28.1 percent against the U.S. dollar during the course of 2009. Furthermore, a more positive investor attitude toward risk taking in emerging-market economies boosted inflows of direct and portfolio investment during the second quarter.

On the policy front many countries in the region had only limited space for countercyclical measures, notwithstanding more prudent fiscal stances during the boom period. Automatic stabilizers worked in South Africa and the

Seychelles, which were among the small number of countries that were able to implement significant countercyclical fiscal policies. A large part of the deterioration in fiscal balances in commodity exporters is linked to both lower volumes and lower export prices for commodities. For the region as a whole, the fiscal balance deteriorated from a surplus of 0.9 percent of GDP in 2008 to a deficit of 4.2 percent of GDP in 2009. Furthermore, monetary policy remains ineffective in bolstering domestic demand in many countries owing to a lack of depth in the financial systems and weak transmission mechanisms.

Lower food and oil prices since mid-2008 contributed to a sharp decline in headline inflation, which has eased to low single-digit levels in many countries (figure A36). By September 2009 several countries in the region were reporting falling headline prices. However, in East Africa, as a result of high food inflation related to recurrent droughts, inflation has remained stubbornly high. Subdued inflation in many countries in the Sub-Saharan Africa region has created room for lowering interest rates. Moreover, lower food and energy prices have relieved some of the pressure on fiscal balances, although sharply lower trade volumes and lower export

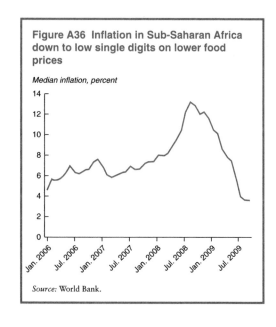

Figure A36 Inflation in Sub-Saharan Africa down to low single digits on lower food prices

Median inflation, percent

Source: World Bank.

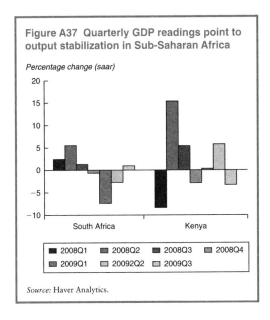

Figure A37 Quarterly GDP readings point to output stabilization in Sub-Saharan Africa

Percentage change (saar)

Legend: 2008Q1, 2008Q2, 2008Q3, 2008Q4, 2009Q1, 20092Q2, 2009Q3

Source: Haver Analytics.

and import prices have slashed trade-related government revenues, which has been particularly acute in the Southern Africa Customs Union countries.

In South Africa output contracted for three consecutive quarters, starting with the final quarter of 2008, then posted 0.9 percent growth (saar) in the third quarter of 2009, thereby ending the recession (Figure A37). Domestic demand remains weak, undermined by declining disposable income, higher unemployment, and high levels of debt. Growth in both government consumption and fixed investment deteriorated in the second quarter, the latter partly attributable to more conservative lending practices. Weaker domestic demand, in particular postponements of capital expenditure by the private sector, led to a sharp contraction in imports during the first half of 2009. This in conjunction with less rapidly falling exports brought the second quarter trade balance into surplus, and helped bring the current account deficit down to 3.2 percent of GDP in the third quarter from 7 percent of GDP in the first quarter.

Nigeria's economy, the second largest in the region, seems to have weathered the crisis well. Notwithstanding lower oil prices and

disruptions in oil production, GDP expanded 4.5 percent and 7.2 percent in the first two quarters of the year, and growth remained strong in the third quarter, largely on account of the non-oil sectors. Agriculture and wholesale and retail trade made positive contributions, suggesting continued strength in domestic demand. However poor performance in the manufacturing, mining, and electricity-generation sectors led to a decline in industrial output. The central bank's recent bailouts of Nigeria's top five commercial banks underscore the weakness of Nigeria's financial system. Together these banks account for 40 percent of all loans, 30 percent of deposits, and 31.5 percent of total assets. These banks had a very large exposure to capital markets and the gas and oil sectors, as well as a high level of nonperforming loans, thanks to poor corporate governance practices, lax credit administration, and nonadherence to the banks' credit risk management practices. The stock market has been severely battered since the onset of the global crisis, with share prices down 57.6 percent and market capitalization down 50.7 percent in the first nine months of 2009.

Kenya's economic growth has been constrained by recurrent drought and ensuing electricity shortages while also suffering the effects of the global economic crisis. When compared with a year earlier, growth decelerated from 4.3 percent in the first quarter, to 2.1 percent in the second quarter, to −0.1 percent in the third quarter, in contrast with growth rates of above 6 percent in 2007, before the election-related tensions. The drought-generated general crop failure affected food security, leading to higher imports of basic foods. Major export crops fell, with tea output down 11.6 percent and horticulture output down 7.4 percent in the first eight months of 2009. Power shortages, higher power costs, and weak global demand caused mining and quarrying, manufacturing, construction, and wholesale and retail trade to contract in the second quarter. On the bright side, transport and communications, as well as the hotel and restaurant sector rebounded as the effects of the postelection violence in early

2008 dissipated. Tourist arrivals rose 42 percent in the first eight months of 2009.

In Ethiopia economic activity has been supported by growth in the agricultural sector, underpinned by an expansion of roads and better market access that have enabled subsistence farmers to enter the commercial sector. The economy was faced with significant external shocks, however. The global recession caused remittances to fall by 6 percent in the first half of 2009 relative to a year earlier, while merchandise exports fell 11 percent. In manufacturing, capacity utilization has been affected by weak demand, shortages of water and electricity, insufficient raw materials and other inputs, and a shortage of capital. Foreign direct investment has also been affected, making it more difficult to finance the large current account deficit. Economic growth is estimated to have decelerated to 7.2 percent in 2009, as remittances, investment, and export growth weaken. Two new hydroelectric dams, one commissioned in November 2009 and the other to become operational in the next few months, will help ease power shortages and remove some of the growth constraints.

Lower demand for minerals is estimated to have weakened performance in southern Africa, and the region was also negatively affected by the recession in South Africa, with which it has close trade, investment, and financial links. Angola's economy also performed poorly: oil output declined to below 1.8 million barrels a day, while falling oil revenues forced the government to cut back on investment spending, and private consumer spending contracted. Lower demand for mining and hydrocarbon products pushed the Democratic Republic of Congo into recession in the last quarter of 2008, and this contraction was extended into the first half of 2009, when output dropped a cumulative 5.8 percent. Strong growth in the agriculture sector helped Mozambique's economic growth to stay at 5.9 percent in the first quarter of 2009 notwithstanding a deceleration in growth in the services sector. Subsequently, growth accelerated to above 6 percent in the second and third quarters.

Growth performance has been stronger in West and Eastern Africa: major economies in the regions have recovered and reform-oriented economies such as Burkina Faso, Mali, Senegal, and Tanzania have turned in relatively strong performances. In Côte d'Ivoire, which has been enjoying a peace dividend following the easing of political tensions, growth accelerated to above 3 percent in 2009, as agricultural, mining, and hydrocarbon output increased. In Central Africa, growth remained plagued by weak performances in the oil sectors of Cameroon and Gabon.

Medium-term outlook

The recovery in growth is projected to be modest and fragile, with output in Sub-Saharan Africa expected to accelerate to below-trend growth rates of 3.8 percent in 2010 and 4.6 percent in 2011. The growth pace will be well below the 6 percent growth rate recorded during the boom years, as a result of lower real commodity prices and slower global growth. Excluding South Africa, the region is projected to enjoy a modest acceleration in growth, from 2.8 percent in 2009 to 4.8 and 5.6 percent in 2010 and 2011, respectively, as global growth recovers; however, this is still below the average 6.6 percent experienced during the boom years. The South African economy is expected to recover modestly in 2010, growing by 2.0 percent, before accelerating further to 2.7 percent in 2011. In per capita terms, GDP in Sub-Saharan Africa is projected to grow 1.9 percent in 2010 and 2.7 percent in 2011.

The rebound in economic activity will primarily be fueled by a recovery in private demand, exports, and investment, with the largest contribution expected to come from exports. However, the overall strength of the recovery will depend on the growth performance in key export markets and investment partners, particularly the United States, the European Union, and China. The projected rebound in growth in these economies, fueled by the inventory cycle and impressive countercyclical policies, is expected to result in stronger external demand for Sub-Saharan African exports and should trigger a modest recovery in investment flows. However growth in external demand is expected to wane in the second half of 2010, as the growth impact of the inventory restocking cycle and fiscal stimulus wanes. Stronger domestic demand will cause import growth to accelerate, with net exports contributing negatively (−0.6 percent) to overall growth. Furthermore, given that recovery in global labor markets will lag, the recovery in tourism revenues and remittances is expected to be modest in 2010. Many countries in

Sub-Saharan Africa have very limited social safety nets, which means that recovery of private consumption will be weaker than in other regions. Indeed private demand is projected to grow by 3.2 percent, partly fueled by higher incomes in export-oriented sectors that benefit from stronger external demand.

Middle-income countries such as Botswana, Seychelles, South Africa, and oil-exporting countries like Angola are likely to register the most dramatic turnaround from low bases owing to weak performance in 2009 (table A12; figure A38). Growth in middle-income countries

Table A12   Sub-Saharan Africa country forecasts
(annual percent change unless indicated otherwise)

	1995–2005[a]	2006	2007	2008	2009[c]	2010[d]	2011[d]
Angola							
GDP at market prices (2005 US$)[b]	8.3	18.6	20.3	13.2	−0.9	6.5	8.0
Current account balance/GDP (%)	−2.2	25.1	15.6	8.5	−4.2	5.9	6.2
Benin							
GDP at market prices (2005 US$)[b]	4.6	3.8	4.6	5.0	3.1	3.3	4.8
Current account balance/GDP (%)	−7.2	−7.1	−12.1	−8.7	−8.5	−7.4	−7.3
Botswana							
GDP at market prices (2005 US$)[b]	6.8	3.0	4.4	2.9	−8.3	4.8	5.6
Current account balance/GDP (%)	8.1	17.6	15.6	7.8	−7.3	−7.2	−7.7
Burkina Faso							
GDP at market prices (2005 US$)[b]	6.4	5.5	3.6	4.9	3.6	4.6	5.2
Current account balance/GDP (%)	−10.1	−11.5	−8.7	−10.4	−9.8	−9.5	−10.2
Burundi							
GDP at market prices (2005 US$)[b]	0.4	5.1	3.6	4.4	2.6	3.7	5.1
Current account balance/GDP (%)	−13.7	−35.3	−26.7	−28.4	−23.2	−21.8	−21.8
Cameroon							
GDP at market prices (2005 US$)[b]	4.2	3.2	3.3	3.1	1.4	2.6	3.2
Current account balance/GDP (%)	−3.5	−0.8	−2.7	−1.0	−6.0	−5.0	−5.5
Cape Verde							
GDP at market prices (2005 US$)[b]	5.2	10.8	7.8	5.9	3.3	4.4	5.4
Current account balance/GDP (%)	−10.1	−6.9	−13.5	−18.3	−23.1	−22.3	−19.9
Central African Republic							
GDP at market prices (2005 US$)[b]	0.7	4.0	3.7	2.2	2.4	2.8	2.7
Current account balance/GDP (%)	−4.4	−7.6	−5.9	−8.5	−7.2	−7.3	−7.6
Chad							
GDP at market prices (2005 US$)[b]	8.6	0.2	0.2	0.2	0.8	2.7	3.0
Current account balance/GDP (%)	−24.2	−7.5	−10.7	−12.2	−20.7	−14.8	−14.3
Comoros							
GDP at market prices (2005 US$)[b]	2.1	1.2	−1.0	0.6	0.5	1.7	2.3
Current account balance/GDP (%)	−6.3	−5.5	−6.8	−11.8	−8.2	−8.2	−8.5
Congo, Dem. Rep. of							
GDP at market prices (2005 US$)[b]	0.1	5.6	6.3	7.1	3.0	5.2	6.9
Current account balance/GDP (%)	−1.7	−4.0	−2.7	−14.5	−13.6	−12.8	−12.0

(continued)

159

Table A12 (continued)
(annual percent change unless indicated otherwise)

	1995–2005[a]	2006	2007	2008	2009[c]	2010[d]	2011[d]
Congo, Rep. of							
GDP at market prices (2005 US$)[b]	3.4	6.2	−1.6	5.8	6.8	11.0	2.9
Current account balance/GDP (%)	−2.2	1.6	−9.3	−2.6	−9.3	3.2	0.9
Côte d'Ivoire							
GDP at market prices (2005 US$)[b]	1.6	0.7	1.6	2.3	3.2	4.0	4.1
Current account balance/GDP (%)	−0.2	2.8	−0.7	2.6	23.6	2.6	0.8
Eritrea							
GDP at market prices (2005 US$)[b]	1.7	−1.0	1.3	1.2	1.5	4.2	4.3
Current account balance/GDP (%)	−15.3	−20.8	−15.7	−16.3	−8.7	−9.3	−10.1
Ethiopia							
GDP at market prices (2005 US$)[b]	5.5	11.5	11.5	11.6	7.2	7.0	7.5
Current account balance/GDP (%)	−3.3	−9.2	−4.5	−5.6	−5.8	−8.1	−6.5
Gabon							
GDP at market prices (2005 US$)[b]	1.0	1.2	5.6	2.3	−1.2	2.3	3.4
Current account balance/GDP (%)	10.6	15.7	13.6	17.1	1.7	6.7	7.8
Gambia, The							
GDP at market prices (2005 US$)[b]	4.4	6.6	6.3	6.1	4.6	5.0	5.1
Current account balance/GDP (%)	−5.3	−13.9	−13.1	−15.6	−18.3	−16.8	−16.3
Ghana							
GDP at market prices (2005 US$)[b]	4.7	6.4	5.7	7.3	4.1	4.6	17.5
Current account balance/GDP (%)	−5.4	−8.2	−12.9	−18.2	−12.6	−15.5	−12.7
Guinea							
GDP at market prices (2005 US$)[b]	3.7	2.2	1.8	3.0	2.0	2.6	4.1
Current account balance/GDP (%)	−5.2	−11.4	−10.5	−15.6	−11.5	−11.1	−11.6
Guinea-Bissau							
GDP at market prices (2005 US$)[b]	−1.4	3.5	2.7	2.9	2.1	3.4	3.4
Current account balance/GDP (%)	−13.5	−18.5	−9.7	−12.5	−16.4	−15.4	−15.3
Kenya							
GDP at market prices (2005 US$)[b]	2.9	6.4	7.1	1.7	2.8	3.7	4.8
Current account balance/GDP (%)	−7.5	−2.3	−3.5	−6.9	−8.3	−7.6	−6.9
Lesotho							
GDP at market prices (2005 US$)[b]	2.8	6.5	2.4	4.5	0.6	2.3	2.8
Current account balance/GDP (%)	−22.0	4.4	13.7	9.8	−3.1	−18.5	−19.6
Madagascar							
GDP at market prices (2005 US$)[b]	3.1	5.0	6.2	6.9	0.9	3.1	3.6
Current account balance/GDP (%)	−8.6	−9.5	−14.7	−21.6	−17.1	−15.8	−15.2
Malawi							
GDP at market prices (2005 US$)[b]	2.4	8.2	8.6	9.7	6.5	5.4	4.6
Current account balance/GDP (%)	−5.7	−4.2	−1.6	−6.3	−3.4	−4.8	−4.6
Mali							
GDP at market prices (2005 US$)[b]	5.8	5.3	4.3	5.1	3.9	4.7	4.8
Current account balance/GDP (%)	−8.7	−3.9	−7.4	−8.5	−6.8	−7.9	−8.5
Mauritania							
GDP at market prices (2005 US$)[b]	3.3	11.7	1.9	2.2	2.5	4.1	5.0
Current account balance/GDP (%)	−3.2	−3.4	−10.9	−16.4	−15.0	−16.3	−17.6
Mauritius							
GDP at market prices (2005 US$)[b]	4.8	3.6	5.5	4.5	1.9	3.5	4.4
Current account balance/GDP (%)	0.1	−9.4	−6.4	−9.0	−8.2	−8.1	−8.8
Mozambique							
GDP at market prices (2005 US$)[b]	8.0	8.7	7.0	6.8	5.0	5.5	5.7
Current account balance/GDP (%)	−15.1	−10.9	−12.9	−11.5	−10.6	−10.1	−9.1

(continued)

	1995–2005[a]	2006	2007	2008	2009[c]	2010[d]	2011[d]
Namibia							
GDP at market prices (2005 US$)[b]	4.2	7.1	5.5	2.9	−1.9	3.0	3.3
Current account balance/GDP (%)	3.0	12.7	9.1	1.9	−1.3	−2.0	−1.2
Niger							
GDP at market prices (2005 US$)[b]	3.5	5.8	3.3	9.4	1.6	4.9	5.3
Current account balance/GDP (%)	−7.1	−8.6	−7.8	−12.8	−17.9	−16.3	−17.7
Nigeria							
GDP at market prices (2005 US$)[b]	4.6	6.2	6.3	5.3	4.3	4.8	5.1
Current account balance/GDP (%)	5.4	15.7	17.7	19.1	8.0	10.6	10.3
Rwanda							
GDP at market prices (2005 US$)[b]	8.3	7.3	7.9	11.2	5.1	5.5	5.8
Current account balance/GDP (%)	−4.6	−6.4	−3.8	−7.0	−6.9	−7.0	−7.1
Senegal							
GDP at market prices (2005 US$)[b]	4.4	2.4	4.7	2.5	2.1	3.4	4.2
Current account balance/GDP (%)	−5.7	−9.2	−11.2	−12.4	−11.4	−10.5	−10.6
Seychelles							
GDP at market prices (2005 US$)[b]	2.8	8.3	7.3	0.1	−10.1	2.7	3.7
Current account balance/GDP (%)	−13.4	−15.0	−29.9	−47.5	−8.8	−16.0	−17.5
Sierra Leone							
GDP at market prices (2005 US$)[b]	4.6	7.3	6.4	5.3	4.0	4.7	6.5
Current account balance/GDP (%)	−12.4	−9.5	−14.3	−16.1	−17.0	−16.6	−16.6
South Africa							
GDP at market prices (2005 US$)[b]	3.3	5.6	5.5	3.7	−1.8	2.0	2.7
Current account balance/GDP (%)	−1.3	−6.2	−7.3	−7.4	−5.0	−5.7	−6.0
Sudan							
GDP at market prices (2005 US$)[b]	6.2	11.3	10.2	6.8	3.8	4.9	5.1
Current account balance/GDP (%)	−6.3	−15.2	−12.5	−9.1	−11.5	−9.6	−8.8
Swaziland							
GDP at market prices (2005 US$)[b]	3.5	2.9	3.5	2.4	0.2	1.1	2.4
Current account balance/GDP (%)	−0.8	−7.3	0.8	−4.3	−8.6	−10.5	−11.5
Tanzania							
GDP at market prices (2005 US$)[b]	5.4	6.7	7.1	7.5	4.6	5.5	6.2
Current account balance/GDP (%)	−6.3	−8.0	−9.4	−9.9	−7.9	−8.5	−8.4
Togo							
GDP at market prices (2005 US$)[b]	3.2	3.9	1.9	1.0	1.7	2.0	3.2
Current account balance/GDP (%)	−9.6	−7.8	−7.7	−11.2	−7.0	−7.6	−7.6
Uganda							
GDP at market prices (2005 US$)[b]	6.4	10.8	8.4	9.0	5.1	5.6	5.9
Current account balance/GDP (%)	−7.1	−4.4	−3.7	−3.5	−4.8	−6.0	−6.4
Zambia							
GDP at market prices (2005 US$)[b]	3.8	6.2	6.2	5.7	5.2	5.4	5.9
Current account balance/GDP (%)	−11.8	1.2	−6.1	−7.6	−4.2	−4.3	−4.4
Zimbabwe							
GDP at market prices (2005 US$)[b]	−2.4	−6.3	−6.9	−14.1	4.7	7.1	6.3
Current account balance/GDP (%)	−11.5	−16.6	−10.3	−26.6	−20.8	−23.6	−21.3

Source: World Bank.

Note: World Bank forecasts are frequently updated based on new information and changing (global) circumstances. Consequently, projections presented here may differ from those contained in other Bank documents, even if basic assessments of countries' prospects do not significantly differ at any given moment in time.

Liberia, Somalia, and, São Tomé and Principe are not forecast owing to data limitations.

a. Growth rates over intervals are compound average; growth contributions, ratios and the GDP deflator are averages.
b. GDP measured in constant 2000 U.S. dollars.
c. Estimate.
d. Forecast.

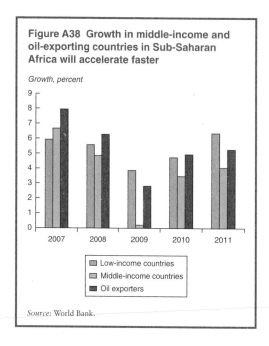

Figure A38 Growth in middle-income and oil-exporting countries in Sub-Saharan Africa will accelerate faster

Growth, percent

Legend:
- Low-income countries
- Middle-income countries
- Oil exporters

Source: World Bank.

is projected to accelerate from 0.3 percent in 2009 to 3.5 percent in 2010 and to accelerate further to 4 percent in 2011, boosted by stronger external demand and a moderate recovery in tourism and remittances. Meanwhile growth in oil-exporting countries will almost double, reaching 4.9 percent in 2010, and accelerate marginally, to 5.3 percent in 2011, helped by stronger demand for energy. For low-income countries, a more moderate acceleration in growth of slightly less than 1 percentage point is forecast, as remittances, tourism, and private capital flows recover more slowly. Indeed, remittances to Sub-Saharan African are projected to rise only modestly, by 1.8 percent in 2010, after having declined by 2.9 percent in 2009, as weak labor markets in destination countries undermine migrants' incomes. In contrast, remittances grew 40 percent over the 2006–2008 period (World Bank Group 2009). Growth in fragile states will accelerate by slightly more than 1 percentage point to above 4.2 percent having weathered the global crisis remarkably, benefiting in some cases from the peace dividend.

Current account balances in middle-income countries will improve only marginally in the next couple of years, as recovery in domestic demand, and in particular investment (with high import content), will boost import demand, causing imports to grow faster than exports. Furthermore the recovery in tourism revenues and remittances will also be moderate because of a weak (even jobless) recovery in high-income labor markets during the forecast period. Current account balances in these middle-income countries are projected to improve by less than 1.5 percent of GDP between 2009 and 2011. Current account balances in oil-exporting countries should improve by 2.7 percent of GDP, with stronger oil revenues partially offset by stronger import demand and higher profit repatriations.

Higher commodity prices and increased trade volumes, along with more robust levels of domestic economic activity, should reduce fiscal deficits in the region. After fiscal balances deteriorated to −4.2 percent of GDP in 2009, fiscal balances are expected to ameliorate in 2010, narrowing to −2.1 percent of GDP, before improving further to −1.7 percent of GDP by 2011 as accelerating output growth raises tax revenues. However, most low-income countries will continue to experience fiscal gaps in excess of 3 percent of GDP. Fiscal balances in oil-exporting countries are expected to improve from a deficit of 5.2 percent of GDP to marginal surpluses over the forecast horizon.

Risks

The major risk facing the Sub-Saharan economies is that the world economy could experience a double dip or economic stagnation. This would undermine the recovery in external demand for the Sub-Saharan economies and would put pressure on commodity prices, undermining government revenues and possibly pushing debt to unsustainable levels. This could in turn force governments to implement procyclical fiscal cuts, increase taxation, or both, with adverse implications for poverty, health, education, and long-term growth prospects. Tourism, remittances, and private capital flows may also decline further, thereby negatively affecting growth and incomes and ultimately causing more people to fall into poverty. Furthermore, safety nets in many countries in the region are very limited, which means that the impact on the poor cannot be cushioned. A jobless recovery in high-income countries would have similar negative consequences for tourism and remittances to Sub-Saharan African countries, some of which depend heavily on these revenues.

The Sub-Saharan Africa region will face a large external financing burden in 2010, equivalent to close to 12 percent of GDP, and growth could fall short of the baseline forecast if unmet financing requirements lead to lower investment and growth prospects. For countries with external financing needs, maturing foreign debt will amount to close to 6.5 percent of GDP in 2010, while the current account deficit including grants is forecast at 5.2 percent of GDP. There is thus a risk in many Sub-Saharan economies, and in particular in low-income countries, that concessional lending will fall short of the need to finance a swift return to growth. In some cases, this shortfall may be exacerbated by institutional capacity constraints, which also limit effectiveness. Given the role that foreign investment flows play in the region, a reversal in these flows not only would directly affect external financing needs, but also would have a severe impact on investment and growth. Given the increased global growth uncertainties, investment flows to the region may be adversely affected.

The fiscal position in some of the smaller members of the Southern Africa Customs Union (particularly Lesotho and Swaziland) may come under severe pressure over the next two to three years, because one of the major revenue sources of the union's revenue pool is related to taxes on South African imports, which have deteriorated rapidly in the aftermath of the global financial crisis.

In countries that experienced rapid credit growth during the boom years, there is a marked risk that nonperforming loans will rise sharply during the economic downturn affecting the financial sector, which in turn would have an adverse impact on the real sector. Countries like Cape Verde, the Democratic Republic of Congo, Ethiopia, Nigeria, Rwanda, Tanzania, Uganda, and Zambia have registered rapid increases in nonfinancial private sector claims (as a share of broad money) and therefore run larger risks. For countries with low capital adequacy, the effect of deteriorating balance sheets on performance will be even more severe.

Notes

1. Fixed investment plummeted across most developing and high-income countries of the East Asia region from the final quarter of 2008 through the second quarter of 2009. For example, investment in Thailand tumbled 40 percent in the first quarter of 2009 (saar), Malaysia experienced sequential falloffs of 35 and 14 percent over the final quarter of 2008 and the first of 2009, while several newly industrialized economies (NIEs) were much more severely affected, with Taiwan, China, suffering four successive quarterly declines, two of which were in excess of 40 percent.

2. The developing East Asia region as referenced in this report comprises the larger countries of China, Indonesia, Malaysia, the Philippines, and Thailand, as well as Fiji, Cambodia, Lao People's Democratic Republic, Papua New Guinea, Vanuatu, and Vietnam. Smaller Pacific island nations generally carry insufficient economic and financial data for inclusion in the database and projections. The importance of high-income East Asian countries—those noted in the text—as well as Australia, should be underscored in the current context of crisis and recovery, because the strong trade relationships among all countries in East Asia tend to amplify the down-phase of recession, but should come to support the rebound and recovery in a similar fashion as recovery evolves over coming months and years.

3. Dollar-based exports picked up to growth of 52 percent for China by November 2009 (saar) from declines of 54 percent in March; to 41 percent for the remainder of the developing region by October, and to 17 percent for the NIEs, also by October of the year. At the same time industrial production for most economies rebounded sharply, for example, to 25 percent for Thailand in September (saar) from trough declines of 48 percent in December 2008.

4. The countries covered in the Europe and Central Asia section of the appendix are those that fall into the World Bank's definition of low- and middle-income

classifications (with 2008 per capita Gross National Income equal to or below $3,855). These 24 countries are Albania, Bosnia and Herzegovina, Bulgaria, Kosovo, Latvia, Lithuania, Former Yugoslav Republic of Macedonia, Montenegro, Poland, Romania, and Serbia (in the Central European subregion); Armenia, Azerbaijan, Belarus, Georgia, Kazakhstan, Kyrgyz Republic, Moldova, Russian Federation, Tajikistan, Turkmenistan, Ukraine, and Uzbekistan (in the Commonwealth of Independent States subregion); and Turkey. Transition countries include all 24 countries, with the exception of Turkey. Among these developing countries, Bulgaria, Latvia, Lithuania, Poland, and Romania are new European Union members. Owing to data limitations, forecasts are not available for Bosnia and Herzegovina, Kosovo, Montenegro, Serbia, Tajikistan, and Turkmenistan.

5. See World Bank (2009b).

6. Bulgaria, Latvia, Lithuania, Poland, and Romania. See World Bank, 2009a.

7. Kazakhstan, Kyrgyz Republic, Tajikistan, Turkmenistan, and Uzbekistan.

8. Armenia, Azerbaijan, and Georgia.

9. World Bank Group (2009).

10. World Bank (2010a).

11. World Bank (2010b).

12. SELIC stands for Sistema Especial de Liquidação e Custodia, or Special System of Clearance and Custody, which is Banco Central do Brasil's overnight lending rate.

13. The low- and middle income countries of the Middle East and North Africa region as presented in this report include Algeria, the Arab Republic of Egypt, the Islamic Republic of Iran, Jordan, Lebanon, Morocco, the Syrian Arab Republic, Tunisia, and the Republic of Yemen. Several developing economies are not covered owing to data insufficiencies, including Djibouti, Iraq, Libya, and the West Bank and Gaza. High-income economies of the broader geographic region, including Gulf Cooperation Council (GCC) members Bahrain, Kuwait, Oman and Saudi Arabia

are covered in this report under the category of "other high-income countries." But as this group has become increasingly more integrated with the developing economies of the region, discussion of economic and financial developments for the group is a feature of this appendix. Among the GCC, insufficient data exists for inclusion of Qatar and the United Arab Emirates.

References

Chen, S., and M. Ravallion. "The Impact of the Global Financial Crisis on the World's Poorest." Vox: Research-Based Policy Analysis and Commentary from Leading Economists, www.voxeu.org/index.php?q=node/3520 [accessed Dec. 9, 2009].

Friedman, J., and N. Schady. 2009. "How Many More Infants Are Likely to Die in Africa as a Result of the Global Financial Crisis?" Research Paper 60 (August). World Bank, Washington, DC.

World Bank. 2009a. "EU10 Regular Economic Report: From Stabilization to Recovery." Washington, DC (October). http://go.worldbank.org/UNCGIKEPH0.

————. 2009b. "Russian Economic Report #20: From Rebound to Recovery?" Washington, DC (November10). http://go.worldbank.org/FKGLSQ4NF0.

————. 2010a. "The Crisis Hits Home: Stress-Testing Households in Europe and Central Asia." Prepared by Erwin R. Tiongson, Naotaka Sugawara, Victor Sulla, Ashley Taylor, Anna I. Gueorguieva, Victoria Levin, and Kalanidhi Subbarao. http://go.worldbank.org/H92ZH3CK20.

————. 2010b. "Turmoil at Twenty." Washington, DC. http://go.worldbank.org/ZQTRLRED70.

World Bank Group. 2009. "Migration and Remittance Trends 2009." *Migration and Development Brief 11*. Washington, DC (November 3). http://siteresources.worldbank.org/INTPROSPECTS/Resources/334934-1110315015165/MigrationAndDevelopmentBrief11.pdf.

Eco-Audit

Environmental Benefits Statement

The World Bank is committed to preserving endangered forests and natural resources. The Office of the Publisher has chosen to print *Global Economic Prospects 2010* on recycled paper with 30 percent post-consumer waste, in accordance with the recommended standards for paper usage set by the Green Press Initiative, a nonprofit program supporting publishers in using fiber that is not sourced from endangered forests. For more information, visit www.greenpressinitiative.org.

Saved:
- 23 trees
- 644 pounds of solid waste
- 10,609 gallons of wastewater
- 2,203 pounds of net greenhouse gases
- 7 million British thermal units of total energy

green press
INITIATIVE